LAUGHING
TO KEEP FROM
DYING

THE NEW BLACK STUDIES SERIES

Edited by Darlene Clark Hine
and Dwight A. McBride

*A list of books in the series appears
at the end of this book.*

DANIELLE FUENTES MORGAN

LAUGHING TO KEEP FROM DYING

AFRICAN AMERICAN SATIRE IN THE TWENTY-FIRST CENTURY

UNIVERSITY OF ILLINOIS PRESS
Urbana, Chicago, and Springfield

Publication of this book was supported by the Santa
Clara University Provost's Office Publication Grant.

Library of Congress Cataloging-in-Publication Data
Names: Morgan, Danielle Fuentes, 1983– author.
Title: Laughing to keep from dying : African
    American satire in the twenty-first century /
    Danielle Fuentes Morgan.
Description: Urbana : University of Illinois Press,
    [2020] | Series: The new Black studies series |
    Includes bibliographical references and index.
Identifiers: LCCN 2020012144 (print) | LCCN
    2020012145 (ebook) | ISBN 9780252043390
    (cloth) | ISBN 9780252085307 (paperback) | ISBN
    9780252052279 (ebook)
Subjects: LCSH: African Americans in mass media. |
    American literature—African American authors—
    History and criticism. | Satire, American—History
    and criticism. | Literature and mental illness—
    United States—History—21st century. | African
    Americans—Race identity. | African Americans
    in popular culture. | African Americans and mass
    media. | African Americans—Intellectual life.
Classification: LCC P94.5.A372 U5635 2020 (print) |
    LCC P94.5.A372 (ebook) | DDC 302.23089/96073
    —dc23
LC record available at https://lccn.loc.gov/2020012144
LC ebook record available at https://lccn.loc.gov/
    2020012145

For my mother, Angela, who taught me how to read and to write, and for my uncle, Kevin McMillan, who was the smartest funny guy and funniest smart guy I've ever known.

CONTENTS

ACKNOWLEDGMENTS

A host of kindness made this book possible. To begin, I must first thank the people I encountered at Cornell University. The staff at the Africana Studies and Research Center, particularly Eric Kofi Acree, Saah Nue Quigee, and Sarah Powers, were vital. They took an interest in this project at its inception, offering warm smiles on blustery days and books I would not have discovered otherwise. Thank you for the home away from home. Mari N. Crabtree, Jesse Goldberg, and Christine "Xine" Yao, I am so grateful for your friendship. Your suggestions and insights make me a more thoughtful writer and our fellowship—in person or across the miles—makes me a more thoughtful person. Gratitude, gratitude, gratitude.

Riché Richardson told me to write about what I love. Without that encouragement, I may not have fully imagined this project. George Hutchinson was critical in keeping the historical at the forefront of the twenty-first century. His framing was instrumental. I thank Dagmawi Woubshet for continuing to inspire me personally and professionally. He shows me how to make space for my whole self in my life and in my writing. I leave conversations with him and only see beautiful possibilities for Black futures. Margo Natalie Crawford is the prototype. I was lucky to sign up for her class in year one and to study under her, to read her words, to pick her brain, and to bear witness to her grace and brilliance; I am blessed now to call her my friend. She is the scholar I hope to be when I grow up.

I am so fortunate to have found community at Santa Clara University. I am thankful for the support of my colleagues in the English department and throughout the university more broadly. Terry Beers, Phyllis Brown, Michelle Burnham, Esther Ruth Cardona, Matt Driscoll, Marilyn Edelstein, Dennis Gordon, Jackie Hendricks, Miah Jeffra, David James Keaton, Michael Lasley, Maggie Levantovskaya, Claudia McIssacs, Aparajita Nanda, Margaret Russell, Brody Sandel, Maura Tarnoff, Robin Tremblay-McGaw, Veronica Miranda, Juan Velasco, and Mike Whalen have offered support and encouragement in a variety of ways throughout the writing process, from reading drafts to suggesting additional texts to inviting me to lecture on portions of the book. Julie Chang, Eileen Elrod, and Brett Johnson Solomon have been generous mentors, offering critical insights, helping me to navigate the university, and keeping me on course. Katy Bruchmann, Amy Lueck, and Julia Voss are dear and true. I appreciate the spaces we've eked out for commiseration and celebration during the process. Thank you for that and more.

C. J. Gabbe, Robin Nelson, and Chan Thai were my first friends way back at new faculty orientation, and I'm so thankful to walk beside you. I am gratified by the love and support you've shown. Without fear of hyperbole, I know I couldn't have done this without y'all. To my Culture, Power, Difference Working Group—Aldo Billingslea, Jesica Fernández, Allia Griffin, Tony Hazard, Mythri Jegathesan, James Lai, Cruz Medina, Anna Sampaio, and Christina Zanfagna—thank you. The wisdom, perspectives, and laughter you've shared with me are invaluable. I've never been a part of the cool kids before, and I am so grateful for our little family.

The students in my African American Comedy course energized my thinking and my writing. In particular, Kelli Bates, Sianna Bethune, Matthew Bettencourt, Maggie Debrovner, Gabrielle Deutsch, Philip DiBoise, Azariah Joel, K. J. Lee, Perla Luna, Lindsey Mandell, Kimmie Meunier, Djenanway Se-Gahon, Derek Sikkema, Sarah Tarter, and Rachel Wiggins opened up new, comprehensive realms of inquiry that made this a stronger book. Special thanks to Julia Joyce and Jasmine Rovaris for their critical work as research assistants, and to Austin Gray for his thought-provoking questions and ideas that helped invigorate my thinking and refine my writing.

Initial funding through Cornell University's American Studies Research Grant allowed my archival work at the Schomburg Center for Research in Black Culture in Harlem, New York. Thank you to the National Museum of African American History and Culture in Washington, D.C., for the opportunity to visit and the space to think. A summer grant from the SCU provost and the University Research Committee allowed me the opportunity to benefit from guidance and feedback from Katie Van Heest, whose insights made for a more polished book overall. I am also deeply indebted to the Santa Clara University Center for the Arts and Humanities for the opportunity to serve as the Frank Sinatra Faculty Fellow and work with W. Kamau Bell. I am thankful to both Kamau and Melissa Hudson Bell for their friendship and for conversations that took comedic theory to practice and opened up new ways of thinking about satiric possibilities.

I owe a debt of gratitude to the University of Illinois Press and especially to Dawn Durante for believing in and shepherding this project. Her insights were fundamental, her guidance invaluable, and her thoughtfulness treasured. Alison Syring saw this book to the end with generosity and care. Walt Evans's final edits and Lisa DeBoer's work on the index were essential. Thank you to my reviewers for their incisive feedback. I am also grateful for those who have offered direction and inspiration along the path to completing this book. GerShun Avilez, Daphne Brooks, Caroline Brown, Brittney C. Cooper, James J. Donahue, Treva B. Lindsey, Derek C. Maus, Sheila Smith McKoy, Myra Mendible, W. Jason Miller, and Roy Pérez were teachers, editors, advisors, and role models. They supported me in ways large and small since this project began.

My parents, Angela and Philip, maintained a belief in me and in my ability to complete this project that was so pure and love-filled and steadfast it felt nearly comical in my more stressful moments. But if they hadn't kept me lifted up in their words and with their prayers, I never could have started this project, let alone finished it. Every word I've ever written is a reflection of my love for you two. My brothers, Carlos and Josh, continue to dream with me. I can't think of two kinder and braver souls. I'm so thankful to be your big sister. My "sister from another mister," Bethann Cleary, is always on my side and always sees me. I don't know what I would do without you. It's unimaginable. My husband, Matt, was my first editor and spent countless hours reading my words, offering suggestions, and listening to my varied trains of thought. Thank you for reassuring me in moments of worry, for beach days and sketch comedy nights, and for your love. You remain "best of husbands and best of men." And finally, to my darling children, Calliope Angela and Rosalie Pearl, who were both born while this project was underway and sometimes rocked in my arms or sat in my lap as I wrote. You two are answered prayers beyond anything I could imagine. I am so proud of who you already are and who you are becoming. I love you and I hope this makes you proud.

The Satirical Mode and African American Identity

Stay with me, son, there is no moral to this tale.
—Percival Everett

Oo, wee! Aw, Lord, this racism is *killing* me inside!
—Dave Chappelle as "Clifton the Colored Milkman"

In a 1993 interview for *SPIN Magazine,* Chris Rock described comedy as "the blues for people who can't sing." I'm especially drawn to this analogy because the blues and comedy, on the surface, seem antithetical expressions of emotion. If the blues are the musical articulation of sadness and grief, what connection might it have with the comedic? The heart of Rock's statement reminds us that blues and comedy, two spheres so associated with ideas of Blackness and Black identity, have a particular utility because they both provide the speaker with formal conventions to describe their own experience and position in a way that *might* let their intention be received by the audience. It is the deceptive simplicity of the mode itself that gives both the blues and comedy their use. The satirical mode emerges in the interstice of the blues and comedy—this sense of what Langston Hughes and others have described as "laughing to keep from crying." Satire addresses the failures and limitations of its contemporary moment with clear intentionality, despite efforts toward veiled temporality, obscured historicity, and denounced centrality of meaning—after all, it's *just* a joke![1]—by some audiences, and even by some satirists themselves.

The fact that the usefulness of satire is often contested ironically lends to its power. Laughter and satire open up the power of Black selfhood by pushing back against the status quo, instead reveling in the inherent absurdity of race and racialization—the way people are separated into racial groups and certain groups are believed to have certain characteristics based on their race—while frequently pretending to do *nothing* except make its audience laugh. It is a hidden, subversive tactic. In *African-American Satire: The Sacredly Profane Novel*, Darryl Dickson-Carr explains, "satire is nothing if it does not aggressively defy the status quo" (1). This defiance of the status quo manifests in an opening up of Black interior space—what I define as the hidden, private realm of Black thought and feeling beyond any expected performance of Blackness. Satirical moments are meant to destabilize the mainstream acceptance of and propagation of the racial status quo and do so surreptitiously by feigning carelessness and pretending to disregard the skill required in humor—one need only look at the slacker-stoner persona of a young Dave Chappelle to know that a good satirist or comedian often makes the joke seem uncalculated and *easy*. The destabilization is key, and if comedy accepts the rules of the social game, satire is predicated on subverting those rules. In doing so, satire creates new realms in which social justice might be enacted by disrupting social expectations and demonstrating the connection between laughter and ethical beliefs. Through a clear focus on questions of racial essentialism, either by disavowing or ironically embracing racial performativity, satire creates a tension that opens up a hidden interior into kaleidoscopic Blackness, those multifaceted, private recesses of Black identity and selfhood that are often unknown to or overlooked by those who would simplify Blackness to render it consumable and commodifiable.

This book addresses the satirical treatment of race and racialization in twenty-first-century African American cultural production. I expand the parameters of satire to focus on the satirization found in African American forms of expression that cross generic boundaries—some of these discourses are satires in the traditional sense, while others engage the satirization of race as a strategy and thus lend themselves to the possibility of satiric readings. The satiric is an intrinsic part of contemporary African American literary and cultural production and is a demonstration of explicit social engagement. These texts, performances, and events do not necessarily engage that which is explicitly funny, although many do; they instead problematize the existing social sphere by highlighting its *absurdity*—both the reality of racialization and the mythology of a "post-racial" that suggests race is now irrelevant—and its reification through the continued centrality and substantiation of white supremacy. These texts revolve around the potential for satirization and *self*-satirization. It is ultimately the post-racial mythology that provokes a sharpened production of African American satire through the necessary articulation of racism's continued existence and the absurdity of "not seeing" racism or race. These texts underscore the ridiculousness of contemporary racialization and post-race to offer satirical readings by revealing critical anxieties about race and critiquing the irrationality of racialization.

The diverse generic forms of these satirical readings disrupt our expectations of a boundary between staged performance and lived experience. In this way, we are reminded that ideas of race are predicated on ideas about racial identity itself as something that can be performed. These satires demonstrate that the expected parameters cannot hold. It is the inherent satirical nature of race itself that blurs the line between the real and the imagined, between the overtly satiric and that which contains satiric potential. As a result, by heightening a sense of racial arbitrariness and meaninglessness, these discourses dismantle the racial hierarchy necessary to substantiate histories of racist treatment naturalized in the national consciousness. I argue for satirical readings marked by confrontational potential, satirical readings that subvert the expectation of the existing racial hierarchy. Ultimately, the utility of satire is found in its upending of dominant ideologies that render race essential and racism natural. These discourses take Blackness back and endow it with the nuance it has always had.

The laughter inspired by satire opens up space to acknowledge kaleidoscopic Blackness—the multiple autonomous ways of being Black—that prevents psychic death, or being objectified and flattened. It is this revelation of kaleidoscopic Blackness through a satirical reading of racialized expectations and stereotypes that uncovers the potential of Black interior space. Indeed, if the mythology of the "post-racial" emerges from the rhetoric of white centrality—where only people of color are expected to move *beyond* racial identity because only nonwhiteness is racialized—kaleidoscopic Blackness, the variety of ways of looking at, thinking about, and asserting one's own Black identity, emerges from the Black interior. I flow here with Elizabeth Alexander's use of the Black interior to imagine life "behind the public face of stereotype and limited imagination" (x) and Margo Natalie Crawford's Black public interiority in *Black Post-Blackness* of "art that is public and tied to the black interior" (168), and I expand into the satiric realm of racial performance and race as performative. By acknowledging and subverting expectations of racial performance, satire opens up space in which the inner realm of Blackness may be revealed. These texts and performances when taken as a whole reveal kaleidoscopic Blackness and demonstrate that twenty-first-century authors, performers, and figures rather than building toward a singular argument about Black identity instead underscore the relationships between the various ways Blackness might be experienced, performed, and lived as self-directed expression. Here "performance" does not imply falseness but instead signals the way Blackness might be viewed in the public sphere. The recognition of kaleidoscopic Blackness is an ethical move that leads to social justice in its revelation of the multiple ways of performing Blackness and being Black, where social justice is the freedom to be, freedom to articulate and perform one's own autonomous identity.

In these twenty-first-century discourses, when the players hearken to recognizable portrayals of Blackness, either authentic or stereotyped, satire reminds us of the inability of these forms to convey the fullness of Black identity. These texts continue the trajectory of the African American literary tradition by reminding us of the always familiar and evoking contemporary meaning through self-investigation that opens up into a communal terrain. Aldon Lynn Nielsen explains in *Black Chant*, "Chant, and this is true equally of such terms as 'song' and 'tradition,' in order to be *heard* as chant, must present itself to us as the at least vaguely familiar, the already heard, for it must have presupposed the possibility of reiteration, response, recall, re-rapping" (30). That Black stereotypes are familiar—that without my needing to name them here, stereotypes and assumptions around Blackness are already known, even if their validity is questioned—is significant because it not only makes the purpose of the satire clear but also reminds audiences of the lingering, and in many cases insidious, nature of these tropes through this "reiteration, response, recall, re-rapping."

However, by invoking these symbols in the national consciousness and working to interrogate and dismantle them, these satires rewrite the script of Blackness.[2] Indeed, that these discourses signify—that they take forms and tropes known to their audiences and re-create and reappropriate them—is not, in and of itself, especially new in a discussion of the satiric potential of African American cultural expression. What is significant, though, is that while earlier texts did much work toward this same examination, they usually also contained a clear, homiletic message to underscore authorial purpose. More recent works instead push the effort to dismantle to the forefront, seeking justice in the subversion itself rather than in placing a didactic message as the immediate and sole purpose. For better or for worse, the onus is now on audience interpretation more than in the past and emphasizes that satire forgoes easy readings both in terms of simplicity of interpretation and the comfort of the reader.

It is not just the reclamation of tropes but also the reclamation of Blackness itself that is undertaken in these works. A satirical reading of these texts, performances, and events detects, refuses, and ultimately subverts an exclusionary hierarchical system of race and the narratives that deny the complex reality of Black life for Black people. I reject the assessment of the contemporary era as having lower racial stakes than the past, or no racial stakes at all, arguing instead for a sense of what I term "laughing to keep from *dying*." As the satirical articulation becomes more overt, so does the potential danger—either physical or psychic—waged in response to the satirist and their in-group audience. Laughing to keep from dying is the survival tactic that operates in two registers—the ability to inspire laughter in those who would cause harm becomes a form of protection in the plausible deniability of *just jokes;* the necessity of inspiring knowing in-group laughter opens up Black interior space that wards off psychic, or even physical, death. Knowing, as Audre Lorde teaches, that the master's tools will never dismantle the master's house, these texts and performers when most successful refuse the language of the oppressor and instead create a new language in a search for a just articulation of a nuanced selfhood.

Even those who acknowledge satire as an incisive form of critique often struggle to name what the ends that justify satiric means may be. I find that the effectiveness of satire is located in its potential for self-making through self-investigation. Racial satirization, found in literature, performance, and the seeming self-satirization of real-world contemporary events, reclaims and revises prevailing tropes of Blackness. This tactic articulates an autonomous selfhood for Black bodies from slavery to the contemporary era—bodies that are systemically disempowered in other spheres. For this reason, it is important to reiterate that this satirical impulse was brought over from Africa and continued to evolve in the New World, rather than springing anew in North America. As a result, it is necessary to start a discussion about contemporary comedy from this shared vantage point of marginalization at its national beginning, with the chattel slave system, and move chronologically to offer context and insight into present-day satirical manifestations.

Although other works have usefully acknowledged the existence of forms of humor in slave culture, few have currently examined closely the trajectory from slave humor to twenty-first-century African American comedy through a focus on the subversive continuing satiric impulse. Glenda Carpio's book, *Laughing Fit to Kill: Black Humor in the Fictions of Slavery* (2008), is an especially important recent contribution to the scholarship on the lasting impact of slavery in the realm of fiction. Carpio engages the long and continuing history of slavery to "explore how different generations of black humorists enact symbolic rituals of redress with respect to the breach of slavery" (11). In doing so, Carpio demonstrates the ways contemporary comedians utilize the imagery and rhetoric of slavery to critique the injustices of the past and their continued impact in the twentieth and twenty-first centuries. While *Laughing to Keep from Dying* begins with slavery and the image of the slave, it focuses on why race, racialization, and racism so frequently continue to form the basis of satirical readings in the twenty-first century in both fictional and nonfictional events. I shift here and am more concerned with the ways that satire opens up the affective potential of Black interior space and leads to an ethical terrain in which autonomous Black selfhood can be actualized. Satire opens an ethical terrain, and justice is tied to this terrain. Justice is bound by ethics, and in many cases the subversive nature of satire reckons with the reality of what justice might look like and what justice might mean by centering the desires of the disenfranchised or otherwise marginalized. This focus on interiority, ethics, and selfhood seeks to expand the existing landscape of critical race theory and explains why satire is not only one of many ways to critique past and present social realms but, especially in the twenty-first century, a necessary one for the individual and communal survival of Black bodies and Black psychic space.

The satirical is a critical framework for articulating Black selfhood in the twenty-first century; the overt depiction of an autonomous self creates a rupture in mainstream conceptions of a racial hierarchy and endows the speaker with a nuanced sense of both the self and collective Black identity. Laughing to keep from dying specifically offers a way to include others, both to form an in-group of those with whom one already identifies and to separate yourselves, as a juxtaposing tactic, from those with whom you do not identify. Further, the levity often fostered by satire offers a way to defuse mounting tensions when autonomous identity formation is threatened. The subversive nature of African American satire and comedy, and its still-disputed utility in political realms, offers a representational strategy that leads to the sphere of justice through the creation of an affective realm that critiques embedded assumptions surrounding race and racialization. Satire cannot be detached from ethics because when it is effectively undertaken it moves us toward social justice, or at least toward considering what justice might look like. Here it is on the level of the individual, in defiance of prescriptive identity and by refusing to adhere to stereotypes surrounding Black identity that engages this ethical terrain. In African American satire in the twenty-first century, refusing traditional respectability politics shifts the concept of ethics away from vague notions of right and wrong and opens up what ethical behavior might really look like in practice—the ethics involved in creating space for authentic ways of being without assigning value to the portrayals. As a result, the individual decisions surrounding autonomous portrayals of Blackness not only lead to justice on the level of the individual—the idea that it is *just* to present yourself in your own terms—but also naturally opens into collective in-group justice that illuminates the many valid ways of being Black. After all, what might justice look like in this context other than the right to exist freely and unmolested, in body and in mind?

The creation of a collective in-group necessary for laughing to keep from dying can be particularly tricky and rests on two presumptions. The first presumption is that the audience is able to decode the authorial intent of the speaker or performer. The audience must understand the satirical motive of the speaker and align themselves with the speaker's perspective; if the audience disagrees with the speaker, its members may discover that they are now the object being satirized themselves. The second presumption is that the speakers hold a comprehensive enough understanding of Blackness not to limit it in their description—to understand that Blackness is kaleidoscopic. This second point combats a tendency toward essentialism that is particularly problematic for a comprehensive discussion of African American literature and culture. In *How to See a Work of Art in Total Darkness*, art historian Darby English explains the difficulty in defining contemporary African American literature, saying, "it is almost uniformly generalized, endlessly summoned to prove its representativeness (or defend its lack of the same) and contracted to show-and-tell on behalf of an abstract and unchanging 'culture of origin'" (7). As English notes, African American literature, culture and, indeed, *people* are often expected to represent a universal of Black cultural experience. The result is a limited scope of acceptance for what the Black experience is from both writerly and readerly vantage points, as authenticity is defined by adherence to expectations. African American satire rejects this limited scope by framing it as laughable.

It is within this space of subversion that kaleidoscopic Blackness most intimately resides—in an awareness of the limitlessness of Black identity in the face of its denial. When effectively enacted, these satirical readings demonstrate the multitudinous nature of Black identity on individual and communal levels, depicting individuals who perform Blackness in both expected and surprising ways; individuals who do not exist as singular stand-ins for a broader community but are simultaneously such a part of their communities that they cannot be fully understood without the context these communities provide. This kaleidoscopic Blackness refutes the "post-racial" mythology by demonstrating new and expanded parameters for racial self-identification and performance, rather than the eradication of race itself.

If there is any benefit to the mistaken avowal of a twenty-first-century "post-racial," it might best be found here: that an unintended byproduct of the insistence that race no longer matters is the creation of a scaffold for the possibility that racial essentialism must no longer matter either. Instead, a focus on kaleidoscopic Blackness permits a degree of freedom for self-construction as it operates in opposition to the mythological deconstruction of race that the post-racial suggests.[3] Instead of rendering race meaningless, as post-racial suggests, a focus on Black interior space leads to questions about the validity of the stereotypes. In this way, a new focus on *racism* rather than *race* as problematic and worth problematizing is feasible.

These ramifications cut across not just race but gender, sexuality, class, and education in consideration of individualized selfhood and connection to community. For many of us, the ostensible post-racial ability to transcend or disavow race is usually connected to our related ability to mimic, however incompletely, an ill-defined white masculine. Ironically, the white masculine is ill defined because, in practice, it is described ultimately by what it is not—not abject, not other, not marginalized. Of course, when those of us who are outside this boundary fail, when we are unable to adhere or do not desire to adhere to this prescriptive frame, the fault is presumed ours, an indication of our undue focus on race, on gender, on sexuality or some other salient facet.

The new respectability politics of the twenty-first century thus sound like the old respectability politics as the object is perceived by the one who is not objectified. If the burden of respectability is ultimately on the marginalized population, then the only ethical terrain respectability leads to is one that continues a cycle of burden and marginalization, where those who have little power struggle to be accepted and seen as similar to those with greater power. Fred Moten asks, "Have you ever suffered from political despair, from despair about the organization of things? What does it mean to suffer from political despair when your identity is bound up with utopian political aspirations and desires? How is identity bound up with utopian political aspirations and desires? How is identity reconfigured in the absence or betrayal of those aspirations? What's the relation between political despair and mourning?" (93) Kaleidoscopic Blackness eschews the respectability that delimits behavior and instead acknowledges *all ways of being Black as valid forms of identity.* What contemporary African American satire seeks to do then is make clear that a supposed post-racial utopia cannot imagine kaleidoscopic Blackness, or any Black futures at all.

While writers and performers of color have always agitated against the limiting parameters of racialization, the difference is that in recent years, joke telling itself has worked even more overtly to push back against this ill-fitting generic contextualization to seek justice on the levels of individual and communal identity. In this way, the satirical emerges as an *unmasked* framework for examining Black identity formation in the twenty-first century—there is a greater emphasis on the message, often overtly stated, than on the comedy itself. It is the innocuous and deceptive nature of satirical joke telling, founded often on plausible deniability, that made it such a useful vehicle for veiled denunciation of unjust social frames in the past. It is reinvigorated as a space for unambiguous critique in this contemporary moment by the absurd post-racial mythology as a persistent albeit unsustainable frame for understanding selfhood. Ultimately, the mainstream insistence on the post-racial is connected to this twenty-first-century explosion of African American satire. The post-racial mythos emerges as a legacy of the racial abstraction that followed the interest in multiculturalism of the 1980s and the neoliberalism of the 1990s, both of which supposedly reached a pinnacle of sorts in Obama's election in 2008 (and his 2012 reelection). However, a different sort of politics has come into play after 2016 where, given the ascendancy of Donald Trump and the presence of alt-right neo-Nazis marching in the street, many proponents of post-raciality have had to relinquish their devotion to this fantasy.[4]

We can see the relationship between satire and selfhood as far back as during slavery, the period when Black people were most overtly and legally disempowered, and how it relates still to the satire deployed during the post-soul era, an era marked chronologically by those born post–civil rights movement, who reckoned with the promises and disappointments emerging from that era. And the satire of this moment is just as crucial as what came before. That Obama's presidency was marked at its end by the ascent of Donald Trump as his successor only reifies this sense of absurdity in view of the supposed promises of both equality and equity in the nation and the actual lived experiences of Black people in the United States.[5] Therefore, the articulation of power through the comedic realm is denaturalized in important ways regarding racial performance, the occupation of space, and self-actualization.

In the articulation of power, both writer *and* performer are significant. By situating their joking within the context of laughing to keep from dying, they seek to inspire revolutionary laughter, or laughter that itself inhabits a tricky space of simultaneous delight and sorrow to inspire justice. This laughter evokes contemplation and self-reflection that challenges the status quo. As author and satirist Percival Everett keenly explains, "Humor is an interesting thing. It's hard to do, but it allows you certain strategic advantages. If you can get someone laughing, then you can make them feel like shit a lot more easily" (qtd. in Shavers). To make someone "feel like shit," you must effectively open up an ethical frame in which they acknowledge their own culpability in your objectification and are then forced to reckon with what accountability might look like. The laughter lowers the guilty party's defense of self-preservation enough for them to register and begin to consider their own potential responsibility. Rather than strict didacticism or moralizing, these works disrupt the standard paradigmatic understanding of race and racialization and, through revolutionary laughter, hold the audience accountable.

The objective Everett offers is particularly useful in consideration of the real-world difficulty in and applicability of satirical humor. Contemporary satirical texts and performances, while they inspire laughter, also compel the audience to reexamine themselves and their complicity within the establishments being satirized. It is important to note here the relation between these two types of laughter emerging in the twenty-first century—the first is the "feel like shit" laughter meant to implicate the offender and hold them accountable, and the second is the "laughing to keep from dying" in which, through the implementation of the satire, the satirist asserts their own humanity, and the humanity of their in-group, in the face of its mainstream disavowal. This utility of the satiric is often directly related to the precision of its target and the ability of the satirist to effectively disrupt social norms and expectations not only of race and racialization but also of humor itself in a revolutionary portrayal of the self. For this reason, it is useful to consider satirists as writers and performers who reflect a sense of rebellious obligation and duty in their written or performed reflections on contemporary political and social events, what James Baldwin described in an interview with Kalamu ya Salaam as the obligation of writers "to be subversive. To disturb the peace" (36). Satirists intentionally subvert an understanding of humor as frivolous and demonstrate that the political and social import of comedy should not be disassociated from the laughter it inspires today.

African American satiric texts, performances, and events in the twenty-first century encourage movement into a new phase while refusing any outright dismissal of previous comedic stances and ideologies surrounding Black identity—it is the repetition with a difference that doesn't erase the past but shifts frames for viewing; it is a reinvention, rather than a razing to the ground. Is it, as Kwame Anthony Appiah describes the logical groundwork for the postmodern, "the rejection of the claim to exclusivity, a rejection that is almost always *more playful, though not less serious,* than the practice it aims to replace" (342, emphasis added)? If so, this contemporary satiric impulse is marked by a broadening space for play where satiric readings could naturally emerge. Here, it is useful to consider the contemporary impulse as acknowledging the salience of Blackness while simultaneously refusing its essentialization as abject as the preeminent factor in self-identity formation.

The contemporary era remains crucial in our understanding of race and racialization. It is a time when the aims of Black communities have become decentralized, or certainly less unified, in interesting ways after the acquisition of de jure rights. It is a time when a fight for justice begins to signal—particularly prior to the necessary Movement for Black Lives in response to the proliferation of filmed instances of police brutality and violence against Black people and prior to the presidency of Donald Trump and a return to an overt frame of racial essentialism (and racism)—an effort to achieve more intangible goals of self-actualization and transcend a binary view of racialization.[6] If we think of contemporary cultural production as what Appiah has described as a "space-clearing gesture" of the post in postmodernism, one that doesn't negate that which came before but instead opens up a venue for new play, we can move toward an understanding of this era that doesn't imply, as some have, that the utility of African American literature and culture has reached some critical, "post-racial" end. Indeed, the articulation of the impossibility of a post-race era may only heighten the need for this satiric production and its engagement with the multiple ways of being Black and performing Blackness.

To understand the stakes and continued relevance of African American satire in the twenty-first century, we must consider the historical context of African American satire, its trajectory, and how the past weighs upon the present. I want to discuss four historical characteristics that directly inform the twenty-first-century satiric impulse and are frequently rearticulated and reimagined in contemporary cultural production: the utilization of humor as a survival technique (as within the slave context), the comedic attention to stereotypes (as on the minstrel stage), the manipulation of racialized expectations (as in narratives surrounding racial passing), and the vulnerability inherent in negotiating the satiric line (as by Richard Pryor). These four characteristics most succinctly contextualize the twenty-first-century satiric sensibility and offer critical historical background for contemporary satiric manifestations. Indeed, the satirical mode and the subversive potential of Black satiric performance is intrinsic, even as far back as slavery. Jelani Cobb notes,

> Black humor out of necessity began as a series of inside jokes. The early records of slavery in the United States are filled with accounts of paranoid slave masters who hear slaves laughing and believe they must be the subject of the joke—a fear that works in the same way a person in a room with two others who are speaking a foreign language becomes convinced that they *must* be talking about him. But as the saying goes, just because you're paranoid doesn't mean you're crazy. (249)

What Cobb identifies as the origins of insider humor is a particularly useful conceptual framework for understanding the history and critical inception of African American satire. African American humor was shaped by the danger inherent to the chattel slave system and emerged as both catharsis and clandestine insubordination. Indeed, this reliance on laughter as a form of revolution is underscored in significant ways in slave narratives and letters from the formerly enslaved[7]—the subject matter was serious, but there are satirical moments meant not only to inspire laughter but to highlight the trauma endured by Black people and to indict white audiences for their silence or passive participation.

Even in moments that initially seem wholly lacking of humor, there was a sense of not only the anticipated "laughing to keep from crying" but also "laughing to keep from *dying*"—here in particular the sense that humor was necessary for day-to-day survival because it reinforced the humanity of both the joke teller and listener while secretly, simultaneously constructing an in-group positioned with more knowledge than their oppressor. In this context, laughing to keep from *dying* required calculation in the telling of jokes—if the comedy was overt, then the target had to seem to be the self-deprecating speaker, while the in-group recognizes this is false. Otherwise, if the target was located elsewhere—on the slave system or slave owners, for example—it needed to be veiled. For the enslaved, when these jokes are waged effectively, it's revolutionary and they *can give you life;* when there's a misfire, the results are potentially disastrous. It is and has always been this laughing to keep from *dying* that expands the individuality of Black interior space into the ethical terrain of collective justice by articulating a selfhood that reaffirms the shared experiences of Blackness within the kaleidoscope of individuality.

In an effort to endure the horrors of slavery not only with their physical life but also with their selfhood intact, the enslaved would often feign a submissive persona, what Mel Watkins describes in *On the Real Side* as "an obsequious *social mask*" (50, emphasis original). This mask was meant to deceive the oppressor and provided the enslaved a subversive form of resistance—and, often, comedic resistance. By purporting to be lazy, foolish, or weak, not only did they foster a dynamic in which they reduced their own productivity (and the master's profit margin) but this subterfuge offered a degree of protection where the seemingly *unknowing* slave would not be viewed as a threat, even when they were. In keeping one's true self hidden, the enslaved could protect clandestine vestiges of their selfhood, demonstrating that even within the context of the slave system there were some things that the master could not own. It is this sort of calculated deception in slavery that laid the groundwork for the continued doubleness of African American satire in the twenty-first century. Indeed, the satiric ability to ridicule the systemic oppression of the slave system and its twenty-first-century aftereffects was and still remains a useful way to demonstrate one's cleverness, feeling, and, ultimately, one's own humanity in the face of its constant denial.

It is important here to emphasize that while the enslaved worked to prove their humanity to white Americans, this was not because there were any doubts raised in their own minds. Indeed, in 1848 when Frederick Douglass wrote to his former master, Thomas Auld, of his escape, "In leaving you, I took nothing but what belonged to me, and in no way lessened your means for obtaining an *honest* living. Your faculties remained yours, and mine became useful to their rightful owner" (*Oxford Frederick Douglass Reader* 104, emphasis original) he incisively states that, even before the chronological marker of Emancipation, African Americans understood that they were being denied the right to selfhood. Yet because possibilities for self-actualization were so limited within the context of the chattel system, the enslaved worked to reify their selfhood in ways to subtly position themselves as advantaged against white people. Writing to Auld "I am your fellow-man, but not your slave" (107), Douglass is able fully to articulate the chiasmic shift he first notes in his *Narrative* from the unnatural imposition of slave to his rightful humanity. Likewise, Sojourner Truth, in her famous speech delivered to the 1851 Women's Convention in Akron, Ohio, dwells in the interstice of race, gender, and slave status and refuses a notion that would deny her humanity due to her inability to fulfill any, or all, of the requisite frames for (white) womanhood.[8] While the enslaved were aware of their own inherent human-ity—and it should come as no surprise that they were, of course—articulating their humanity in surreptitious and substantive ways remained the challenge.

Moments of satiric dissent offered a necessary sense of self in the face of slavery's attempts to diminish and deny selfhood. While the use of satire of-fered moments of psychic freedom from the brutality of the chattel system, it also reinforced many of the negative stereotypes surrounding Blackness that persist to this day, their subversive usurpation forgotten or lost to main-stream historical accounts. The belief in the inherent laziness and stupidity of the slave was, in many cases, the result of being fooled by carefully crafted diversion tactics against suspicions of insurrection or discontent. Yet for the enslaved, this was a way to express displeasure under the guise of naiveté. This methodology extends into twenty-first-century African American satire as satiric personas adopt and revamp the existing tropes and ideologies.

Much of the commentary about humor in slavery usually begins and ends with a focus on apocryphal jokes of unknown origin attributed to nameless enslaved individuals and the later retelling of these jokes on the minstrel stage during Reconstruction. But what if we consider that satire was utilized in subtle and significant ways in slave narratives as an entry point to understanding contemporary satire? Most firsthand accounts of slavery are not traditionally considered *humorous,* for clear reasons, and are analyzed instead for their political and social import. To think about slave narratives in this way is useful, but to *only* do so is a disservice—in a desire to assure modern audiences of the intelligence and mental strength of slaves in the face of much modern reluctance to address the history of the chattel system at all, this simplistic treatment ultimately minimizes them, turning them from multifaceted and complex into ascetic.

As a result, many contemporary audiences cannot, or refuse to, imagine the reality of the trauma of slavery because they cannot imagine a slave that resembles a human in the first place. We must acknowledge the satire and the verbal play found in slavery's resistance to remember that without the outlet of humor, death is imminent—killed either under the weight of an oppressed self or by the master's lash over unrestrained insolence. Wrested humor not only offered an opportunity to prove one's intelligence in the face of the oppressor but the joke telling may also unexpectedly undercut the laughter and renders the mood somber rather than light. Carpio writes that the laughter inspired through slavery "is disassociated from gaiety and is, instead, a form of mourning" (7). In these twenty-first-century satirical readings, laughter is not disassociated from gaiety but instead exists simultaneously with mourning to create a psychic funereal space in which joy and sorrow—concurrent tears of joy for the gift of life of the person being memorialized and tears of sorrow at the overwhelming reality of their absence in death—emerge in tandem. The manifestation of these jokes does not imply that slavery was not an atrocity or that it was laughable in any way but instead heightens understandings of the trauma experienced through the demonstration of this critical survival technique. This subversive joking as self-making reaffirms the utility of satire as an ethical move in African American literary and cultural experiences. Pleasure exists in this space: the pleasure of being understood, the pleasure of defining oneself, and the pleasure of naming one's ancestors in one's own language.

Even after abolition, American society was structured to systematically marginalize Blackness—indeed, to move Black bodies to the margins both geographically and socially—in new ways in a realm of shifting definitions. A sense of (un)freedom manifests in persistent criminalization and targeted imprisonment, lynchings, continued and continuing police brutality, and chain gangs, to name only a few such spheres. Yet as society moves away from the chattel system, the roots of this marginalization fade and are replaced by a comfortable, absolving cultural amnesia that instead suggests that distance and vague sympathy suffice in thinking about slavery. Yet, sympathy is never enough. Instead, empathy is required for modern American readers[9] to understand not only the significance of the suffering attached to slavery but how this suffering continues to contextualize the present. It is painful but necessary—it is not, as has been argued, needlessly opening the scars of the past but instead examining and medicating the still-raw wounds that were never addressed enough at the start to heal in the first place.[10]

I turn from slavery to the satiric impulse in minstrelsy as the forms and functions of satire became even more overt acted out on the stage. In *Darkest America*, Yuval Taylor and Jake Austen rightly explain, "Despite the appearance of black minstrelsy as a servile tradition, there were elements of *liberation* in it from its very beginning, and these were instrumental to its popularity" (27, emphasis original). Certainly then, despite the shame tied to minstrelsy today, there is a direct trajectory from the minstrel stage of the nineteenth century to the African American stand-up comedy of the contemporary era in its efforts to create liberation through the self-actualization of the performers through an ironic—although not always read as such—embracing of stereotypes of Blackness. Indeed, this performance underscores the intelligence of the performer in their ability to identify and mask the irony of the joke telling, to play the buffoon while negotiating a sophisticated critique of the oppressor.

Minstrelsy undertaken by African American performers had a subversive element and was often structured as Black comedy for Black audiences even in the presence of white viewers. What this means is that while the white viewing audience may laugh at the expected tropes of Blackness as performed, Black performers and audiences laughed at the foolishness of white audiences for believing in the myth of docile Blackness. As Eric Lott describes it, minstrelsy could in some contexts be read as "a derisive celebration of the power of blackness; blacks, for a moment, ambiguously on top" (29). Can this be construed as momentary justice? If we embark on a reading that embraces this possibility, then minstrelsy and the minstrel stage may have created space for an ironic emancipatory performance in which these actors could avail themselves of the negative stereotypes of Blackness in a gesture toward establishing communal selfhood. If a Black performer knew the portrayal was false—and, again, in most cases they surely did—the performance ultimately may have been a critical lens through which the performer and the performer's in-group could bear witness to the reality of society. Indeed, here the performance would indicate that the viewer, rather than the object being viewed, was the fool worthy of ridicule.[11] Of course, whether or not the audience was willing to accept this meaning is a different issue.

On the minstrel stage, the performers knew these caricatures were offensive, and yet one possible reading indicates that choosing to perform these roles acknowledged the prevalence of these ideas surrounding Blackness and a simultaneous delegitimizing of them for Black people. Perhaps the innovator of this performance—or, more specifically, the performance within the performance post-Reconstruction—was African American blackface actor Bert Williams.[12] In his performance, charcoal-enhanced Blackness became both literal and figurative mask, as Bert Williams delegitimized stereotype as fiction by indicating that he was a laughable darky while wearing it, but expressly *not* without it—a message that was meant to be lost on white audiences, but not Black. Even seemingly self-deprecating humor emerging from disparagement—from the audience's belief in its own superiority as compared to the subject of the comedy—could offer an ironic protection and a momentary reprieve from the weight of actual lived experiences of racism. This perception of the performance as inconsequential and merely a joke was ultimately important in reifying an in-group understanding of dynamic Black selfhood.

The multiple facets of this satirical performance were not intended as just an in-joke or a punching-up laugh at the expense of those at the pinnacle of the racial hierarchy. This clandestinity was absolutely necessary for survival. Even as minstrel performers made white audiences laugh, not only were their tenuous *livelihoods* but their very *lives* on the line. In 1902 Louis Wright, a minstrel performer with Richards and Pringle Company, was hanged following an interrupted performance. As he and his fellow actors walked through the St. Louis streets, white bystanders launched snowballs at the men and taunted them. In response, Wright turned and allegedly cursed the men. Shortly thereafter, the performers took to the stage, where the taunts erupted into a riot during which Wright was reported to have drawn a pistol and fired into the crowd, with others returning his fire.[13] Wright was arrested, subsequently taken from the jail, and then lynched. His battered and beaten body was shipped back to his mother's home in a pine box (Watkins 100–101).

The public nature of this trauma sheds particular light on the necessity of doubleness in Black satire, which we can see in close examination of the chain of events. What is especially interesting is not that Wright was lynched for supposed insubordination but that he was not publicly punished for his *defiance before his minstrel performance*. As the story is recorded, Wright was attacked in the street verbally and with snowballs, and he responded in kind. Yet this defensive maneuver was allowed and did not result in any clear punishment or immediate violence—he was given the false opportunity to make amends through his performance of these negative tropes of Blackness. Was it the promise of the minstrel mask that offered his temporary protection? Even that expected portrayal was insufficient for Wright, and the performance could no longer be undertaken once the reality of his personhood and humanity was made manifest through his continued refusal to conform to his expected role. It was once this veil was removed—once he disallowed the attacks on the stage and would not perform the stereotypical role of subservience and docility—that his Black body was viewed as a legitimate threat and made a public example.

The threat inherent in losing the minstrel mask meant some performances were necessarily so subtle that, stripped of context and intentionality for twentieth- and twenty-first-century audiences, they seem to lose their subversion and are taken as legitimate acts of servility. Certainly, now while racial performativity takes on new forms, this oversimplified specter of minstrelsy remains. It can be a precarious and risky situation for the satirist. When performers rely on old tropes and stereotypes of Blackness without this proper context, the results can be disastrous; when proper context is given and care is taken to prioritize meaning, the reality of laughing to keep from dying is amplified.

In the early twentieth century, existing conversations about racial performance continued. However, these discussions shifted from the mockery of blackface minstrelsy to include degrading concerns surrounding racial purity, miscegenation, and the potential ease of transgressing the color line—topics that underscore the absurdity of race and lend themselves to satiric readings. We witness narratives that eschew racial essentialism and demonstrate the fallibility of race by proving how easy it is to utilize racial assumptions for one's own benefit—to perform on the minstrel stage, to be sure, but also to engage in deception and play within race itself through stories of racial performance, racial choice, and racial passing. This is not, of course, to say that narratives surrounding racial passing *only* occurred in the twentieth century. Indeed, one of the earliest accounts, that of Ellen and William Craft, appears in the antebellum nineteenth century. Their escape to freedom was orchestrated through an understanding of the expectations of passing and a disruption of the binary upon which it operates. The light-skinned Ellen fixed her hair under a top hat and donned the attire of a sickly white planter traveling with "his" faithful slave, actually her husband.[14] Knowing that slave catchers would be searching for Ellen passing in a more obvious disguise as a white woman, the Crafts wisely played social and gender constructions to their advantage—William Craft records that his wife "made a most respectable looking gentleman" (210).

A look at these stories of twentieth-century racial performance and passing reminds us that essentialism was critical to a social understanding of Blackness. For this reason, the narratives surrounding passing, and racial performance more broadly, offer particularly interesting ways to reinscribe imagined racial difference and racial performance in their satirical reading. It is also why these conversations so often stoked implicit fear. In 1931's "Crossing the Color Line," Caleb Johnson writes, "One out of every ten persons in the United States bears the visible tinge of the 'tar brush,'[15] according to the last Federal Census. No statistics are available, naturally, of the number of persons who do not acknowledge their Negro ancestry but pass for white in their home communities and elsewhere, but it is a large and rapidly increasing number" (121). Johnson perhaps did not intend to fill his words with such satirical potential, but it is difficult to read this passage otherwise. The fearmongering in this statement is tangible—that it is impossible to quantify the increasing number of individuals passing for white while knowing with certainty that the number is "large and rapidly increasing." The title itself, "Crossing the Color Line," seems to indicate a visible demarcation that must be transgressed with no backward glance as if, like Lot's wife, those who do may find themselves turned into a pillar of salt for too fondly remembering their past.

Nevertheless, the context of these narratives is simultaneously meant to offer *some* relief from an impending terror mode because it allows that racial passing occurs, but also argues that the color line is impervious once crossed and that racial categorization is ultimately solid and secure—people are Black, or they are not. However, real-life accounts of passing by African Americans demonstrate the true permeability of the color line and provoke the satiric laughter of introspective self-making that comes from acknowledging the ridiculousness of racialized assumptions. For instance, in "I Investigate Lynchings," written by NAACP leader Walter White, he explains,

> The lynchings were not so difficult to inquire into because of the fact already noted that those who perpetrated them were in nearly every instance simple-minded and easily fooled individuals. On but three occasions were suspicions aroused by my too definite questions or by informers who had seen me in other places. . . . One other time the possession of a light skin and blue eyes (though I consider myself a colored man) almost cost me my life when (it was during the Chicago race riots in 1919) a Negro shot at me thinking me to be a white man. (254)

White acknowledges the dangers of both the white and the Black gaze while simultaneously articulating the ease of engaging the pass. Even in his recollection of danger, there is a wry realization of the ridiculousness of racial stratification, where he nearly met his own death because he presented as phenotypically white despite his own identification as "colored."[16]

These conversations surrounding passing focus on the eye as the ultimate deceiver where passing relies on expectations of race as presentation and expectations of presumed racial stasis. In this way, whatever "racial terror" is evoked by the possibility of passing is ultimately the fault of a white supremacist system that creates parameters that are, in a given set of circumstances, so simplistically understood and manipulated—it is not Black desire but white foolishness that opens up the space for passing.

Later twentieth-century satirical performances of race often placed ideas about racial difference and their comedic possibilities at the forefront. Richard Pryor is perhaps the most direct forefather of contemporary African American satirical production, and often actively heightened rather than feigned trivializing the significance of race in his material. What is most striking about his persona as comic is that he is consistently and unabashedly willing to make himself the joke even in the midst of his own introspection. While much has been made of Pryor's irreverence, he also enacted clear and unambiguous "punching up," where audiences identify that the status of the comic is lower than his subject—even when his subject was marginalized groups, he bore the greater burden of the target. In the case of African American comedic performance, this sense of punching up may lessen the fears of "airing dirty laundry" or unfair racial simplification. Pryor was all too willing to point out his own individual flaws to make larger points about racialization and the compounding impact of racism on Black collectivity.

As his comedic persona evolved and shifted, Pryor allowed the traumas of his own life, whether growing up in a brothel, familial loss, or rampant drug use, to become the framework for understanding his comedic persona and thereby illuminated personal and communal Black interior space. Watkins argues that "Pryor's cockiness and assertiveness was balanced by an introspection and vulnerability that permitted him to jest not only about the less manly or commendable aspects of his own personality but also about the less militant or exemplary aspects of black life in general" (558). As a result, audiences initially misread the meaning and lowered their inhibitions, and were led unawares to the realization of their own involvement and identification with the seeming laughing matter itself. Here, with Pryor, we see a covert shift to implicating the audience, which is accomplished by his overt focus on first-person narration.

This frame of vulnerability as an aid to understanding is most prominently on display in his sketch "Bicentennial Nigger," the closing track on the album of the same name. In it, Pryor adopts the persona of a Black man who has been alive since the Declaration of Independence and is now celebrating the bicentennial of the United States of America. His tone is affable as he recounts the history of the Atlantic slave trade and the history of chattel slavery and the related traumas of Black experiences in the United States. At the end of the set, he continues his forced jovial laughter, acknowledging, "Y'all prob'ly done forgot about it, yuk yuk yuk." His voice shifts unexpectedly out of character and back to Richard Pryor's as he gravely announces, "but I ain't gon' never forget it." This abrupt, jarring conclusion is not only the end of the set but the end of the album itself. Pryor ends an ostensibly light comic album by shifting to a direct assessment, through humor *initially*, of slavery and its lasting impact, seeking justice by eschewing the oversimplified "happy slave" trope and asserting his own connection to ancestral trauma and ancestral memory. While he laughs throughout, the laughter is clearly feigned, misplaced, and insincere. Here no joke is being told by way of the climax of the set and no humor is found in the satiric treatment of this serious subject matter. Pryor anticipates the twenty-first-century focus on message even in view of the comedic vehicle.

Forced, inappropriate laughter is meant to highlight that perhaps there are even some subjects that cannot be made into jokes, or certainly that the lasting impact is no laughing matter. It disarms through laughter and then, in the removal of the comedic mask, renders the laugher complicit. This transferal explains why even audience laughter begins to dwindle as the music to the "Battle Hymn of the Republic" swells. When Pryor shifts back to his own voice at the conclusion and forcefully asserts that he will never forget the history of African Americans, the laughter and music both abruptly end—there is no comedy here. Now audiences are not only forced to reexamine their understanding of the past set, a mere two-and-a-half minutes long, but also to consider the entire performative nature of the album in its entirety and their laughter throughout. Indeed, Pryor's own laughter is uncomfortable and uncanny—obviously feigned and grotesque in its insincerity. Pryor's decision to step away from this persona at the end, his assertion that he "ain't gon' never forget it," refuses what would be otherwise a death impulse. Instead, this momentary retreat from comedy becomes the act of self-making as Pryor articulates the experience of a people removed from their rightful originative home who now experience existence in cramped spiritual interstices, forced to labor as slaves or as clowns for the amusement and flourishing of a nation to which they have been continuously denied the full rights of citizenship. This is a jarring indictment from a satirist, particularly one at the height of his career, who could certainly choose to keep these traumas unspoken, or at least refuse to center himself in the crosshairs of these painful ancestral remembrances. Yet his aural shift from slave persona back to Pryor again eschews his own death or the possibility of being flattened by racist imagery that discounts racist history.[17] Pryor's vocal shift from the "Bicentennial Nigger" back to himself demonstrates a personal and public relevance that can only exist affectively through a performance of vulnerability. In this way, it is the strength behind the laughter, the vulnerable and dangerous reclamations of the grotesque and stereotypical, that offers a possibility of communal justice.

In what follows, I consider Black histories and Black futures to examine the continuing relevance of satire in African American cultural expression in the twenty-first century. The literature, performances, and events chosen are those that offer significant cultural commentary or are themselves critical cultural touchstones of the twenty-first century in view of ideas surrounding Blackness and Black identity. Each text offers a way to think about the ideology of laughing to keep from dying that emerges in the twenty-first century because of its widespread popularity, reach, or representative nature within its respective genre. These texts demonstrate the contemporary pervasiveness of the satiric mode and its related ability to reveal Black identities within the frame of kaleidoscopic Blackness. While not every text or event may be instantly thought of as satirical in a traditional sense, these are pieces that lend themselves to satirical readings in their contemporary context either because of their wry engagement with the ridiculousness of racial assumptions and their awareness that these assumptions work to stifle the selfhood of the racialized or because of their inadvertent reliance on racial assumptions to an extent that renders the portrayals in the work itself absurd. It is the capacious nature of satire, this possibility for reading African American literature, performance, and events as enacting a strategy of satirizing to reveal the inherent absurdity of and frustrations with continued racism and racialization, that offers context for twenty-first-century African American cultural production.

Chapter 1, "'The Storm, the Whirlwind, and the Earthquake': Slavery and the Satiric Impulse," addresses the use of satire as a survival technique during slavery and the infatuation of the twenty-first century with the imagery of slavery for new satirical production. By acknowledging the ways that the enslaved used satirical reckoning to articulate covert selfhood in the face of its widespread denial, we can see that the figure of the slave becomes shorthand for racism and injustice to varying degrees of effectiveness for a wide variety of writers, including Jourdon Anderson, Suzan-Lori Parks, and Quentin Tarantino. These texts raise questions surrounding autonomous Black identity formation and the extent to which laughing to keep from dying might offer a sense of justice for the past and in the present.

Chapter 2, "'Race Is Just a Made-Up Thing': Abject Blackness and Racial Anxiety," continues to examine the possibilities for autonomous Black self-hood in view of Black interior space. For this reason, in their efforts toward justice, satires in the twenty-first century demand a move to a critical under-standing of race. I place in conversation texts and events as diverse as Keith and Mendi Obadike's eBay selling of "Blackness," Percival Everett's *Erasure*, the transracial passing performance on Donald Glover's *Atlanta*, and Touré's *Who's Afraid of Post-Blackness* to explore their indictment, or lack thereof, of a mainstream public for their perceived readiness to accept simplistic por-trayals of Blackness. These works reveal the psychic trauma enacted when the autonomy of Black interior space is discounted and disallowed. Here, laughter inspired by effective satire creates a potential means for escaping psychic death.

Where these texts and events often work covertly to uncover autonomous articulations of Black interior space specifically and of race more broadly, they are often at a greater risk of misconstrual. Chapter 3, "'When Keeping It Real Goes Wrong': Vulnerability and Satiric Misfires," addresses the is-sues that arise when satire misses its intended mark through what I argue are moments of misrecognition, misrepresentation, or misreading, and how these moments may lead to a problematic laughter that inadvertently reaf-firms rather than subverts troubling mainstream expectations. I focus on the satirical efforts of Chris Rock, Whoopi Goldberg, Dave Chappelle, and Leslie Jones to argue that the vulnerability founded in Black interior space may of-fer a means to avoid the most egregious misfires by reminding audiences of the speaker's own humanity, requiring the audience's active participation in discerning meaning from nuance, rather than accepting the joke on its face as uncomplicatedly infallible.

Chapter 4, "'How Long Has This Been Goin' On, This *Thang*?' Centering Race in the Twenty-First Century," examines Jordan Peele's horror movie, *Get Out*, alongside Issa Rae's HBO series *Insecure*, and in conversation with horror films and Derrick Bell's *Faces at the Bottom of the Well* to highlight the limits of laughter and the deliberate efforts in the twenty-first century to refuse racialized assumptions and embrace self-making, and the necessity of Black friendships and communities in establishing Black selfhood. These friendships offer strength and self-certainty necessary to refuse racial es-sentialism and are connected to the twenty-first-century desire to establish spaces for authentically and autonomously expressing Black selfhood. Ulti-mately, *Get Out* and *Insecure* offer an unlikely pairing that demonstrates new possible directions for unapologetic satire and satirical readings as political and social commentary in the twenty-first century.

Perhaps even more than in years past, African American satire is especially in need of greater analysis as a conscious and deliberate effort to examine not only the play of the satirical but of the dynamic reach and applicability of African American literature and culture more broadly. The conclusion, "Black Futurity and the Future of African American Satire," returns to Dave Chappelle and rearticulates a sense of twenty-first-century African American satire as focused not necessarily on inspiring easy laughter but instead on opening up space for Black selfhood and self-making. Ultimately, a post-Obama, *post*-post-racial United States demands that our satirists offer us productive ways to express Black identity and imagine ourselves in a world that seems increasingly self-satirizing. The twenty-first century requires our satirists offer productive ways to express autonomous Black identity—whatever that Black identity might be.

Critical consideration of the past is necessary for a deeper and more impactful understanding of the contemporary era. How our ancestors resisted, and even *that* they resisted, is a necessary framework for understanding resistance today. As a result, any discussion surrounding twenty-first-century African American satire must begin with the ancestral trauma of the past, starting with the chattel slave system. Revisiting these traumas can be painful, and can on the surface seem antithetical to even the potential for laughter, but as has been said, we need to know where we come from to know where we're going. The use of satire in these slave narratives and narratives about the image of the slave demonstrates a particular tenacity that should offer hope for present generations and remind us of the power of laughing to keep from dying to ward off the physical, spiritual, and psychic deaths that would otherwise disallow kaleidoscopic Blackness and consume Black people. And it explains why we are consistently drawn back to these narratives and images as a starting point. The satire undertaken in slavery was an active revolution, and it inspires the revolutionary laughter that keeps us alive in the twenty-first century.

"The Storm, the Whirlwind, and the Earthquake"

Slavery and the Satiric Impulse

> We should never forget slavery. We should talk about
> it every morning and every day of the year to remind
> this country that there's an enormous gap between its
> practices and its professions.
> —John Hope Franklin

> Slavery . . . is not funny. Like, it's not funny, you know
> what I mean? But if you can *make* it funny? Like, you
> gotta make it *real* funny.
> —Keegan-Michael Key as "Vandaveon"

I tried to avoid beginning this book with slavery. On its face, slavery seems anachronistic in conversations about satire and the twenty-first century. I worried that it might come across as too reductive or essentialist, or perhaps even melodramatic. After all, in the twenty-first century there are no former slaves still living in the United States, and African Americans are ostensibly freer than at any other point in the nation's history: as we are so constantly reminded, slavery was abolished. Yet I found myself irrepressibly pulled back to slavery as a frame for critically considering contemporary satire. What I discovered in this engagement is that I am certainly not alone. The deeper I delved into discussions about the twenty-first century, the more apparent it became that slavery was an unavoidable frame, and one that continues to inscribe meaning onto the lives of African Americans. The editors of *The Psychic Hold of Slavery* note that "our inability—or unwillingness—to 'get over' slavery emerges in relationship to contemporary philosophical debates about whether slavery serves as the distinguishing feature of black social life" (Colbert et al. 3). Indeed, notions of slavery and the slave inform a contemporary understanding of Blackness both owing to and despite the national reticence in naming the atrocities of the chattel system or apologizing for its horrors—the silences surrounding slavery only inadvertently remind us of its impact.

One of the most interesting ways that slavery is reemerging is in a renewed interest in nineteenth-century historical accounts in the twenty-first century. From the 2013 film version of *12 Years a Slave,* Solomon Northup's harrowing 1853 account of being captured in the North and sold into slavery, to Donald Trump's 2017 vague evocation of Frederick Douglass where he spoke of Douglass in the present tense despite his 1895 death, audiences in the United States desire narratives of the slave even as they question the continued significance of slavery itself, yet they become uncomfortable when these images are overtly conjured. It is slavery that defines the nation, and it is the figure of the slave that defines Blackness for the nation: it is not only what one has ancestrally witnessed but also the frame through which one is witnessed today through incarceration rates and suspicions of inherent criminality. Literal individual slave ancestry is irrelevant because the slave ancestry of the *nation* is the cultural paradigm for Blackness, debate surrounding whether it should still be notwithstanding. It is for this reason that the twenty-first-century satirist returns to the figure of the slave, and a critical examination of twenty-first-century satire requires an inclusive analysis of satirical inclinations at the beginning of African American cultural experience. The danger in ignoring these linked ideas is in potentially solidifying a reflexive belief in a contemporary moment that is only remarkable as a result of its own exceptionality, and a past that is easily pathologized as lacking nuance and humanity—too stoic, too oppressed, too humorless to be recognizable for modern audiences. This simplified removal of irony and absurdity does a disservice to any comprehensive understanding of the African American experience as lived in actuality because the satiric itself is a foundational part of the African American literary, political, and social tradition even and especially as far back as slavery.

To understand the nature of African American comedy and satire in the twenty-first century, it is necessary to begin by considering the utility of humor more broadly for the enslaved and, importantly, the continued hold of slavery on the contemporary satirist. Slavery and the figure of the slave still matter so much to the idea of the self in the nation—both for its Black and non-Black inhabitants—and physical Black bodies serve as tangible reminder of the legacy of the chattel system, our presence en masse seeming to be residual physical evidence. The presence of Black people reminds the nation of its sin even as the nation refuses to explicitly name the sin *as* slavery, and so these bodies remain contested and fraught. Margo Natalie Crawford argues in "The Inside-Turned-Out Architecture of the Post-Neo-Slave Narrative" that "remembering the trauma of slavery is often inseparable from the need to twist and turn this lingering pain *inside out*" (69, emphasis original), and it is this turning *inside out* that opens up a space for laughing to keep from dying—the laughter in a place of solemnity and trauma, of what would otherwise be social death and dying. It is this laughter that might lead to justice as autonomy, where justice is freedom to be without limitation or oppressive parameters that would punish or otherwise discourage establishing selfhood.

To be clear, satire alone is not able to enact justice. Satire doesn't make demands—it reveals the social context and asks its audience to determine the next course of action. Satires open up space for laughter and for calculated silences. In consideration of slavery, these silences emerge in two contexts. The first is in what is *not* said but already known and understood where, if we are engaged, we can begin to imagine what justice might look like. It is in thinking about what justice and freedom mean in a twenty-first-century context that leads to the ethical terrain in which we consider how justice might be enacted. The second context is the self-conscious silence these satires create for audiences who are initially uncertain of how to respond. These satires often inspire the sardonic laughter that awkwardly breaks the uncomfortable silences after audiences reckon with their own culpability. This laughter recognizes continuing injustices in society, whether the satirist specifically names these injustices or not, and forces audiences to reckon with them. In this context justice might be best described as the right to express one's own identity without its authenticity or representation being questioned, a right that has often eluded African Americans in mainstream publics. Justice within the realm of laughing to keep from dying is not tit for tat, as justice is often erroneously described. It is reparative, not retributive. This is not to say, of course, that vengeance does not have its pleasures. Indeed, a retributive frame may emerge through the satiric mode in the twenty-first century, although it is frequently seen in more nuanced ways—objectification of the oppressor or demands for payments that the speaker knows will not come are common—rather than any expectation of violent quid pro quo. In the context of laughing to keep from dying, retribution is secondary to a refocus on self-articulation and self-determination.

Perhaps nowhere is the connection between African American satire, laughter, and possibilities for justice more defined than in the use of the image of the slave in the twenty-first-century. What follows addresses the subtle naturalization of satirical humor by the enslaved as a survival technique in the eighteenth and nineteenth centuries, the reasons contemporary African American satirists have returned to the ideologies and imagery of slavery and the slave in the twenty-first century, and the possibilities for justice within the ideology of laughing to keep from dying. Indeed, it is the humor—subtle and intermittent though it may be—evoked in these narratives that reaffirms the seriousness of slavery itself in its ironic juxtaposition. For this reason, not only was humor valuable to the enslaved within the context of the chattel system but it remains a valuable touchstone for satirists in the twenty-first century as they engage the context of continued racism and racialization today through the figure of the slave. Moreover, where the figure of the slave becomes a sort of racial shorthand for Blackness, twenty-first-century recognition of slavery as if not an atrocity, at least a national embarrassment, frames the figure also as shorthand for injustice. As a result, these texts and performances demonstrate the varied efficacy in using the figure of the slave to highlight changing contemporary spheres of injustice as they compel audiences to rightly question what justice for the past might look like.

I begin with Jourdon Anderson's letter "To My Old Master," a nineteenth-century exercise in truth-telling through the deployment of satirical silences, arguably one of the first texts to evoke satire within slavery to articulate selfhood to such powerful effect. Anderson responds in a satirical affirmative to his former master's request that he return to the plantation to work after the Civil War, sardonically enacting silences and understatement to remind readers of what they already know or suspect of the horrors of slavery, thereby indicting his former master while simultaneously couching his truth-telling in plausible deniability. I move from here to neo-slave satires with a focus on damali ayo's performance art and satirical manual, *How to Rent a Negro,* which articulates the ways slavery continues in the twenty-first century through its psychic toll on Black minds and bodies. Through this text, ayo demonstrates the persisting relevance of the chattel system on the United States through intraracial relationships and the continued use of slavery as a shorthand. Similarly, through the trope of "renting a negro," ayo imagines a new realm where if the justice of freedom of expression is disallowed, then retributive monetary payment for psychic trauma may suffice.

Suzan-Lori Parks's *Venus,* which re-creates the historical narrative of "The Venus Hottentot" with a twenty-first-century emphasis on autonomy (or a lack thereof), reminds us of slavery's lasting reach and the limits of racialized autonomy. I end with Quentin Tarantino's film, *Django Unchained,* to examine the stakes when slavery is enacted as a trope with little attention to affect. Tarantino is particularly significant here because his use of the image of the slave, his eagerness to engage African American film tropes and vernacular sensibilities, and the mainstream success of his appropriations unintentionally offer a satirical reading in its over-the-top and racially simplistic absurdity; it problematically implies that race and racism are synonymous, naturalizing racist terror and essentializing Blackness to close off possibilities for a more comprehensive and just Black identity.

This affective potential of satire continues to matter so much for a just articulation of selfhood, and it is the specificity of these communities that offers particular context to African American satire and comedy in the present. I focus here on a notion of communities because, again, while there may be no monolithic Black *community*, Black Americanness is intrinsically linked to the ancestral trauma of slavery, even without its members having experienced literal slavery in a twenty-first-century context. It is a communal experience that marks Blackness in this nation; it is a communal experience that is particular to Americanness and to *Black* Americanness in form and function. It is through the figure of the slave, when enacted effectively, that we might approach a better understanding of kaleidoscopic Blackness and the multiple ways of being Black where Blackness is not merely one thing but has certain similarities of history that may frame the way it is experienced and performed in the public realm.

The Continued Significance of Slavery

It's clear, then, that the nation continues to understand itself through the re-memory and memorialization of slavery. It is Black identity against which the nation at large defines itself—*not* Black, *not* abject, *not* slave. The need for slavery in nation building precipitated racial categorization as contemporarily understood by serving as a justification for the chattel system and the excuse for attempting to strip humans of their humanity. In this way, race must be understood as not only a *social* construct but a *political* construct as well. If racialization as understood in the Western world emerged as a necessary justification and legal frame in which chattel slavery could occur—if the desire to enslave did, in fact, beget race—then there is no escaping the continued significance of slavery today because of the continued significance of race today. It is for this reason that I resist the idea that slavery is an unnecessary and overdetermining factor in the contemporary lives of African Americans—the reality of Black life in the nation is marked explicitly by the history of slavery and the invention of race and racialization as its justification. Slavery offers the initial content and continued context, and there can be no possibility of justice without reckoning with the continued significance of the slave.

For this reason, there also needs to be an emphasis on the nature of *living* history at the heart of any comprehensive inquiry into cultural production. In its engagement with the iconography of the slave, African American satire continues the line represented by the Sankofa bird of the Akan tribe of Ghana that looks backward as it continues its forward progression and declares, "go back and get it." Rather than locating discrete and distant points on a line, we must consider the ways the past, present, and future work in concert, and the way the present reclaims and reanimates the past and anticipates the future. We must disabuse ourselves of the idea that the historical is grounded in static memorialization only. Manning Marable further elucidates the necessity of a more substantive and evolving application of history when he explains,

> We all "live history" every day. But history is more than the construction of collective experiences, or the knowledge drawn from catalogued and stored artifacts from the past. History is also the architecture of a people's memory, framed by our shared rituals, traditions, and notions of common sense. It can be a ragged bundle of hopes, especially for those who have been relegated beyond society's brutal boundaries. (3)

Marable's definition, that history is "framed by our shared rituals, traditions, and notions of common sense," refuses the inclination to treat the past as something that has, in fact, *passed*. Yet even within this nuanced notion of a historical present, Marable is right to express concern that as we move away from imagining the historical as lodged soundly in the past, there is a risk of the new relevance tending toward the oversimplified—that a new context may breed euphemism rather than humanism. The denial of the nuances of a historical Black self is a tacit and unconscious denial of Black humanity that has far-reaching implications on our understanding of present Black personhood; we must understand our past to understand our present. We must "go back and get it."

Satire both within history and as present practice offers nuanced, subversive performances of race and what it means to be racialized as a way to deconstruct the white supremacy and white gaze that define Blackness by white expectations. What this means, then, is that when Blackness is proven malleable by those endowed with it, whiteness is no longer privileged for its ability to force ascribed parameters on everyone else. In consideration of satire and comedic output in the twenty-first century, what might laughing to keep from dying through slavery mean both in periods of de jure disenfranchisement and during a contemporary period where social rights—and, some have argued, social justice ideals—have been supposedly obtained? If social justice ideals in this context look like self-making on individual and communal levels, how might laughter open up this space in the context of the re-memory of trauma? Here, when revolutionary laughter breaks through the silences, it becomes a spirit-filled funereal exercise in which mourning and rejoicing occur simultaneously; it offers the peace necessary for clear-eyed self-making in the wake. It is a laughter that may even ward off the literal bodily death produced by the brutality of the chattel slave system but also the slow-acting "dying on the inside" enacted by the stripping away of selfhood. The satiric in the twenty-first century returns to the imagery and rhetoric of the slave and slavery to examine contemporary realms of power and powerlessness through cultural shorthand.

For this reason, it is important to reiterate that even as early as the nineteenth century, African Americans were aware of the power of satire and signifyin(g), the verbal play that dwells in the interstice of what is (or is not) explicitly said, as a mechanism for self-actualization—this is no new feat and satire is a part of African American cultural heritage. I am reminded here of Frederick Douglass's 1852 speech, "What to the Slave is the Fourth of July?" in which he addresses the affective potential of irony, explaining,

> At a time like this, scorching irony, not convincing argument, is needed. O! had I the ability, and could I reach the nation's ear, I would, to-day, pour out a fiery stream of biting ridicule, blasting reproach, withering sarcasm, and stern rebuke. For it is not light that is needed, but fire; it is not the gentle shower, but thunder. We need the storm, the whirlwind, and the earthquake. The feeling of the nation must be quickened; the conscience of the nation must be roused; the propriety of the nation must be startled; the hypocrisy of the nation must be exposed; and its crimes against God and man must be proclaimed and denounced.

It is the honesty unveiled by irony, by ridicule and sarcasm, that might conquer hate and injustice by revealing it and leading to an ethical terrain, not by merely reveling in a sense of congeniality or united laughter but because there is a disruptive possibility that creates spaces for self-making. Here it is the immediacy and the power of the sardonic that, in Douglass's estimation, might serve as indictment when waged with intentionality. The comedic during this period of slavery is often addressed in terms of its subtlety, and so Douglass's identification of the *need* for irony as a form of social justice—that, in the case of abolition, it might *only* be irony that fully agitates against the status quo—is striking. Douglass elucidates the idea that both the possibility and the practice of laughter may contain the revolutionary potential that opens into an ethical realm in which the conscience of the nation may be awakened for freedom.

Slavery is contemporarily conjured within satire through the evocation of its historical facts and functions, including reinterest in nineteenth-century documents of slavery, and in the transplantation of the historical onto the present in what can be termed neo-slave satire.[1] In this way, we see that what Saidiya Hartman describes as the "afterlife of slavery" not only impacts the quotidian experiences of African Americans in the twenty-first century but also becomes a shared language through which a twenty-first-century conception of Blackness continues to evolve. If we contend that the contemporary era is founded on the myriad ways of performing and experiencing one's own Blackness, then this idea of the reality of slavery as a universal and foundational piece of Black *experiences* takes hold. What this means is that personal experiences of slavery are perhaps irrelevant; it is the framework that slavery provides in understanding racialization as predicated on a series of relationships of hierarchical difference that matters in the articulation of race today, and that lends itself so neatly to the continued satirization of ideologies surrounding race. Ultimately, as the racial hierarchy defies frames of justice, the figure of the slave signifies injustice in its personification. The slave as an image then becomes a clear symbolic representation of the horrors of racism and, when utilized effectively, demonstrates a contemporary need for justice outside the frame of contemporary de jure freedoms—that ethics and legality are not synonymous.

As a result, we witness a return to slavery through an overt rearticulation of the imagery of slavery or through the rhetoric of continued appeals to white or racialized power structures. GerShun Avilez notes that within the contemporary era, there is a destabilization of "not only the racism that is embedded in White American identity, but also the asymmetrical power relations, which the rhetoric sets in place, that come to define U.S. racial identity" (30). Indeed, it is revolutionary laughter that offers one potential avenue for destabilization. The interest in contemporary motifs of slavery in satire shows the continued relevance of slavery as a frame for satirical discourses of race and justice by revealing the importance of the rhetoric itself to underscore the instability of the racial binary—the use of rhetoric to reframe and reclaim the past to alter modes of contemporary understanding.

Whether it is the reemerging overt interest in slavery as rhetoric or image, or broader appeals to and critiques of systemic power by those who have been otherwise rendered voiceless, the satiric mode contemporarily engages notions of Blackness as abject by revealing the *changing same* strictures on Black bodies and Black lives. In this way, there are broad critiques of white supremacy and of stereotypes of Blackness. What these contemporary texts and performances reveal is that African American satirists are resisting more than ever the limits outwardly placed on Blackness specifically through the reclamation of the figure of the slave and by lifting the veil of the comic mask in their own articulations of dissatisfaction with their tenuous relations to power.

Slavery necessitated a particular reticence, and silence itself serves a purpose—the choice to be silent or to silence others either counteracts or enacts hegemony. These calculated silences on the part of the oppressed, taking the form of what one chooses to say or not say to the oppressor, and how one keeps interior identity clandestine, work against erasure by altering the existing narratives surrounding slavery. It is here that the continued utility of the figure of the slave emerges. In many cases, nineteenth-century accounts of slavery utilized understatement and intentional silences as a rhetorical distraction—the true, veiled meaning could be located in what was *not* being said. These moments worked to restore subjectivity to the objectified by creating space to articulate the narrative for themselves and to refute traditional shallow representations. These silences can be interpreted as satirical gestures as they subvert expectations of power dynamics by withholding some reality from those who believe that they know all and own all. Satire underscores the absurdity of slavery and opens up into the potential of revolutionary laughter, of laughing to keep from dying. It is here that silence highlights both what remains to be said and what audience members are called upon to imagine for themselves as they wade through these calculated silences.

Even more specifically, the use of subtle satirical absurdity in narratives written by slaves and in twenty-first-century narratives evoking the image of the slave highlights the gravity of slavery by drawing our attention to the preposterous extents and mental gymnastics to which oppressors must attend in justifying the slave system and refusing the ethical terrain. In a twenty-first-century context, slavery takes on a second life through the process of re-memory, where understanding emerges in the mind of the person doing the remembering, but also in how the memories are disseminated into the broader political and social realm, into what becomes public memory. Contemporary satirical artists, for example, utilize the firsthand accounts of slavery in their ancestral memories alongside stories prevailing in the public realm and then engage in the process of re-memory to translate these narratives into a twenty-first-century context not only to emphasize the humanity of their antebellum counterparts—an idea that should go without saying but often requires a reminder—but to consider if it is even possible to achieve ancestral justice for these ancestral figures by creating space in which the objectified might speak. In doing so, these artists operate in more overt terms than possible in a nineteenth-century context to restore subjectivity to those who have been historically denied it. These calculated silences and omissions of the past give way to thinking about the *appearance* of passivity; the sounds of silence create space to reclaim and redistribute voice for the objectified.

In thinking about voice in these narratives, it is imperative that we move from notions of fearful reticence as the *only* response to slavery in its time because so many of these silences and moments of understatement were structured not out of fear, or not only out of fear, but as intentional space where the enslaved could lead their listeners or readers to the most productive conclusion without stating it outright. These tactics were brave and risky, and not motivated by base trepidation alone. We must think about resistance in slavery and resistance *as* reclaiming slavery in terms of Henry Louis Gates's articulation of "signifyin(g)," what he calls "the figure of the double-voiced" (*The Signifying Monkey* xxv). The idea of the satirical mode attached to slavery is intimately established in this double-voice, the possibility of remembering otherwise and speaking otherwise—saying, or not saying, what one means. In this sense, the figure of the slave becomes not only the signifier but the signified. It is Black representational rhetoric and the recognition of kaleidoscopic Blackness.

Silence operates as a supposed masking of emotion that forces us to recall and enact re-memory to fill in the lacunae. What this means is the satires that evoke slavery, both contemporarily and throughout history, utilize silences to compel audiences to reckon with the national (sub)consciousness surrounding slavery. The silences ironically intensify meaning by directing the focus of this re-memory and forcing audiences to consider what justice might look like in spaces where injustice cannot even be articulated. Gates continues, explaining, "Thinking about the black concept of Signifyin(g) is a bit like stumbling unaware into a hall of mirrors: the sign itself appears to be doubled, at the very least, and (re)doubled upon ever closer examination. It is not the sign itself, however, which has multiplied . . . only the signifier has been doubled and (re)doubled, a signifier in this instance that is silent." (44). This connection to an understanding and re-memory of slavery and *silence* through satire is significant. It is not only what is said but what is left *unsaid* and how we ultimately respond to it that frames these critiques.

Historical Engagement

The significance of the spoken/unspoken dichotomy is elucidated in Jourdon Anderson's 1865 letter to his former master, which has gained prominence again in the twenty-first century, in which Anderson engages the satirical in a response to the request that he return to the plantation to work after slavery.

What might the interest in this particular nineteenth-century letter in the twenty-first century indicate about our (re)investment in the satirical treatment of slavery in a modern context? It seems to demonstrate our desire for nuanced depictions of the figure of the slave and a broad refusal of traditional oversimplifications that render the enslaved passive. In this letter, Anderson responds to his old master's postbellum request that he return to the plantation to work by asking for payment for his years of previous unpaid labor and requesting clarification of the terms of his potential employment. While the nature of the terms that the former master offers are unclear, Anderson's response weaves skillfully the witty and the sober as he satirically suggests his willingness to return to the plantation, given a certain set of provisions and repayments he knows his former master will be unwilling to provide. Anderson is able to navigate this potentially dangerous territory through a reliance on understatement and occasional silences and omission. The significant understatement and lacunae throughout his letter, coupled with a presumption of increased safety—*safer,* but not wholly *safe*—owing to geographical distance and the legal abolishment of slavery in the United States, render his letter if not fully above reproach then surely retaining enough plausible deniability for protection through his feigned naivete. Although Anderson does not engage in a full-length satiric endeavor—his tone vacillates throughout as he negotiates his new freedom in view of his enslaved past—it must be one of the earliest, and most grossly unexamined, pieces of African American cultural production that not only lays out the parameters for what justice might realistically look like but that also contains direct moments of satire, or that at least lends itself to a reading within a satiric frame.

Anderson remarks at the outset of his letter to his former master, "I have often felt uneasy about you." Considering his later account of the master-slave relationship between the two men, which removes any possible consideration of the "kind master" mythology, as well as our understanding of the chattel system, this "unease" can only be understood as an intentional understatement. Later in Anderson's articulation, we learn that his master was consistently cruel, including attempting to shoot the freed man as he left the plantation at emancipation. Indeed, emancipation afforded African Americans nominal freedom only within a comparative frame of the past. Anderson expresses tacit knowledge of the subtle shift in his status by limiting the terms and emotionality with which he speaks about their past relationship. By using the qualifier "uneasy," he rejects the request of his former master in unspecific and vague terms. Adopting that position, he protects himself, veiling his denotation through obscured language while the connotation remains clear—the language appears, on the one hand, weak and indirect, even as it solidly refuses his former master's entrance or ownership of him or his labor any longer. In "Signifying, Loud-Talking and Marking," Claudia Mitchell-Kernan explains, "To loud-talk is to assume an antagonistic posture toward the addressee. When it is used to censure, it reveals not only that the loud talker has been aggrieved in some way; it also indicates, by virtue of making the derelict public, that the speaker is not concerned about the possibility of permanently antagonizing his addressee" (325). As opposed to "loud-talking," the understatement here signals an antagonistic posture while retaining the plausible deniability that loud-talk rejects.

The understatement or lack of specificity is not meant to obscure but instead to highlight satirically audience's existing knowledge of slavery and the slave–master relationship. He does not need to tell us why he is uneasy; we already know. Therein lies the productive potential of satire in contested spaces. What *isn't* said reminds us that some things remain unspeakable; what *isn't* said proves there are still horrors available for immediate recall for both the author and the audience without naming them. It also reminds us that while freedom is just, it cannot offer justice for the past. It is this act of *not* saying—this satirical signfiyin'—that offers a possibility for selfhood as it refuses to do the work for us that we can and should do for ourselves, particularly when this work or these words place the speaker in even greater danger. He dismisses the need for any white-authored preface to serve as validation for his account of his own history, instead vouching for himself by addressing his former master's crimes and the context of their relationship without initially naming the crimes.

Anderson continues, "I thought the Yankees would have hung you long before this, for harboring Rebs they found at your house. I suppose they never heard about your going to Colonel Martin's to kill the Union soldier that was left by his company in their stable. Although you shot at me twice before I left you, I did not want to hear of your being hurt, and am glad you are still living." His assertion that he assumes the man's death while presumably—and quite probably sarcastically—expressing relief that his former master still lives may elicit the wry revolutionary laughter of the darkly satirical impulse; it may evoke laughing to keep from dying, which allows him to reassert his master's treachery in a way that retains plausible deniability of any ill intent. In this moment, Anderson makes clear his new positioning as autonomous from his former master. Although he is (not yet) ready to name his former master's crimes against him, he is also unwilling to protect his former master by maintaining silence about crimes against *whiteness*. Here is the tacit acknowledgment by the formerly enslaved—by naming first his master's hidden acts of treason, crimes against whiteness and the nation, he establishes a frame in which his subsequent claims might be accepted and understood, because his former master is now identified as a war criminal and scoundrel. If silence was considered tantamount to the slave system, as the presumed allegiance of the enslaved to their master was necessary for survival, then Anderson, under the guise of stating his concern for his master, reveals his former master's treachery and treason. Once again, the steady, unassuming tone and shifting focus provides Anderson the opportunity to deny any ulterior motivation.

Here, Anderson takes the position of central power where his own narrative has primacy. Interestingly, once his response is published in the newspaper, Anderson's narrative is contextually validated through the recognition of the media. In this way, it not only reaches a more immediate audience but it publicly denounces the behavior of his former master while simultaneously positioning him as perhaps even benevolent in his forgiveness and in the absolution he extends the man. While this generosity may be exaggerated or feigned, Anderson articulates a morality that his former master lacks and, as such, asserts a sense of humanity his former master cannot claim. This is a subtle but powerful articulation of justice and selfhood, which reminds both nineteenth- and twenty-first-century audiences of the necessity of cleverness for physical and psychic Black survival throughout history. Anderson's articulation pushes back against damaging tropes of the noble savage or the kind master—the skillful doubleness in his meaning is critical. The sarcasm reveals the horrors of the slave system in what is said and what is silent in this ironic juxtaposition.

Nevertheless, there is a possible reading here in which plausible deniability takes hold—*was* Anderson glad to learn that his master was unharmed? This statement, following his exposure of Colonel Anderson's "harboring Rebs"—a treasonous act in the context of the newly reunited nation—is filled with clear potentiality even as his language is ambiguous. What protection might there be in a united nation that a fractured one denies? That he is willing to name his former master's war crimes while still positioning himself as sympathetic to Colonel Anderson's humanity is a feat that can only be accomplished through skillful circumlocution. The lacuna between what Anderson says and what he hopes to accomplish are filled through reader awareness of the history of expected behaviors surrounding Blackness. Is it possible, then, that Anderson is feigning ignorance when he announces without hesitation that his former master was unabashedly treasonous? It is difficult to read this passage without giving credence to that probability. In fact, his articulation is predicated on the trope of the docile, master-loving Sambo, to which he knows Colonel Anderson subscribes, as he switches from naming these crimes and then expressing joy that his former master has been left unharmed— taken together, a subversive gesture on the part of Anderson to reify and reclaim the negative trope to his clear satirical advantage, and one that anticipates future Black satirists in his lineage.

Without the letter of validation necessitated for slave narratives—although, again, publication in a newspaper does serve a significant role—and without the use of authorial pseudonym, Anderson is offered no implied protection by white abolitionists, and so his writing needs to be as specific as possible while retaining the silences that protect him from endangering himself. Even with the aid of an unnamed amanuensis, his engagement with his own understanding of his history reiterates his humanity in the terms of white citizenship. To this end Anderson creates a new frame that seeks to solidify his own autonomy and position in the United States. He writes,

> I am doing tolerably well here. I get twenty-five dollars a month, with victuals and clothing; have a comfortable home for Mandy,—the folks call her Mrs. Anderson,—and the children—Milly, Jane, and Grundy—go to school and are learning well. The teacher says Grundy has a head for a preacher. They go to Sunday school, and Mandy and me attend church regularly. We are kindly treated.

Anderson's insistence on familial naming and honorifics, those that specifically gesture toward more nuanced understandings of Black humanity and class status than are traditionally discussed in the context of identity formation in a chattel slave system, serve to assert his humanity and the articulation of his own selfhood—in terms of justice, it is the *least* he is owed from the world at large. This is not, of course, to imply that the evils of slavery can be eradicated via emancipation, through postbellum truth-telling, or through naming alone, but instead that staking a claim to one's own autonomous selfhood might open up justice in Black futures. His effort here is twofold. By claiming it for himself, Anderson is able to reassert his personhood by placing himself in the context of other citizens without overtly naming race— either his or theirs—as a salient quality. He instead dwells in the interstices of respectability politics to declare his family legitimate in clear defiance of his former master's sensibilities. One can imagine his former master's indignation on reading "the folks call her Mrs. Anderson," as Anderson situates himself as satirically meaning no disrespect in a mere statement of fact. This positioning is so significant as it stakes a claim to those trappings of humanity that were denied African Americans by their oppressors, and even by abolitionists who frequently fought for the end of slavery itself without advocating for, or even anticipating, the equality of the races.

In fact, it is Anderson's forceful and unapologetic positioning of himself and his family as equal to his former enslaver that makes the most overt claims to justice in the present and perhaps even to a possibility of retroactive justice for atrocities of the past. Anderson writes,

> [P]lease state if there would be any safety for my Milly and Jane, who are now grown up, and both good-looking girls. You know how it was with poor Matilda and Catherine. *I would rather stay here and starve—and die, if it come to that—than have my girls brought to shame by the violence and wickedness of their young masters.* You will also please state if there has been any schools opened for the colored children in your neighborhood. The great desire of my life now is to give my children an education, and have them form virtuous habits. (emphasis added)

The audaciousness of what he says—and what he doesn't say—is staggering. Anderson takes a somber tone as he refuses to name the danger his daughters would face, knowing that his audience—both the newspaper audience and his former master—are aware of the rapes and abuses suffered by women under the plantation system, and that emancipation serves as no assurance that these traumas would be disrupted.

Again, it is the act of *not naming*—the unspeakable things unspoken, to conjure Toni Morrison—that most plainly opens up the ethical terrain of the letter. This silence is the rhetorical crux of the letter, not only because he rightly assumes audience ability to discern his meaning but also because it is too painful for him to describe the events that took place. There is no laughter here, but the tactic underscores the revolutionary laughter of the sarcastic moments in their juxtaposition, and both are important to underscore the unparalleled horrors of slavery, even through satire; there is heightened emotionality throughout the letter, but the seriousness of the inhumane treatment in the slave system is highlighted through the juxtaposition of this overt, clear-eyed refusal versus earlier moments of lighter rhetorical play. In other words, there are surely deaths that laughter alone cannot prevent.

This moment where laughter is refused creates pseudo-silence as both the intended reader and the broader newspaper audience are able to instantly conjure these terrible images. His shift from seeming joviality to stoicism in these moments—similar to Richard Pryor's shift from seeming joke-telling to the implicit condemnation of "but I ain't gon' never forget it" in "Bicentennial Nigger," where Pryor's laughter literally gives way to the final, overwhelming silence of the end of the album—highlights Anderson's understanding of his past and his future. In fact, it is his use of the slyly comedic rather than the openly retributive that ironically works to highlight the seriousness of slavery and its inability to be repaid—it is the seeming incongruence that resonates, and when he returns to the grim tone to which audiences are accustomed, it reifies the impact of slavery on its survivors. This moment is brief but bold. There is no laughing to keep from dying because these deaths have already occurred. There are costs that can *never* be repaid and crimes that even vengeance cannot erase. The humorous turn draws in his readers, but this serious move makes manifest the necessity in writing and should remind twenty-first-century audiences of the lasting significance of slavery *even after* emancipation. He is signifyin(g) on his former master, daring his master to name these actions—"you know how it was"—and how this "violence and wickedness" might have taken form. These silences create the space where authorial intent meets audience understanding. It triggers recognition; even the former master's denial would require admitting that the frame exists and is always already known because he would have to admit knowledge of what was unsaid. Indeed, this may signal reasons for its popular reemergence contemporarily as it underscores the humanity of the slave. It shifts away from notions of the slave as either superhuman or subhuman, both of which are damaging constructions that deny empathy to the person who was enslaved and overwhelm our conceptions with an abstract figure of the slave.

Twenty-First-Century Slaves

Anderson's letter is important to our continued understanding of slavery. The letter represents a brief moment where Anderson has some ability to refuse his former master and corroborate well-suspected plantation secrets for a broader audience. In the public forum of a newspaper, his voice operates as a stand-in for the countless other enslaved and formerly enslaved who were disallowed the space and opportunities to speak. Performance artist damali ayo likewise creates space for the voiceless to speak as she reimagines slavery in an overtly twenty-first-century context. Based on her 2003 performance-project website, her 2005 book, *How to Rent a Negro,* satirically provides a venue for the selling of Black bodies, riffing on national history by endowing the African American participants with autonomy in their own sale for personal profit and reparations for unpaid debts. She explains,

> As we all know, the purchase of African Americans was outlawed many years ago. Now, black people are once again a valued and popular commodity. These days those who boast of black friends and colleagues are on the cutting edge of social and political trends. The roles of owner and owned have evolved, preserving the spirit and sanctity of the old relation-

ships without the hassles of long-term commitment, high prices, or their unpleasant features. (2)

Once again, the imagery of the slave emerges in the spaces between what is actually said. These "unpleasant features" force us to reckon with our own knowledge of the physical and psychic trauma of the chattel system and further insert it into a contemporary context. The assertion that her Rent-a-Negro business preserves the "spirit and sanctity" of former master-slave relationships, juxtaposed against the lack of these "unpleasant features" begs the question of what was inherent to the system and how it translates to a twenty-first-century context. And this seems to be the point. Here ayo shifts our understanding of commodification from the literal ownership of Black bodies for physical labor to the impermanent but ongoing renting of Black bodies for compounding emotional labor to underscore the continuing demands made on African Americans by an insatiable public sphere. By framing these rentals in terms of what has changed, ayo highlights the fundamental ways that race relations have not.

In ayo's estimation, Blackness is still commodity, and its value lies in its utility for white consumers—most performatively signaled in her use of the word "negro" as identifier. The terminology is especially interesting, not only because it exists as a rather outmoded classification of Blackness, but because of its malleability. The term itself now occupies a sort of liminal space between a racial slur and a more innocuous racial descriptor. It became less used beginning in the 1970s, when "Black" as an identifier became more prominent. Certainly, the appearance of "negro" in the title reminds readers of the twenty-first-century connection to historicity and to the term itself as a classification that implies abjection, and it is because of this connection we are jarred out of a complacent treatment of slavery as relegated to the mere past. The title *How to Rent a Negro*, despite its focus on renting rather than the permanence of *buying*, still marks a return to "negro" and addresses the entanglement of past and present, forcing us to reckon with the changing same of racialization.

In this way, as ayo notes, the "spirit and sanctity" of the relationship remains the same. It is this merger of past and present that matters so much in the explication of Black identity formation in the twenty-first century. It is a merger that reflects the self-satirizing changing same in the national understanding of race—the inability of these "renters" to separate the actual lived experiences as felt and articulated by Black people from the simplified tropes and ideation of history; a tacit desire to reify Black subservience in the simplest terms available. Even if the roles have evolved, the trauma lingers and frames contemporary interactions and expectations. What does the commodification of Blackness—of literal Black bodies[2]—mean in a twenty-first-century context? When Black physicality is no longer legally sold and purchased in a chattel slave system, *what* then is the commodity? Here, the haunting ancestral desire for and feelings of entitlement to Black labor now manifests as expectations of emotional labor; the overt racial abjection makes way for a liberal-racist ideology that pretends to eschew overt racism while it continues to deny Black selfhood and is more concerned with the use value of performative Blackness as modish accoutrements to whiteness.

In creating an argument for "renting one's self," ayo does not overtly name any psychological value to the selling of oneself, perhaps because there is not one. Monetary reparations serve as a potential stand-in for any other possible justice. But, in ayo's satirical estimation, this demand "takes place on a daily basis, virtually at any time, in nearly any location . . . without the consent or compensation of those being rented" (2). Instead, these intentionally structured silences create the spaces that refuse subjugation and imply a way to deconstruct the expected racial hierarchy—it quite significantly allows African Americans to own a portion of the fantasy as well, by imagining a form of reparations for the unpaid debt not just of slavery but of the continued burden of representational expectations.

If characteristics of African American personhood are being used as signifier without permission, and it is unavoidable that this commodification will continue, ayo suggests that by playing into these expectations and desires African Americans might profit from their own marginalization. In fact, she reserves a large portion of the text for instructing the Black would-be rented of ways to maximize their profit. She hastens readers, "Your ancestors didn't endure all that suffering so you'd forget about it. Use it to your advantage. There are ways you can evoke slavery, with savvy to the satisfaction of all" (122). This is not merely evoking the memory of slavery but a re-memory of the figure of the slave that permits a subversive illusory justice through satiric play while also subtly acknowledging that what was endured cannot be undone. Once again, there is no suggestion of returning harm with harm but instead she satirically imagines the changing same as holding possibilities of present justice as she shifts assumptions surrounding the benefits slavery affords—and *who* might benefit—in the twenty-first century.

This process of re-memory is critical in contextualizing both the past and the present. In some ways, it is easier to think of the slave as lacking the voice and selfhood we attribute to our contemporary age because it reassures us that this could never happen here or to us; whether we are descended of the enslaved or slaver, denying the humanity of the slave offers a false sense of protection or absolution. As a result, when we think of the silences surrounding slavery, we aren't able to think of them as subversive measures that veil the Black interior and retain a secret space that whiteness cannot see or own. However, this duplicity was a necessary survival technique because it positioned African Americans to appear subservient while allowing the space for private self-actualization at the expense of their oppressor—African Americans playing a prescribed role to indulge in the fantasies of white populations while retaining their own masked nuanced selfhood. A connection between the past and the present helps to explain some of the unease ayo's work inspires as it disrupts notions of the slave as not only inherently lacking radical potential but also lacking humanness.

Unsurprisingly, online responses to ayo's business-as-performance-art were uneven. In addition to praise for the inventiveness of her form or satirical rejoicing at the potential profit to be made, there were also predictable slurs and threats made against ayo herself, with accusations that her endeavor was "worse than slavery" (179). However, ayo's response makes most explicit the difference between slavery and current racialization and is one of her most powerful statements surrounding the trajectory of race relations in the United States: "It's not quite the same as being chained, starved, and overworked while living in subhuman conditions and healing from your latest whipping. Really, when you compare the two, I doubt you'd choose slavery" (179). It is the space of contested humor, the recognition of the absurdity of the comparison, where the potential for revolutionary laughter emerges. *Of course,* ayo's satirical play isn't worse than slavery—such an accusation attempts to shift the blame to the descendants of the enslaved for their lack of reverence as they attempt to mediate their emotions surrounding the lasting impact of slavery itself. Both ayo and her audience know this fact implicitly. What ayo does is create a darkly satiric response to the continuing legacies of slavery in contemporary society and consider what, if anything, present-day justice might look like in view of historical prologue. She reminds us, in this way, of Derrick Bell's articulation of the permanence of racism, manifesting in a changing same of racialization founded on the slave system—not slavery itself, but connected to the racist ideation that justified slavery and continues to justify the de jure and de facto secondary treatment of African Americans.

By evoking the real, systemic violence and physical labor experienced under the slave system and distilling it into the emotional labor of a twenty-first-century context, ayo reminds us that the difference between slavery and the consistent commodification of Blackness today is one of degree as both mean to exert power and superiority over Black people; to push back against this relentless exertion of power, ayo highlights the act of choosing as a potential frame for justice. *How to Rent a Negro* interrogates possible spaces of autonomy in the interstice of past and present Black identity. It is this possibility of choice—the choosing of Black identity formation and performance—that has such resonance in bridging the historical distance between slavery and the twenty-first century. In this way, slavery is an unavoidable factor of present Black existence as it provides context for racialized expectations, and it is the recognition of this unavoidability that might lead us into an ethical terrain where contemporary justice might be attained without implying that this rectifies the evils of the past.

Reappropriations of Slavery

In *How to Rent a Negro*, damali ayo satirically imagines a realm in which a frame of traditional abjection could turn into a benefit. However, even if we willfully sign on, is it possible to control our own commodification if we cannot control the means of our own distribution? Is this what justice looks like? It seems unlikely, even within the realm of satire. Suzan-Lori Parks imagines the problems and promise inherent in this idea in *Venus,* where she conceives the behind-the-scene story of the historical Saartjie "Sarah" Baartman, a woman from the Khoikhoi tribe of southwestern Africa who was exhibited as a "freak" in nineteenth-century Europe. The continued interest in this play highlights the recurring appeal of the slave in the twenty-first century and underscores the variety of forms this reappearance takes—not only firsthand accounts or contemporary extrapolations but also the continued utility of the neo-slave narrative and a desire to revisit historical figures in a twenty-first-century context. Not only have nineteenth-century accounts of slavery been reanimated contemporarily, but this twentieth-century reimagining has seen a revitalization in the twenty-first century, quite literally, through its recent revival (original production in 1996, off-Broadway revival in 2017). This play satirically imagines a Black object with assertive subjectivity—the object moves toward subjectivity not by refusing to be degraded but instead by using degradation to reveal truths about her oppressor's lack of humanity.

Although this play takes place outside the geographical Americas, Parks is an African American playwright, and she infuses the narrative with broader questions of enslavement and justice that have recurring contemporary significance for the nation. In this reimagining, Parks grants audiences insight into not only what Baartman *might* have experienced prior to her sudden and premature death but also how audiences might have been engaged and what passive culpability looks like. The play opens with the announcement of the death of Baartman, and scenes are numbered in reverse chronology—audiences are immediately made aware of Baartman's impending death, and are left to reconcile this information with the presentation of her living, doomed body. Parks is interested in the traditional exploiters and, even more, the possibility that exploitation can ever be a reciprocal arrangement or if it can ever lead to anything but the destruction of the exploited. This connection between exploitation and destruction is perhaps made most clear during the intermission. A scene runs concurrently with the intermission—"Scene 16: Several Years from Now: In the Anatomical Theatre of Tubingen: The Dis(-re-) memberment of the Venus Hottentot, Part I"—distorting the expectations of traditional form in a play. This scene stages the autopsy of Baartman and the subsequent quantification and qualification of her body. Here is a moment where the Black body is explicitly an object; she is afforded no respite from exploitation and there is no sense of autonomous peace, even in death. The stage directions read, "*Scene 16 runs during intermission. House lights should come up and the audience should be encouraged to walk out of the theatre, take their intermission break, and then return*" (95). What, then, to make of this direction that the audience "be encouraged" to leave and return? By choosing to follow, or even by choosing to ignore, this instruction, audiences become participants in how to frame their engagement with the play itself. Here, even the choice to do *nothing* cannot be passive—doing nothing is perhaps, ironically, the act of resistance itself. And, as the action of the play itself continues on regardless of the absence or presence of audience members, either choice signals complicity in the choice to watch or the choice to turn away. Far from an actual break, as spectators we give tacit approval of what we witness; if we refuse to watch, the action continues with our passive consent as we've done nothing—and, as we are witnessing the re-memory of history, *can* do nothing—to stop it. The intermission gives audience members a cursory sense of freedom of movement—they can leave, of course, but they will miss the continued action of the play. Like the Venus of Parks's imagining, while there may be some options for movement provided, only one possibility is tenable even as Parks encourages audiences to leave. This false choosing subverts expectations and refuses to give audience members relief or consolation—there will be no snacks in the lobby, no bathroom break, and no chit-chat with friends about where to go for drinks at the play's end. Instead, Parks intends for this to be and to feel like a *captive* audience.

There is discomfort in the realization that there is simply not enough that can be done to redress historical evils. As the intermission is the autopsy itself, Parks seems to remind audiences that even if we pull ourselves away from the action, the damage has been done, the death has been enacted, and the body broken and clinically examined. This intermission also offers Parks a further opportunity to signify on the structure of the play itself, where the intermission distracts from acknowledging the reality of Baartman's treatment—here Parks takes us beyond the horror of this display and reminds us that even in Baartman's untimely death she still remained an object to be seen.[3] There is no sense of reparative justice to be found, but Parks forces her audiences to reckon with their own complicity by demonstrating how easily disenchanted by and detached from atrocity we can become, disabusing us of comforting ideas of twenty-first-century altruism and naturalized activism. Even choosing here becomes an unsatisfactory form of reciprocity that reminds us that Baartman has never received justice and that justice can never be served.

Ultimately there can be no justice found here because if the Venus's desire to commodify herself and to find joy in her own consumption signifies on old tropes of Black objectivity, it does not change the reality that she is exploited and thereby doomed. The play begins with the death of the Venus, so even in this reimagining, the fantasy is tethered to the reality of her circumstances. Even her contemporary autonomy is limited, and despite her participation any frame she creates is still at variance with her literal imprisonment—whatever pleasure she is able to eke out does not ultimately become any lasting joy for the imprisoned. I am reminded of an NPR interview with comedian, author, and *Two Dope Queens* podcast host Phoebe Robinson in which she recounts being in a writing workshop where a white classmate wrote a story about a slave who refuses freedom because she was in love with the master's daughter. Robinson explains, "I kind of had to speak up and be like, you know, I don't think any slave would be like: 'Hard pass on freedom, I'm going to keep picking cotton so I can hook up with this chick twice a week.'" This clarification cannot be overstated. There is a recurring fantasy in the American popular imagination of slaves and masters falling in love, as if the unequal power dynamics and the inherent brutality of the chattel system wouldn't preclude such a thing. Once again, the refusal to consider the humanity of the enslaved leads to frames in which implausible relationships and affairs seem possible because the slave becomes mere object or vessel for the nuanced subjectivity of others. Perhaps nowhere is this belief more tightly held than in the numerous fictional accounts of Thomas Jefferson and the enslaved Sally Hemings, and the encounters that began in her teenage years and while Jefferson was in his forties. The situation cannot be construed as consensual by any stretch of the imagination, but this hasn't stopped films like *Sally Hemings: An American Scandal* or the book *Thomas Jefferson Dreams of Sally Hemings* from envisioning it as a tragic love story. What Parks does is remind us that, in the case of the Venus, imprisoned acquiescence does not imply consent and certainly does not mitigate exploitation and cannot lead to freedom. She reminds us that seeking justice requires a level of autonomy that some frames simply cannot provide even when imagined in the twenty-first century.

Overlaying the Present and the Past

If we think about the representation of the slave and potential exploitation, Quentin Tarantino's *Django Unchained* (2012) is an important film to consider. This is particularly true in terms of its active eschewing of the subtleties of silence and, problematically, Black public interiority. Even though it is not an African American film, or even necessarily a satire in the traditional sense, Tarantino has deliberately inserted himself into conversations surrounding Blackness and Black performance, imagining himself as a voice for a particular Black experience, even a voice for quantifiable Blackness itself. Moreover, the distortion of history for the purposes of imagined revenge coupled with the use of the image of the slave as a contemporary symbol lends the film to a satirical reading. That Tarantino chose slavery as the backdrop for this revenge plot demonstrates that slavery and Black trauma have been made to function as accoutrements, reminding us that while the image of the slave contains meaning, for many it remains malleable. In this way, the film's utilization of fearsome Blackness in slavery without addressing the private motivations or desire for self-actualization that would contextualize the performance is a failure indicative of Tarantino's own inadvertent self-satirizing impulse; without interior space to open as motivation for Django's seemingly revolutionary behaviors, the film only makes sense as a satire, although perhaps not in the way Tarantino intended. Not only this, but the implication that the horrors of slavery can be made right through revenge ultimately reveals Tarantino's inability to imagine justice in meaningful ways even as the material conditions of African Americans evolve in the nation.

Django Unchained simultaneously reimagines both the spaghetti western and slave narrative and merges them into a fantasy of male revenge. I am reminded of Patrice O'Neal's set in his *Elephant in the Room* stand-up routine, in which he satirically bemoans the failures of the post-racial by explaining a year before *Django*'s premiere, "I'm mad at [Obama] because I thought I'd have a white slave by now! I thought it was vengeance day!" Tarantino seems to expect and validate this retaliatory frame and reimagine it in a slave context. Yet despite its overt imagery of the slave, I still hesitate to call this film even a neo-slave production because the narrative does not attend to the implications of race outside a trite conception of Blackness as chattel, nor does it effectively center Django as its protagonist—although this is where its inadvertent satirical content most directly emerges. Indeed, although Will Smith was initially picked to play the lead, he turned the role down after he determined that Django was not the true hero of the story. Instead, as Smith rightly noted, the hero is Christoph Waltz's King Schultz, with Django acting as mere sidekick (Child). The film ostensibly places Django at its center, but its plot acts as a predictable vehicle for white saviorism. Although the narrative circles around Django's efforts to find his wife and take her to freedom, it is only through the tacit permission of and space created by Schultz that Django is even able to participate in his own supposed narrative. Here, there is no preface to Blackness, but instead an overreaching preface to whiteness with Blackness as reluctant prologue and unsatisfying conclusion, only once the white characters literally cease to exist on the screen.

As ayo incisively demonstrates through her satiric performance art, there is a clear reluctance even in revisionist history to imagine Black joy, or even Black choice. Nevertheless, Quentin Tarantino has been outspoken in his belief that with the Django universe, he conjures pro-Black performativity because Django kills again and again, with increasing levels of desensitizing violence, going so far as to say in an interview, "I've always wanted to explore slavery, but I guess the reason that actually made me put pen to paper was to give black American males a Western hero, give them a cool, folkloric hero that could actually be empowering and actually pay back blood for blood" (Tarantino). Even overlooking the problematic use of "males" as a noun to dehumanize actual Black men, Tarantino seems to discount and erase the existing revolutionary folk heroes of African American lore, including the blaxploitation film *Joshua* (1976), written by and starring Fred Williamson, in which a Black Union soldier kills the white men who killed his mother during the Civil War. Instead, the problem here is that Tarantino is preoccupied with the opportunity to insert *his voice* as a savior into the existing narrative under the guise of filling in a silence that no one requested he fill and that doesn't exist in the way he imagines it. In this way, Tarantino constructs *Django* as not only a revenge fantasy centered on slavery, but the implication that "black American males" need a "cool folkloric hero" as if these heroes don't already exist throughout Black American history indicates Tarantino's own subscription to the belief that figure of the slave is racial shorthand.

It is only through Schultz's cunning and determination that Django is emancipated from a line of shackled slaves and begins on a journey to free his wife and take his own liberation. But in the end, it is Schultz who kills the "big bad" primary antagonist—Django doesn't even get the anticipated masculine catharsis of killing his wife's abuser—and it is Schultz's self-serving focus that ultimately most endangers both Broomhilda and Django, even putting Broomhilda's freedom at risk, stating that he "couldn't resist." Indeed, very little time is devoted to Django's interior space or motivation, instead focusing on cheaper laughs surrounding Django's connection to stereotypical Black culture—his flashy choice of attire, dancing horse, and culturally significant lineage (he and his wife, it turns out, are ancestors of Shaft). Does Tarantino mean for these moments to be satirical comments on expectations of Blackness? There are no signs to indicate it goes that deep. Instead, by creating a fictional "badass" slave, Tarantino merely plays into stereotypes of fearsome Black masculinity and subtly undermines the actual lived experiences of slaves and former slaves who were in most cases unable to fight in the same overt and violent manner as Django, but fought in significant ways to resist, nonetheless. In this focus on Django's fantastical exceptionalism, Tarantino effectively erases actual resistance in slavery. This move is expressly *not* the reclamation of slavery undertaken by Parks, or even ayo, but a troublesome continuation of the white gaze as framing the slave experience. Tarantino has made multiple revenge fantasies for groups to which he does not belong—*Inglourious Basterds* (2009) and *Once Upon a Time in Hollywood* (2019) imagine taking down Adolf Hitler and Charles Manson, respectively, for instance—and *Django* likewise seems to indicate an ideology that seeks retribution without considering the stakes, that imagines that independent good men or the punishment of solitary bad guys somehow equates justice. Yet even on the level of the individual, there is no introspection or consideration of Black interiority that would allow us to imagine that this film offers justice or salvation, and no silences or sardonic laughs to encourage us to extend the line from slavery to the present day, no matter how Tarantino attempts to frame it in interviews.

Throughout the film, there are no meaningful silences in which we can consider Black interior space or what justice might look like. There is no laughter that makes audiences consider their complicity or the continuation of racism and racialization today. There is no veil to be lifted. Instead, what we witness is bluster that frames Django as anachronistic and unique, rather than symbolic of existing antebellum agitation for selfhood. In fact, Django is so exceptional that he not only seems out of step with the past but out of place in the future—it is difficult to imagine the child who would be wooed to idolize Django in his unrecognizability. Ultimately, the film unintentionally focuses on the seeming exceptionalism of the one as juxtaposed against the implied mediocrity of the rest, and demonstrates Tarantino's inability to imagine a realm in which a Black hero exists outside the context of a white gaze—this is a film about a white savior, rather than heroic Blackness or Black self-actualization fulfilled. Tarantino unfortunately highlights the limits of his ideas of liberation because he utilizes Blackness only insofar as it functions as accoutrements to white cool. Tarantino's *Django* serves the interests of its director and his ideal and intended audience—primarily viewers who are white liberals, like Tarantino himself, who can imagine this revenge fantasy as symbolically just, who are eager for cultural productions that engage race without invoking contemporary racism, and who find absolution in the passive viewing of a film about slavery.

In some ways, this revenge fantasy merely revises the respectability politics and ideas of Black exceptionalism that were presented prior to the civil rights movement and implies that if only the enslaved had been more cunning or less subservient, then the end of slavery could have been ushered in more quickly. Prior to the inconsistent post-racialization of film and literature in the twenty-first century, much of the treatment of slavery and discussions of what can broadly be referred to as *the* Black experience revolved around respectability politics that uplifted Black people and sought to prove Black worthiness to a general public. Django's exceptionalist performance is merely the other side of the same coin—Django is still a racially essentialized Black character who ultimately proves his selfhood through violence rather than performative nonviolence. The fundamental characteristics of the politics of respectability—proving one's worth through one's behavior and adoption of the sociocultural norms and expectations of the culture at large—are reinforced for a new generation as Django's existence is still validated specifically by his (re)actions and extraordinariness. *Django* offers no new frame for understanding Blackness—or whiteness—and instead the new tropes Tarantino promotes bear a suspicious resemblance to the old tropes that have always existed.

Perhaps nowhere is Tarantino's faulty understanding of the actual experiences and legacies of slavery more on display than in the Mandingo fighting scene, a moment in which Django and Schultz witness two enslaved men made to fight to the death for the entertainment of the masters. Tarantino refuses to interrogate the apocryphal story and ultimately positions the chattel system in the realm of unnecessary mythology—is it necessary to invent new traumas of slavery, particularly if they teach us nothing about our past and give us no insights into our present condition?—never asking himself why slave owners would be willing to routinely destroy their own *property* for sport, why these men would so emphatically work to kill one another to survive as enslaved, or even to whom voice is given in his articulation of this battle. Audiences may even recognize that this proposition makes no sense, but Tarantino offers enough realism without reality to encourage doubt. Ultimately, the problem with Tarantino's reimagining of slavery is in his sense that slavery needs heightening through melodrama and the addition of gore to an already bloody scene in order to be made meaningful for modern audiences. He is so concerned with what he might have to add to the idea of slavery that he not only eschews the silences that allow audiences to make the connections that might lead to justice, but he also ignores the existing conversations about slavery. This move does not, ultimately, endow Django with any real autonomy or highlight Black interior space, nor does it discomfort audiences into recognizing their own complicity. Without subverting these ideas, the racialized roles ultimately are reified in a traditional white gaze.

Key and Peele satirically reimagines these tropes in their "Slave Fight" sketch—an unassuming in-joke that utilizes the same staging and set coloring to mirror and then undercut the depiction presented in *Django*. In this sketch, the eponymous comedic talents Keegan-Michael Key and Jordan Peele portray the two slaves forced to fight to the death. Rather than the gruesome and jarring violence of *Django*, the comedians focus instead on the overwhelming assertions of performative masculinity in the film—here, the slaves plot to get out alive, but are confounded by which one should take a dive, arguing in hushed tones: "Let me get you," "let me get *you*." When Peele suggests, "We'll back up, and you run at me real fast, and do a bunch of spins and kicks and flourishes, and then I'll just knock you out—one punch—and then you're dead," Key responds, aghast, "I'm sorry, so you can look cool? No, thank you." It is this highlighting of the ridiculousness not only of the image of Mandingo fights as a notion but also the improbability of the willingness of slave participation in a deadly game that is significant and, in this three-and-a-half-minute sketch, offers a more nuanced depiction of identifiable slave humanity than Tarantino's film, and evokes the revolutionary laughter that engages the Black interior and ideas of Black selfhood. Tarantino luxuriates in the realm of the absurd, yet his idea of absurdity reifies the status quo of racialization rather than impacting ideas of how Black selfhood was articulated in past and present realms.

In *Django*, Kerry Washington's meager role is also peculiar in the context of a twenty-first-century engagement with slavery. Django's wife, Broomhilda, is silenced in favor of what ultimately becomes a buddy film focused on Schultz and Django. This is not the silence that creates space for new ways of thinking about Blackness, but is instead a silence that stifles and shuts down nuanced development. Broomhilda is little more than a damsel in distress, the Olive Oyl to Django's Popeye, and as such the casting is peculiar—although Washington signed on for *Django* before ABC's *Scandal* became a runaway hit, the minimal performance requirements seem better suited for a novice actress rather than one who, if not A list, was certainly well established at this point in her career. Washington's charismatic presence endows the role with more gravity than it merits; her character is written as a display of many of the physical performances for which *Scandal*'s Olivia Pope is often parodied—widening her eyes dramatically and quivering her lip. Yet unlike Olivia Pope, we see no real motivation on the part of Broomhilda. In fact, even when she is being punished, the cause is never fully elucidated because it is inconsequential to her character; the violence of the punishment only serves to explain to the audience why Schultz and Django must continue on their sojourn. Broomhilda needs saving from the brutality inflicted on her by other men and becomes the catalyst for retribution.

Yet Broomhilda's faults here are not due to Washington's lack of effort; she emotes earnestly in a role that seems to provide her little with which to work. The problem stems from Tarantino's effort to sensationalize the reality of chattel slavery in the United States despite the fact that its reality needs no sensationalizing, and his unwillingness throughout many of his films to provide silences that allow his characters the space for actualization or to be anything other than representational, let alone for audience processing. Through this imagining, stereotypes of Blackness are propagated through the implication that those Black characters who do exert power are inherently post-racial—that somehow Django and Broomhilda are racialized only in the presence of whites (the savior Schultz notwithstanding, of course)—and when they are free, the trauma of slavery is lost to the destruction of Candie's plantation as they ride off into the sunset unrestricted, the assumed burden of Blackness now lifted, as if they wouldn't be persona non grata throughout the nation. This assumption suggests that the horrors are relegated to history. If Django and Broomhilda can ride off into the sunset, then there is some happily-ever-after sanctuary to be found for Black bodies in the nineteenth century. But even a cursory understanding of slavery or antebellum racialization disallows the belief that our duo can find contentment given what lies behind and what lies ahead in terms of an inevitable pursuit after the bloody scene they leave in their wake.[4]

Particularly for Broomhilda, to whom we are introduced being shoved naked into a hole, this lasting freedom seems especially unlikely and is a stark erasure of the ways that race and gender are still meaningful both in antebellum and contemporary social spheres. Moreover, that any specifics of Broomhilda's experience are disregarded other than those that place her in direct line with Django's wants and needs is especially troubling. While this may be common for the damsel in distress, structuring Broomhilda in this way only reifies the belief that the enslaved are necessarily men, and that the experiences of women aren't worth mentioning. Similarly, by placing Django and Broomhilda in the company of other more accommodating and even gleeful slaves—such as Samuel L. Jackson's notorious Stephen—or passive, unobtrusive slaves, liked those witnessed swinging casually in the Candieland trees,[5] their exceptionalism comes at the cost of the further erasure of the lived experiences of real slaves, who are implied to be tacit accomplices to the slave system. Tarantino shows very little interest in depicting the historical context of slavery and instead takes it as a given that his audience will somehow simultaneously accept both the historicity and the fantasy without clear indications on when either is being enacted.

Both *Scandal* and *Django Unchained* premiered in 2012—*Scandal's* first season began airing in April, while *Django* was released on Christmas Day. That these two narratives emerged in the midst of the Obama presidency— indeed, during his campaign for reelection—is no surprise. With the election of a phenotypically Black president, the mythology of the post-racial seemed to take hold for some. If 2008 was the year that the post-racial was preeminent in the popular discourse, 2012 and the beginning of Obama's second term were when its claims were purportedly proven for those who wanted or needed to believe. *Django* and *Scandal* both speak to a potential of racial erasure that the post-racial implies, with *Scandal* ultimately and emphatically refusing racial meaninglessness even in the twenty-first century. *Django*, however, suggests that racial oppression can be overcome through sheer determinism and power of will. Somehow, in a film that ends with two quasi-free—free adjacent?—slaves making their way through parts unknown in the Deep South, audiences are to believe that love conquers all despite the fact that there is no way that Broomhilda and Django could literally blow up a plantation at the end and then move through any part of the nation unobserved and unbothered, an idea undercut by all the preceding drama and conflict of the film itself. The implication seems to be that most slave uprisings were unsuccessful because there was never a slave so exceptional and resultantly so successful as Django, with Broomhilda as accessory.

Ultimately, the reanimation of slavery in the contemporary moment reifies the significance of the figure of the slave in Black selfhood both in and out of time. Yet the bombast of *Django* undercuts the ways that silence was cleverly enacted in slavery as a form of resistance. It distracts from the fact that kaleidoscopic Blackness was hidden from public view as a survival tactic by implying that slaves were either brave, like Django, or master-obsessed cowards, like Jackson's foil, Stephen. In "A Resistance Too Civilized to Notice," William D. Pierson posits:

Too often in the history of American slavery we assume acts of effective resistance are best defined by organized violence because rebellion and revolution are thought by American culture to be the highest, most worthy, most manly forms of protest. But such a vision is far too narrow for African American studies since traditional African cultures held different values based on differing forms of political science. Indeed, in some ways it might be said that the institutions of traditional African politics were sometimes simply too civilized to be understood by Western categorization. (349)

This articulation is so important in our understanding of the powerful possibilities and potential failures of revisiting and reclaiming slavery and the slave in the twenty-first century. This engagement with slavery fails to recognize other realms for what revolution might look like outside traditional Western frames and, as a result, discounts the multiple forms of resisting throughout history and multiple ways of being in favor of a lurid portrayal of revolution that lacks nuance. It is why Django is the *only* slave in the film who we see offering any real resistance or expressing active and actionable disgust with the status quo and why Django as *ideal* slave figure becomes a frame for social justice that cannot hold in reality. Tarantino imagines justice as retribution without considering what material conditions have or have not changed for African Americans in the twenty-first century. What does freedom look like? What justice could an enslaved person rightly imagine then, and what can their descendants hope for now? The blood and gore are certainly the primary impulse for Tarantino in his oeuvre, but the utilization of the slave—this seeming personification of injustice in the context of the nation—muddles even this message as it is haphazardly overlaid with historical context and meaning.

Satire remains a critical mode in the expression of the joys and sorrows of the African American experience. What would it mean if we didn't enact satire in the retelling of our traumas? Laughing to keep from dying in the face of grief not only serves an ameliorating purpose to persuade those who might be convinced to help relieve our pain. In fact, in some cases, the use of satire specifically, and even laughing, eschews the ease of both the satirist and the audience, relishing instead in the discomfort of the absurd treatment of trauma. Saidiya Hartman explains, "a history of the present strives to illuminate the intimacy of our experience with the lives of the dead, to write our now as it is interrupted by this past, and to imagine a free state, not as the time before captivity or slavery, but rather as the anticipated future of this writing" (4). We return to slavery because it frames the Black present and gives context for Black futures. The seemingly incongruous use of satire in the description of trauma serves to regulate emotions and offers a sense of stability in moments of intense re-memory—through an emphasis on nuanced Black identity in past and present forms, satire at its most effective mediates our process of recall so we are not overcome and overwhelmed by the sheer grief of it all. It highlights our resiliency, both individually and collectively.

The image of the slave also, significantly, reminds us—if undertaken effectively and if we allow ourselves to be convicted—of the debt that cannot be paid. What's done is done. There is no payment, monetary or otherwise, that can erase the harm of the past or the ancestral trauma experienced in the present. This does not mean that a desire for justice in the present moment is frivolous. Instead, thinking about the calculated silences and potentials for revolutionary justice in twenty-first-century satires opens up an ethical terrain—a space where we not only must consider the rhetoric of the satirist but also our response to the matter itself—in which we begin to conceptualize justice, without the didacticism that would tell us exactly what justice is. The burden is squarely on the audience to make meaning.

During slavery, the use of satire and the comedic not only offered plausible deniability as a protective veil but also reaffirmed the wit and shrewdness of the one making the satirical joke—in a society in which Black people were forbidden knowledge and education, the use of satire reasserted one's ingenuity and cleverness, rendering the oppressor the fool. In the twenty-first century, it serves much the same function of protection and liberation, of community building among those who *get* the deeper meaning and a tenuous inversion of the racial hierarchy over those who don't. The continued fascination with slavery as a frame for understanding extends from the shared community and from the ancestral trauma of historic racialization, and the changing same of race today. The following writers and performers examine what reclaiming Blackness means in view of expectations of Black performance. The focus remains on the impression of Blackness as commodity and consumable and the continuing and very real danger of psychic death. To refuse to reclaim these limited ideas of Blackness already insidious in the public sphere would be to bear witness to the deaths of our ancestors—in the kaleidoscopic glory of the various ways they enacted and experienced revolutionary laughter and revolution itself—again and again.

CHAPTER 2

"Race Is Just a Made-Up Thing"

Abject Blackness and Racial Anxiety

> I grew up in Chicago in a white neighborhood.
> It messed me up. Then I moved to a black
> neighborhood and it was too late. 'Cause I
> went from being the only black child in an all-
> white neighborhood to the only white child in
> an all-black neighborhood.
> —Marina Franklin, *The Awkward Comedy Show*

Twenty-first-century satires and self-satirizing moments bring continuing racialization and contemporary discomfort in discussions about race to the forefront. These satires demonstrate that race *does* matter just as much as it *doesn't* matter—that we can realize race holds no inborn significance and implies no identifiable biological difference while still acknowledging and resisting the ways that race frames our lives and interactions. It is in that tension that the subversive potential of satire most intimately resides. These conversations are framed by ideas of representation and representational space in order to strip away notions of racial essentialism while highlighting the damage that assumptions of racial performance can do to an articulation of Black selfhood. The ostensible lower stakes of racialization in the twenty-first century and the presentation of the "post-racial" as a desirable public mythology heighten this sense of simultaneous racial meaningfulness and meaninglessness. Twenty-first-century narratives reveal continued anxieties surrounding both Blackness and whiteness in the assumption of the "lower stakes" of the present day. It is this anxiety that contemporarily precedes not only satire but satirical readings of texts and events that imagine race out to an absurd conclusion.

In this contemporary context, there is often an emphasis on the idea of Blackness as potentially worthwhile in limited ways; here Blackness is abject, to be sure, but also cool and trendy—Blackness with a particular use. One of the most overt contemporary public satirical endeavors that engaged Blackness as valuable in this sense was the sale of Keith Obadike's "Blackness" on the internet auction site eBay in August 2001 by conceptual artists Mendi and Keith Obadike. Before ultimately being closed by the website for "inappropriateness," Obadike's "Blackness" reached a bid of $152.20 from an initial opening bid of $10.00. Obadike described his work in essentialist, objectified terms, explaining, "This heirloom has been in the possession of the seller for twenty-eight years. Mr. Obadike's Blackness has been used primarily in the United States and its functionality outside of the US cannot be guaranteed. Buyer will receive a certificate of authenticity." What is interesting here is not only the selling of "Blackness" itself in the twenty-first century, but the purchase of it. What were buyers hoping to gain? It's perhaps too easy to say that potential buyers were bidding on this "Blackness" as a lark; if we reduce this to *just a joke,* we must still ask ourselves whence the humor is derived. Certainly, eBay purchasers are often drawn to the silly, the niche, the kitsch, but how can those qualities be extracted from the literal and figurative purchase of Blackness? And, most importantly, are these bidders aware that *they* are the actual objects of mockery? Any laughter this piece inspires can only occur from recognition that the Obadikes are riffing on the existing stereotypes surrounding Blackness and Black performance for which they themselves are not responsible. Mendi and Keith Obadike's exhibition reveals and critiques the desire to continue to own *Blackness*—an effort not only to quantify Black identity but to naturally refuse the humanity of *Black people.*

Similar to damali ayo's later performance piece, the Obadikes' work makes us consider the limited parameters by which Blackness is described and to wonder about the actual ramifications for Black bodies and for Black people. Particularly in the twenty-first century, when the African American relationship to power is denaturalized in ways it hasn't been before, what are the consequences of this expectation for Black identity? In "Pedagogy and the Philosophical Anthropology of African-American Slave Culture," Stephen Nathan Haymes explains,

> The human anxieties, which preoccupied the pedagogy of slave culture, emerged out of a specific historical reality in which the slave's humanity as a black was denied. Prompted by these anxieties, the slave culture's exis-

tential concerns struggled to affirm or assert the slave's recognition of his or her humanity, which was learned within the slave quarter community. However, in contrast to Western philosophy of education, it understood that being human is not something one becomes through education but, rather, is what one already is. (191)

Indeed, this performance of selling Blackness requires interrogating the idea of Black humanity. It subtly positions public Blackness as something different from Black interior space. When Obadike sells his Blackness, it is clear that he is expressly *not* selling himself. The two are separate entities—his Blackness is related to but distinct from his understanding of self. He is selling the part of himself that, in his articulation, seems most quantifiable, most collectible, and, strangely, seems to have simultaneously the most capital and risk in the United States—his Blackness renders him both cool and endangered, hip in its feigned undesirability. Moreover, because it has been defined insufficiently by others throughout history, his "Blackness" can be sold without its original owner actually losing or revealing those hidden recesses of Black interior space. Here Obadike has the last laugh, and this laughing to keep from dying wards off the spiritual demise that would otherwise come from being flattened and objectified. By naming *thingness* as Blackness, and offering it up for sale (even receiving bids!), Mendi and Keith Obadike highlight the impossibility of the post-racial to present a new way of contextualizing Black identity in the contemporary era, instead demonstrating the power in the reclamation of the ideas surrounding Blackness, both positive and negative.

Here I deploy satirical readings of texts and events that engage notions of Black identity and racial essentialism by either intentionally performing a limited portrayal of Blackness or by inverting notions of Blackness to distance oneself from the damaging effects of these expectations. These texts and events remind us, sometimes inadvertently, that our racial expectations are unreliable and limiting, while also acknowledging that they continue to linger and operate in the service of racism itself in important ways. Ultimately, these works reveal the potential psychic trauma experienced when Black interiority is disallowed. The revolutionary laughter inspired by effective satire may create a means to escape psychic death. I place the film *Precious* and the novel on which it was based, *Push*, in juxtaposition as depictions of racial essentialism to think about moments in which Black interiority may open up space for kaleidoscopic Blackness to emerge despite its seeming denial. Considering Barack Obama's "dad jeans" controversy and *Atlanta*'s "B.A.N." episode offers insights on the ironic refusal and acceptance of racial essentialism and the ways that audience perception may limit one's ability to shirk these restraints. Percival Everett's novel *Erasure* and Touré's *Who's Afraid of Post-Blackness* reckon with the psychic toll of prescriptive Black identity. These texts demonstrate that essentialism continues to operate as damaging racial shorthand to circumscribe our articulation of self and remind us of the power of audience belief on the acceptance of self-articulated identity.

It is necessary here to address nontraditional satires—texts that are not written in the satiric mode but still lend themselves to satirical readings by virtue of the social absurdity they underscore and serve inadvertently to critique—not only because they reveal the continued relevance of assumptions surrounding Blackness and move the discussion from theory to practice but also because they remind us that satire is founded on audience perception, perhaps even more than authorial intention. Moreover, the nontraditional satiric texts and events chosen—specifically *Push* and *Precious,* Obama's "dad jeans," and *Who's Afraid of Post-Blackness*—became such critical and quickly flowing pieces of the zeitgeist that their implications surrounding race are particularly resonant. That is, these texts and moments seemed to offer an explanation for identity, and identity crises, in the twenty-first century and, importantly, served as the satirized inspiration for future critiques of racial anxiety. Indeed, Touré's *Who's Afraid of Post-Blackness* serves as touchstone for a number of the vital essays in *The Trouble with Post-Blackness* (2015), edited by Houston A. Baker and K. Merinda Simmons, in the critical takedown of the popular use of the term "post-Black" itself.

There is a need for a more comprehensive understanding of the ways that not only Blackness but race in general is performed in consideration of and despite racial stereotypes, which forces us to question whether a move past race into the "post-racial" or "post-Black" so frequently addressed in view of Obama's presidency is possible or even desirable. These texts acutely indicate that race matters, but that it matters in unexpected and nontraditional ways. These texts and events, in their satirical content or satirical readings, illustrate the fallacy of believing racial essentialism and underscore its wide-reaching impact in both fictional imaginings and in the actual lived experiences in the twenty-first century. Here, Blackness and non-Blackness are descriptors but also operate as metaphors to demonstrate the insufficiency of race as a schema in the twenty-first century. This is an important move away from an accepted understanding of racialization that places an undue burden on the marginalized for their continued marginalization. Conflict arises in these satires from the failures of society to move past an oversimplified and erroneous understanding of both race as a problem and racism as inevitable. Richard Dyer argues, "As long as race is something only applied to non-white peoples, as long as white people are not racially seen and named, they/we function as a human norm. Other people are raced, [white people] are just people" (1). These contemporary texts and events actively refuse this obfuscation. Instead, they engage a tension where race is acknowledged as a social construct *and* there are undeniable real-life effects of racialization and a continuing belief in essentialized Blackness.

Expectations of Black Performance

I want to begin by considering *Push* (1996), a novel by Sapphire, and the film, *Precious* (2009), based on it. Both grapple with the seeming incompatibility of Blackness and whiteness and, through an ironic and apparently essentialist view of abject Blackness, imagine the unsustainability of the racial binary. Although neither was created in the traditional satiric mode, both *Push* and *Precious* utilize exaggeration and racial essentialism to such an extent that they inadvertently lend themselves to satirical readings and ask us to grapple with the inherent absurdity of race and racialization, and the lengths to which those who are marginalized might go to make space for themselves in a society that circumscribes their selfhood. Indeed, it is the reliance on stereotypes as representational space that allows a clear satirical reading of the book and especially the novel—the satiric mode is founded on the relationship between the audience and the text, and so in many cases it is less about authorial intention and more about audience perception. In this way, while Sapphire did not intend the text to be received as a satire when published in 1996, this reading emerges particularly in concert with the even more popular film and in view of other contemporary texts and performances—including the Obadikes' eBay exhibit, damali ayo's website and book, and even the overtly comedic in *Key and Peele* and *Chappelle's Show*—that offer more-nuanced depictions of Black interior space in the face of the mainstream attempts to circumscribe Black identity. These two works necessarily underscore the potential disjuncture between authorial intent and audience perception in understanding a work as a satire and remind us that simply displaying the trauma of Black abjection is not the same as critically revealing it in the aim of restorative justice. Not only this, but each work reveals the necessity of Black interior space in self-articulation in the ways Precious understands herself and is able to make meaning—or not—in her life.

Particularly in the case of *Precious*, it is important to consider a satiric reading because while the book gestures toward possibilities of liberation through Black nationalism and radical Black self-love, the film refuses to examine Precious's Black interior space and instead primarily leaves behind naturalized assumptions of Blackness as abject. Indeed, irrespective of any satirical potential, both the book and the film have received such immense acclaim from audiences and critics that they not only continue to inform contemporary understandings of racial essentialism but they reveal preexisting notions of race and racialization and are overtly satirized in contemporary comedic texts. Likewise, while I acknowledge that both *Push* and *Precious* offer few moments of a nuanced or realistic portrayal of Black womanhood—instead trading in more simplistic understandings of reductive Blackness and what has been described as "trauma porn" to the extent that even the arguably more nuanced *Push* itself has been parodied in Percival Everett's *Erasure* and elsewhere as an example of limited portrayals of Blackness—I am here interested in the ways the novel works to imagine white representational space and possibilities for Black self-love. In fact, *Precious* can be most effectively read as a satire, or certainly as self-satirizing, when we consider its departures from its novel's source material.

Push introduces readers to Claireece P. Jones, "Precious," a 1980s Harlem teenager described with characteristics meant to signal her abjection—she is Black, female, overweight, illiterate, and poor. She is also, we soon learn, physically, mentally, and sexually abused by both of her parents. When she is introduced to readers, she is pregnant for the second time, and both of her children are products of incestuous rape by her father. Interestingly, Precious seems to attribute her own difficulties in life not to her surrounding circumstances but instead to the skin color that she believes creates her circumstances. She explains, "My fahver don't see me really. If he did he would know that I was like a white girl, a *real* person, inside" (Sapphire 32). Precious continues to imagine herself associated with both literal and figurative whiteness not because of an aesthetic desire to be white, but primarily because she believes that whiteness begets personhood and that *it is through whiteness that she will be made visible.* Whiteness represents not only protection but limitless opportunity. Yet instead of presenting Precious's internalized colorism as mere pathological self-hate, Sapphire juxtaposes these moments with Precious's interest in Louis Farrakhan and notions of Black radicalism and Black pride. By showing Precious's dichotomous internal feelings and revealing the revolutionary power of her Black interior space—her initial rejection of her own dark skin next giving way to her burgeoning acceptance of some aspects of Afrocentrism—Sapphire's protagonist demonstrates a method by which African Americans may articulate positive selfhood in the face of the self-hate fostered through American society, where communal Black identity may lead to individualized feelings of self-worth.

The 2009 film, *Precious: Based on the Novel* Push *by Sapphire,* directed by Lee Daniels, removes the revelation of Black interior space and thus erases the most overt ways by which Precious identifies with Black nationalism and any pride surrounding Blackness as communal or individual identity more broadly. The film purports to be an authentic look at Black interiority, but by expunging Precious's interest in Afrocentrism and her interactions with Black role models, the film ultimately implies that she is merely dissatisfied with her own physicality and gives no clear indication why she should not be. Precious's desire for whiteness is implied to be tantamount to Black interiority and a function of her own self-hate or lack of selfhood—that *of course* a Black girl would dream of being white, and this desire requires no further elaboration or analysis—where her freedom is tantamount to whiteness. The erasure of Precious's burgeoning Black pride, particularly in the removal of Black nationalist emblems and her connection with the original Afrocentric version of Miz Rain, hinders the film and makes it seem to enact the absurdity of the satiric mode to display the pathology of a poor Black girl rather than a more complicated explication of the ways in which Blackness itself is frequently pathologized to a damaging extent. Instead, in the film, Precious's problems can all be located in her family life, without any greater condemnation of the larger social setting.

In *Push,* readers are introduced to Precious's discomfort with herself as she sits in her math class, entertaining a rather asexual, suburban fantasy of her math teacher. She describes Mr. Wicher in descriptive terms both neutral and vaguely derogatory, saying, "He a skinny little white man about five feets four inches. A peckerwood as my mother would say" (4). She continues by explaining, "I like [Mr. Wicher], I pretend he is my husband and we live together in Weschesser, wherever that is" (6). Unlike a traditional schoolgirl crush, Precious fantasizes about Mr. Wicher not because she finds *him* attractive or even powerful—indeed, based on the description, it is clear that she does not—but instead because she is attracted to the privilege of suburban placidness she presumes to be attached to his whiteness. She imagines being married to him and living in "Weschesser," or Westchester, a wealthy, predominantly white county north of New York City to escape the limitations prescribed to her by her existing setting. Consequently, Precious removes herself from her own racial and geographical identification, fantasizing a companionate attachment to whiteness as her escape. What makes this moment especially compelling is not that she seems to have a crush on her teacher, a rather universal and traditional school-age trope, but that this desire has less to do with physicality and more to do with the privilege attendant to the presence of whiteness, discrete from his physicality, revealing at the outset Precious's specific racial anxiety. This distinction is important and reveals the nuanced ways in which Sapphire both acknowledges whiteness as offering significant mobility in contemporary society and also mocks it as having naturalized or inherent desirability outside this privilege.

This infatuation with whiteness continues when Precious is suspended from public school and enrolls in Each One, Teach One, an alternative school. As she meets her new classmates, she describes one particular student, Rita Romero, as "slim, not pretty but she *got that light skin that stand for something*" (61, emphasis added). What light skin "stands for" is left unarticulated but might be inferred, as Precious overtly refuses any naturalized equivalence between light skin and beauty. By stating instead that the skin stands for something, she indicates that she is acutely aware of skin as a signifier of *mobility*, again separate from any Westernized sense of beauty or desire. Precious negotiates her own understanding of a line between beauty and the light skin that *stands for something*. She does not subscribe to a belief that whiteness is inherently beautiful. She remains infatuated with whiteness as a symbol of opportunity based on her own personal observations, not because she is dissatisfied with her own racial appearance for any other reason. Likewise, it is interesting to note that the name and description of Rita Romero signify that she is not white presenting; she is identified as Latinx. Sapphire makes this distinction to reinforce the fact that Precious is infatuated with whiteness as a sign of upward mobility, rather than whiteness as signaling personhood.

Precious's fixation on whiteness and away from Blackness is most directly addressed and critiqued in the book through her interactions with Miz Rain. These interactions force Precious to fully confront her own issues with color and to reinscribe her own Blackness as something worthwhile and powerful. Miz Rain is Precious's teacher at Each One, Teach One, and the first aspect that Precious notices about her appearance is her hair. She explains, "I look Miz Teacher's long dreadlocky hair, look kinda nice but look kinda nasty too" (39). Even before interacting with Miz Rain, Precious notices the potential for a "transgressive" beauty in Black pride—"kinda nice . . . kinda nasty"—as represented through Miz Rain's natural hairstyle. She continues her description of Miz Rain by articulating that, "She dark, got nice face, big eyes, and hair like I already said. My muver do not like niggers wear they hair like that! My muver say Farrakhan OK but he done gone too far. Too far where I wanna ax. I don't know how *I* feel about people with hair like that" (40). Her immediate transition between Miz Rain and Louis Farrakhan—a satirical moment to signal that for Precious, Black people "with hair like that" are connected to a "gone too far" militancy, presuming an aesthetic connection to the political—seems to indicate that Precious instantly associates Miz Rain with a pronounced performance of Afrocentric Blackness and Black nationalism. This moment is especially important in laying the foundation for Precious's ultimate self-acceptance through a communal identity, as Miz Rain becomes her greatest mentor and advocate, and Each One, Teach One forms a surrogate family.

Farrakhan's presence as a figure through which Precious derives strength is overtly addressed throughout the novel. Precious explains, "First thing I see when I wake up is picture of Farrakhan's face on the wall. I love him. He is against crack addicts and crackers. Crackers is the cause of everything bad. It why my father ack like he do" (34). Her love of Farrakhan placed next to her disdain for her father again reinforces that this is not merely a story of Black as bad and white as good. The further assertion that "Crackers is the cause of everything bad" is a particularly clear indication that she is not simply engaging in white idolatry: she sees a distinction between the ideology of whiteness as goodness and generalized "crackers" as people who are evil.[1] This distinction allows Precious the opportunity to see the power in herself, rather than only subscribing to racialized self-hatred. The inclusion of figures of Black radicalism—even initially in the problematic figure of Farrakhan—coupled with Miz Rain's physical appearance necessitates a more nuanced understanding of the interplay between the issues occurring within Precious and those surrounding her regarding racialized expectations. Whether audiences are willing to participate in this nuanced reading, of course, is variable and unpredictable, and so this meaning may be lost in the midst of variable audience perception. The film depicts a voyeuristic journey through a worst-case scenario environment of compounding trauma.

Unfortunately, the possibility of this nuanced reading is actively removed from the film version in an effort to appeal to a mainstream audience—in a desire to let audiences watch the film without feeling implicated, the film is stripped of the book's interest in convicting society, and this narrative lack of conviction lends itself more directly to a reading in which, rather than satirically indicting the viewers, the film self-satirizes its own subject matter. Certainly, a book allows engagement with interiority that a film may not—the internal monologue of the book takes preeminence that it cannot in a movie—but even with this recognition, the film seems to actively avoid considering Precious's thinking outside mainstream expectations of what a girl who looks like Precious and who lives in Precious's circumstances might be anticipated to think by outsiders. There is nothing new here and no outward accountability.

Not only does the film shift the villains from society at large (including Precious's parents) to a more localized target of Precious's parents in isolation, but Precious's burgeoning Black pride is effectively erased. *Precious* begins with the protagonist wishing she had a light-skinned boyfriend with good hair. This is the audience's first encounter with Precious, and there is no information provided to explain *why* she wishes for a boyfriend described in these terms. The implication then seems to be that Precious is attracted to light skin for aesthetic reasons, rather than offering any context for anything societally or culturally endemic—she merely hates her own dark skin, and there is no further explanation or insight provided. She is reduced to a mere type—another self-hating Black girl, and who could blame her, filmmakers seem to ask, when Blackness is obviously so abject? Jim Emerson explains in a review of the film as John Waters–inspired camp, "The one thing that genuinely troubles me about [the film] is not that some people have taken it seriously (it's serious *and* funny), but that they have taken it literally." Indeed, Precious's life is so terrible and her options for selfhood so continually foreclosed that her very existence seems to suggest a worst-case scenario that exists in the lives of at least some Black people. The audience is shown a young woman who is dissatisfied with her life and is given no tools through which she can begin to repair her battered self-esteem. Instead, she is simply a tragic figure to be pitied or ridiculed. Or worse, she is a stand-in for an entire pitiable race and gender, her own self-discontent signaling public Black interiority.

The tragedy of *Precious* is underscored for audiences familiar with both the novel and film because all of the ways in which the character finds pride in Black bodies in *Push* are removed. The posters of Farrakhan are notably and inexplicably absent from her wall, instead primarily replaced by images of the white models whose bodies Precious idealizes and fantasizes she inhabits. Without these moments of Black nationalism to balance out these daydreams of white femininity, the film only displays Precious's desire to become a white girl, absurdly showing her looking in the mirror and seeing a white teenager reflected back, without any subtlety to indicate *why* she wants to be white. Instead, the presumption is that she desires to be "beautiful"—which is visually represented through blonde, blue-eyed whiteness—a much more facile explanation that teaches none of the lesson of the novel itself.

In a particularly disturbing scene, Precious steals fried chicken—a basket in the novel but portrayed as an overflowing bucket in the film—on her way to Each One, Teach One. As she flees the restaurant, she passes by a sign reading "Elijah Muhammad Lives." The sign is prominent and visible in its entirety. Without any other Black nationalist imagery, this visual appears apropos of nothing, seems to have no connection to Precious's thinking, and is easily missed; if it is seen, it is absurd in its near-comic juxtaposition. It's as if the filmmakers attempted to delicately hark to the Black nationalism that audience members familiar with *Push* perhaps expected without alienating mainstream viewers by demonstrating any interest in it on the part of Precious herself. The sign is a shallow and vague concession, at best. Elijah Muhammad died in 1975, and the film gives us no indication that he "lives" in Precious's realm, particularly as only momentarily juxtaposed against her chicken theft.

Likewise, a troubling erasure of Blackness and Black pride occurs through the presentation of Miz Rain, portrayed by biracial[2] actress Paula Patton, who shares none of the physical features of her literary counterpart. The filmic Miz Rain is light-skinned with rather Eurocentric features, and straightened, shoulder-length hair. This near-whitewashing of Miz Rain is perhaps the most conspicuous erasure of Precious's encounters with positive depictions of Black identity or a Black nationalist sensibility from the film. This erasure is especially significant because Miz Rain is a lesbian, a revelation that Precious receives with trepidation in the book. In the film, it is much easier for Precious to accept Miz Rain's sexuality when she resembles her purported physical ideal. Even Miz Rain's partner is similarly light-skinned. Consequently, the more complicated issues of sexuality and self-pride are razed from the film. Similar to the allusion to Black nationalism through the "Elijah Muhammad Lives" poster, Miz Rain's wall features a prominent poster of "For Colored Girls . . .," Ntozake Shange's powerful choreo-poem, as if to allude to a more nuanced understanding of the interplay of race, gender, and sexuality (or perhaps to simply remind audiences of producer Tyler Perry's at-the-time-upcoming 2010 film, *For Colored Girls*). Yet without these ideas overtly addressed, Precious is a flattened character whose fantasies of whiteness end not because she learns to love herself with the help of Miz Rain and Black radical thought but instead because she realizes that those dreams are unattainable. This is an entirely different didactic unfolding, and one that only reifies the existing racial hierarchy. In fact, the film's message diverges so much from the book that it must be understood as inadvertently satirizing the book itself, imagining trauma with no insights provided other than the reliability of racialization to limit possibilities, for it to be understood as in conversation with the book at all.

Ultimately toward the end of the novel, Precious begins the metacognitive process of thinking about her own thinking about race. She explains her inner-strength by deliberately placing herself in opposition to whiteness, stating, "I just don't always want to be crying like white bitch on TV movies. Since I ain' no white bitch. I understand that now. I am not white bitch. I am not Janet Jackson or Madonna on the inside" (125). This moment is critical in understanding Precious's connection to whiteness. The inclusion of Janet Jackson may be initially surprising and seem misplaced, but for Precious whiteness was never primarily about physical appearance but instead about *treatment* and *mobility*. This statement is entirely absent from the film and indeed would be incongruent with all other information presented about Precious's understanding of her place in the world. By portraying Precious as merely yearning for a stereotypical appearance of white femininity for aesthetic reasons, the film strips the protagonist of her most important and significant ways of understanding and loving herself and refuses the compelling kaleidoscopic potentiality of Blackness when freed from the hierarchical notions of racial inferiority. Instead, it seems to imagine that it is only by loosening herself of her own images and ideas of Blackness—indeed, almost every phenotypically Black person with whom Precious comes in contact violates her in some way—that she might achieve actualization and selfhood. This is a damaging portrayal of self-identity but also seems to indicate expectations of Blackness as a limitation more broadly.

The Limitations of the "Social Construct"

We see a similar sense of the presumed limitations of Blackness, undertaken with comedic results, in Donald Glover's *Atlanta* episode, "B.A.N." Normally, the thirty-minute comedy-drama focuses on Glover's Earn Marks and his cousin, rapper Alfred "Paper Boi" Miles, played by Brian Tyree Henry, as they aspire for financial security and professional prominence in Atlanta, Georgia. The show offers a nuanced depiction of Blackness within communal and individual identity frames and is notable for its emphasis on the homosocial bonds in Black masculinity. This episode, however, shifts the focus from the plot proper and instead zooms in on Paper Boi during an interview on B.A.N., a fictional BET surrogate. He is one of the guests on *Montague,* hosted by Franklin Montague, an African American pundit and the personification of respectability politics. Montague is juxtaposed against Paper Boi's politically incorrect rapper persona as they discuss the latter's controversial rhetoric. Yet the even more compelling segment on *Montague* is a special report on a man named Antwoine Smalls, an African American high school student who identifies as a "transracial" white man. Christening himself Harrison Booth, Smalls explains, "Well, I've always felt different. I go to the store, the movies, and just be thinking to myself, why am I not getting the respect I deserve? And then it just hit me: I'm white. And 35." What audiences witness here is not an instance of *passing,* because this person is not ultimately *misread* or *accepted* by anyone as white, but instead a related performance of racial essentialism without the racial ambiguity or phenotypic sameness that passing in all its forms necessitates. Smalls presents as a young

African American man with dreadlocks and brown skin—importantly, he is not even remotely able to pass for white based on our understanding of the phenotypical presentation of whiteness and of what whiteness is meant to represent. Because he is unable to "look white" in a traditional sense, for Smalls this association with whiteness, or pushing back against Blackness, manifests itself in loose, belted jeans—"dad jeans," as a shift away from Black masculine performance—and a less flashy appearance. He adds a blonde wig at the end of his interview, an overt comedic gesture on the part of the creators, but the style of clothing remains the same and is potentially an even more striking assessment of expectations of Black performance and abjection as well as how non-Blackness can be quantified as a space framed by the possibilities of mobility.

Smalls states that his family resists his transracial identity, explaining, "I don't think they get it because they don't realize that race is just a made-up thing." The irony of his statement in this context is potent. Here, it is clear that race is simultaneously meaningful and meaningless, even in its denial—Smalls can only reject his racialized identity because he accepts it as valid and aims to attain a more privileged one. This move by Smalls isn't antiracist. It isn't even "post-racial"—it ultimately subscribes directly to the racist system of a racial hierarchy as we know it, even as it assumes a possibility of racial choice. Race is "just a made-up thing," except that Smalls knows whiteness has value and provides respect and mobility. Imani Perry argues,

> In truth, the racism we see in the United States is more appropriately called "correlational racism," in which disfavored qualities, or for preferred groups, favorable qualities are seen as being highly correlated with membership in certain racial groups and dictate the terms upon which individual members of those groups are treated, as well as the way we evaluate the impact and goals of policy, law, and other community-based decision-making. (17)

What is especially intriguing about Perry's assessment of correlational racism is that whiteness is, ultimately, viewed as a void in American society. The favorable qualities of whiteness are hard to discern because they are vaguely defined in terms of what they are *not* by way of comparison to marginalized groups—whiteness as *not* abject and *not* object; whiteness as relative subjectivity. In this way, satirical portrayals of both Blackness and whiteness speak to a social truth that "the perceived fiction of black men's illegitimacy as proper American men is preferred above the truth of such a perception as a self-legitimizing projection of bourgeois white male arrogance" (Wallace 33); this portrayal on *Atlanta* requires audiences to define whiteness and, in doing so, to make whiteness strange. It attempts to quantify what whiteness might mean within the same parameters created for Blackness. Ultimately, by addressing this idea to an absurd extent, many contemporary satires force our disavowal of the conventional silence surrounding race by imagining what racial essentialism might look like if whiteness were made observable. Without it, we are forced to suffer under the "scopic function of racialist regimes" (Wallace 40) that reinforces the parameters of Blackness as fearsome and always threatening in its abjection, while leaving whiteness as abstract, undefined, and ultimately filled with possibilities. We recognize Smalls's inability to pass or to perform as white not because he is *not* white but because he *is* identifiably Black.

This incompatibility between attempts to self-define race and audience acceptance of racial identity recalls, in some ways, the controversy surrounding Rachel Dolezal and her attempts at white-to-Black passing. In June 2015, it was revealed by her biological parents that Dolezal, who at the time was the head of the Spokane, Washington, chapter of the NAACP and an African American studies professor, was actually a white woman passing for Black. The internet erupted with jokes, memes, think pieces, and genuine curiosity and befuddlement. The nation was riveted, of course, by the strange passing itself and by the ways Dolezal seemed to equate Blackness with accoutrements and stereotypes—from the weaves to the bronzer to the specificity of her articulated *oppressed* experiences—but it is perhaps more useful to critically consider her performance of Blackness alongside the strange *context* of her attempted passing. One particularly melodramatic aspect of passing narratives is the heartbreaking fact that the passer's family has to participate—through silent familial concealment they let the passer go, presumably forever. In prominent passing narratives, individuals intentionally sever ties with their family, and families struggle to allow the pass, recognizing the mutual sacrifice on both the part of the passer and the witnessing family—this is certainly recurrent at least in fictionalized accounts, as nonfiction tales of successful passing are scarce, for clear reasons. As a result, what might be most interesting is not that Rachel Dolezal chose to pass. This may not be surprising if we refuse to naturalize the racial hierarchy and white supremacy and also if we consider she made quantifiable gains privately and professionally as an African American woman. What is worth greater consideration is that her family revealed her pass and that they chose—years after she began the pass—to do so. In fact, their choice to "out" Dolezal's racial heritage explicitly breaks the conventional rule of *not* divulging the passer's secret identity in Black communities.

Given the contentious relationship, it is impossible to name their motivations with certainty, of course, but their public contestation of Dolezal's passing raises questions surrounding the contemporary ability to defy racialization. Despite the controversy, Dolezal told Matt Lauer on *The Today Show* that she still openly identifies as Black, even recently giving birth to a son she's named Langston (after Hughes) and changing her own name to Nkechi Amare Diallo. While this has been criticized as an astounding display of white privilege—indeed, in most cases Black Americans don't have the public opportunity to opt into a nonphenotypic definition of race at their pleasure, and certainly not if their socially constructed racial identity has been revealed—her decision to openly flout a national understanding of race offers a useful entry point into contemporary conversations about racial instability. How then can contemporary satire define race or resist racialization without, as both Smalls and Dolezal did, falling into the trap of reasserting stereotypes surrounding both?

Blackness as Fearsome Commodity

Expectations surrounding race permeate public and private spheres in multiple ways, and this continued focus on race as essentialized and something to be performed *accurately* or *authentically* demonstrates our tacit internalization of and acceptance of these tropes. In 2009 then-president Barack Obama threw out the first pitch at the MLB All-Star Game. Although there were no concerns that Obama might be embarking on a postpresidential second life as a pitcher, the ball cleared the plate and didn't bounce—usually viewed as the two casual requirements for success for nonprofessionals offered the opportunity for public sports play. Later, Obama told Fox reporters, "This is as much fun as I've had in quite some time." The moment in many ways marked Obama's status as "traditionally presidential" in the face of the racial anxieties of the nation—he was masculine, athletically inclined (but not *too* athletic), and enjoyed the national pastime (notably a sport that isn't *too* connected with Black athleticism in the national consciousness in the way that basketball or football is). However, what became a peculiar talking point wasn't Obama's participation or his reasonably successful pitch but his appearance. Clad in a black Chicago White Sox jacket, Obama wore a loose-fitting, slightly tapered pair of jeans—a sort often publicly referred to as "dad jeans."[3] What earns jeans the moniker of "dad jeans" is their focus on movement and roominess; in an age of skinny jeans and dark wash, "dad jeans" prioritize practicality and comfort over tailoring and trends—they are decidedly *un*cool. Even years later, Obama was forced to defend his choice of pants, explaining in 2013 to Ryan Seacrest, "The truth is, generally I look very sharp in jeans. There was one episode like four years ago in which I was wearing some loose jeans mainly because I was out on the pitcher's mound, and I didn't want to feel confined while I was pitching and I think I've paid my penance for that." Yet despite his assurance that he usually looks "very sharp in jeans" and the countless images of Obama and First Lady Michelle Obama dressed to the nines in their formal attire—the former in tailored suits and immaculate tuxedos—conversations surrounding Obama's appearance were often seemingly marred by the "dad jeans" misstep.

What is particularly interesting about Obama's connection to "dad jeans" is that many in the general public interpreted it as a tacit statement on the man's virility and masculinity. Former vice-presidential nominee Sarah Palin said, "Look, the perception of Obama, of him and his potency across the world is one of such weakness. People are looking at Putin as one who wrestles bears and drills for oil. They look at our president as one who wears mom jeans and equivocates and bloviates." It seemed then that for some, Obama's pants marked him as an ineffectual leader—that the jeans' apparent lack of sexuality stripped him of some inborn *right* to performative manhood and to masculinity that leadership is often thought to require. For Palin, this fashion faux pas provided the leverage necessary to wage criticism against Obama for their political disagreements in ways made obvious and tangible to a general public. Although Obama's decision to wear "dad jeans" and Palin's response were not undertaken in an intentionally satiric mode, they speak to a sense of self-satirization within racialization—the heightened representationality of the personal, innocuous choices of Black people. Here, suddenly, Obama became a joke—a seemingly self-satirizing figure. The specific policies or international relationships in question went unmentioned because they were redundant; the jeans were his unsatisfactory behaviors made manifest.

Yet postpresidency, Obama's appearance and personal performance of self have shifted in interesting ways. First, he and his wife took an immediate vacation to the British Virgin Islands and to Virgin Group founder Richard Branson's private island. On this occasion, Obama experienced what is collo-quially called a "glow up," described as a coming into oneself and, resultantly, becoming more attractive from the inside out. Obama was photographed, smiling widely, kite surfing with Branson, feet in the sand with his wife, and wearing a backward baseball cap. Upon returning to the United States, Obama was photographed shopping with his wife and wearing sunglasses, a trim brown-leather jacket, and well-tailored dark-wash jeans. This may have been the first time Obama's personal, casual style seemed to surpass the sartorial heights of his formalwear—with a look that evoked *Star Wars'* Han Solo's signature style and Lando Calrissian's swagger, Obama was poised, trendy, and performatively masculine.

It's compelling to think about the possible meaning of this stylistic trans-
formation from his presidency to his return to civilian life through a racialized lens. Indeed, it's difficult to imagine its appearance in a fictional satire
with any less clear significance. Traditionally, after leaving the White House,
the public may note devolution away from presidential appearance—we see
former politicians growing beards, forgoing weekly haircuts, and generally
engaging in activities and grooming habits that would be unexpected or
seemingly inappropriate in office. For Obama, this pendulum swung heavily. If we view the more stylish Obama as his authentic self—and indeed,
he himself has made claims that this *new* sartorial sense was *always* his
aesthetic—what might have been the impetus for his stifling it while in office? It could be that Obama was aware that even, or *especially,* the office of
the presidency was no respite from the easily conjured fears and anxieties
surrounding Black masculinity, where "the black man historically has been
perceived as the bearer of bestial sexuality, as the savage 'walking phallus'
that poses a constant threat to an idealized white womanhood and thus to
the whole U.S. social order" (Harper 9). By wearing these "dad jeans," Obama
muted the threat of a fearsome Black masculine, sartorially eschewing his
connection to Black male sexuality.

Obama's presidential style can be imagined as a conscious effort to perform
presidentially in a way that defiantly disrupted the traditional expectations of
Black masculinity. By dressing in a way that seems to refuse expectations, he
tacitly indicates his own refusal to perform a racially prescribed role; he also
simultaneously reminds us of the ever-present idea that Blackness is connected to physical and sexual excess by performing this refusal, quite literally,
on the pitcher's mound. Wanda Sykes articulates this anxiety brilliantly as she
satirically imagines Barack Obama's internal monologue and provides some
anticipation for his later shift to a more performatively masculine style in her
2009 stand-up performance, *I'ma Be Me.* In it, she describes what she notes
as Obama's looser and more casual posture and walking style after the 2008
election. She notes, "He didn't do that shit during the campaign, did he? Naw,
he was stiff as a motherfucker during the campaign! It's like he was count-
ing that shit down in his head, like, 'OK, 1, 2, wave, smile, 1, 2, wave, smile.
Whatever you do, do not touch your penis. Touch your dick, it's all over. Do
not touch your dick." It's interesting to note here that the height of the "dad
jeans" fiasco, the MLB first pitch event, was in his first year of presidency.
Sykes locates Obama's understanding of racial anxieties on the conjuring of
the Black phallus—that by even gesturing toward or accidentally brushing
against it, he might remind the nation of their already present fears surrounding Black masculinity and the figure of the Black male, thereby destroying

his political aspirations. It may be, then, that these preeminent concerns surrounding race and racial performance demonstrate the inherent hypocrisy of the post-racial era, the inability of the frame to hold, revealing instead the racism built into the post-racial mythology. Resultantly, Black people are expected either to fully reject or fully embrace preeminent stereotypes surrounding Blackness. Obama's real-life "glow-up" offers useful context for the preeminent focus of twenty-first-century satires on the instability of race. These satires unearth the fallibility of racial essentialization by illuminating its untenability and instability in practice. Moreover, twenty-first-century satires demonstrate a need for a more nuanced engagement with Black interior space by revealing the psychic trauma possible when essentialized notions of race take preeminence.

Although it is easy to accuse those who are being racialized of paranoia or sensitivity, essentialized ideas of Blackness are often so predominant in their reliance on abjection that they are easily conjured—they are so expected that they are thought to be true even in the face of limited evidence. Percival Everett's novel *Erasure* (2001) reminds readers of the insidious nature of these assumptions, the ease of their transmission, the psychic damage they can do. The novel operates with a clear awareness of the calculated and conventional reticence around race, pushing anxieties surrounding the public reception of a self-determined Black identity to the forefront. If whiteness is always assumed in American literature through an absence of signifiers, then Blackness must be called into being. This calling in of Blackness is particularly important in consideration of contemporary satirical interest in racialization. Racial essentialism might be eschewed, but this does not mean that race becomes invisible. Instead, there is a satirical acknowledgment of the failures and limitations of language to define race in satisfactory ways—where Blackness is not whiteness, whiteness is not Blackness, and no other possibilities or classifications bear general reflection. In this way, race is not reliant merely on what can be seen. Instead, within the contemporary satiric imagination, race relies on virtuality—not what is physically present but what is *presumed* to be present. What is assumed then acts as surrogate for a more complicated understanding of race and selfhood.

In *Erasure,* the protagonist, Thelonious "Monk" Ellison, is an African American writer who is struggling to write for the general public. His books, written in dense, academic jargon, are suffering from the preconceptions of the readers and publishers alike. These are not tales of poverty, of race and racism, of danger, and do not demonstrate essentialized concepts of Blackness in a consumer market. Monk is likewise distressed by the popular and critical success of Juanita Mae Jenkins's novel *We's Lives in da Ghetto*—a thinly veiled stand-in for books like *Push* and its ilk, which he feels benefit from a particular negative portrayal of Blackness and Black identity. It is out of a frustration begetting anger that he adopts the pseudonym Stagg R. Leigh and writes *My Pafology,* later titled *Fuck,* a novella focused on a grotesque and violent Black male protagonist, Van Go Jenkins, and an over-the-top ghetto and its downtrodden residents. While initially embracing a tactic similar to Obama's efforts to distance himself from these harmful tropes, in the creation of *My Pafology,* Monk ultimately runs headlong into these ideas and is subsumed by the imagery. In doing so, he ostensibly indicts a public readership of its oversimplified and ultimately harmful construction of Black masculinity, yet we soon realize his rage holds no revolutionary potential for either individual or communal justice in its lack of focus and it ultimately reinforces these tropes, rather than offering either catharsis or retribution.

The novella within the context of *Erasure* offers a critique of the market literature and images that limit and box in Blackness. Monk describes himself as being almost possessed by the novella: "I remembered passages of *Native Son* and *The Color Purple* and *Amos and Andy* and my hands began to shake, the world opening around me, tree roots trembling on the ground outside, people in the street shouting *dint, ax, fo, screet* and *fahvre!* And I was screaming inside, complaining that I didn't sound like that." (61). The juxtaposition of *Native Son* and *The Color Purple* with *Amos and Andy* is particularly revealing, as the former two bear little in common with the latter in terms of tone, mode, mood, or content. Instead, they concern the lives of imagined Black people from whom Monk has always sought to distance himself, and so his rage stems from his discomfort not with the individual tropes themselves but with their collective meaning alongside his own ready recall and ease of replication. Gillian Johns incisively notes,

> Everett's satire reaches for more than a critique of such stories on their own terms, it bitingly extends to readers (and, moreover, writers like Monk) who would compartmentalize them and believe themselves above suspicion regarding their invention, display, and consumption. That is, if we have been duped into Monk's "readerly" approach to *Fuck,* his own "blindspots" allows us to miss the irony that the "ghetto" tale featuring a black male "other" who rapes women rolls off the tongue of the self-professed highly educated, thoughtful writer who has the interesting hobbies of fishing and woodworking and who has never felt comfortable with black English. (91–92)

Everett is not only demonstrating the insidious nature of these negative portrayals but also that no one is without guilt in their promulgation, including and *especially* those who feel holier-than-thou, like Monk. Not only are the readers at fault for readily consuming these portrayals, but Monk himself is culpable through his own immediate exploitation of Blackness broadly and Black masculinity specifically without offering any real satirical context.

The contemporary satirical approach necessitates this kind of internal critique, not just for Monk but for readers as well. This is such an important move because it shifts decisively away from the idea that racial parameters or even racism itself are inherent and natural evils or that they stem from individual behavior—the currently popular idea that racism will die out with an unspecified "old generation" that indicts no one and requires no contemplation or self-examination—and instead frames racism as an interplay of a social dynamic fostered and even encouraged by passive personal acceptance. Importantly, while *Native Son* and *The Color Purple* (and *Push,* for that matter) may have portrayed some aspects of Blackness in troublingly stereotypical ways, they do offer useful agitations that demonstrate the humanity of African Americans within the frame of a white supremacist understanding of race and *without* subscription to respectability politics. These protagonists, Richard Wright and Alice Walker indicate, deserve their selfhood not because they are *good* but because they are *human*—even in their abjection, these characters reveal the potential of kaleidoscopic Blackness and resist anti-Blackness; their Black interior space demonstrates nuance and complexity and the individuality that holds significance for communal identity without implying that it simply represents *all* Black people. When Monk crafts *My Pafology,* he has no such discernible didactic aims, and neither the character he creates nor the audience he imagines is held culpable.

What is particularly significant about *Erasure* in this case is that Monk's failure—at best, a failure to engage in a focused satire, at worst, an emotional failure of enacting a temper tantrum rather than enacting the satiric mode—ultimately underscores the public naturalization of Black identity in simplistic, essentialized terms. I think here of Monk's early encounter with a woman he meets in the waiting room at his sister's health clinic. He immediately presumes the woman's lack of sophistication before being impressed by her engagement with Jean Toomer's *Cane.* Monk narrates, "I didn't know what to say to that. I scratched my head and looked at the other faces in the room. I felt an inch tall because I had expected this young woman with the blue fingernails to be a certain way, to be slow and stupid, but she was neither. I was the stupid one" (21). In this moment Everett brilliantly demonstrates, through the perhaps unlikely vessel of Monk—pre-*My Pafology* creation—that these stereotypes of Blackness have nothing to do with the lived experiences of Black people or with Black interior space. Instead, they have everything to do with how Blackness is reductively imagined by many, and how stereotypes were and continue to be sites for trauma to be (re)enacted, in a dehumanizing reliance on the same tropes—tropes that circle around ideas of stupidity and brutality.

Monk's novella is well received as a window into typical, wretched Black life because these images of Blackness are always already available and, as a result, reified. Yet despite this interaction, Monk still immediately creates *My Pafology,* a text that reinforces all of the previously held beliefs he notes here as fallacious. Monk's frustration stems from the longstanding social ease with which Blackness is commodified, rather than with Juanita Mae Jenkins's or any author's individual attempt to profit. In Monk's ostensible attempt to point out the ease with which this commodification takes place and the absurdity of these portrayals of fearsome Blackness, by adding no discernible commentary to these limiting portrayals of Blackness, he ultimately reinforces them and highlights racialization—and the subscription to stereotypes surrounding race—and strengthens its status as inextricable from public consciousness.

Because Monk's portrayals lack agitation against the traditional schema, the audience of *Erasure* is prevented from accepting his half-hearted retroactive declaration that his work is satire and the audience of his novella cannot identify it as such at the outset. It becomes even less possible when the novella is presented under the pseudonym Stagg R. Leigh, a name taken from the real-life and mythological "bad Black man" Stagger Lee of folklore. Monk assumes the Lee/Leigh persona, and while the readers of *Erasure* may discern a statement about how these negative tropes of Blackness can consume actual Black people, the readers of *My Pafology* merely see their conceptions of Blackness reaffirmed in the shallow performance that Monk-as-Stagg offers. When considering the ways in which fearsome ideas of Blackness exist regardless of the willing participation of the Black subject, this is particularly troubling. About Ralph Ellison's *Invisible Man* Maurice O. Wallace argues, "the black masculine virtuality obtains in the affective power of shadows" (35). This power of shadows creates the space in which Leigh takes form. Similar to the context for Precious in the film, it is the flimsy outline presented that makes space for audience assumptions founded on negative tropes and then proves these preconceptions correct by offering no moments of resistance or even introspection for either the characters or their audience. There is no space for the opening of Black interiority here. Blackness is paradoxically situated within American culture as that which is quantifiable and commodifiable by all, yet simultaneously alien and hidden—something so outside the norm that its motivations and behaviors are dehumanized, becoming animalistic.

The shadow then obscures the possibility for a nuanced understanding of Blackness and instead represents Blackness as what cannot be seen but is fearsome in its assumed, boogeyman-like presence. In *Erasure,* this mythic Stagg R. Leigh is empowered by forced clandestinity—his persona is maintained through this power of shadows. Stagg then is most convincing not simply because Monk subconsciously believes and accepts the stereotypes, but because accepting these stereotypes requires the least amount of his effort and effort on the part of his audience. In this way, it is significant that it is not only the oft-maligned general public that legitimizes Stagg's existence but also the liberal and educated elite, and *Monk himself.*

Thus, while Everett effectively uses satire to censure mainstream perception, Monk's very personal anger overwhelms his text and he consequently lacks the critical stance necessary for a full evaluation or condemnation of race in American society. Monk explains to his agent, "Look at the shit that's published. I'm sick of it. This is an expression of my being sick of it" (Everett 132). While Monk's anger is understandable, Everett shows the articulation as problematic and damaging, where Monk indicts the world around him but never himself: costuming himself in Black stereotypes results in nothing but his own fleeting feelings of smug superiority. Ultimately, Monk achieves nothing more than momentary catharsis in his writing. The satiric potential of his novella is rendered null as he furthers the Stagg R. Leigh charade. When an editor hopes to meet with Stagg, Monk asks his agent to "Tell her I'll call her. . . . Tell her Stagg R. Leigh lives alone in the nation's capital. Tell her he's just two years out of prison, say he said 'joint,' and that he still hasn't adjusted to the outside. Tell her he's afraid he might *go off.* Tell her that he will only talk about the book, that if she asks any personal questions, he'll hang up" (153). Monk is careless here and seems to anticipate no ramifications in this portrayal, ironically despite his own acknowledgment that it is literature and art that ultimately proves the validity of these stereotypes in the minds of the audience. His simplistic performance of abject and fearsome Blackness, both in the creation of the novella and in the creation of his authorial persona, offers only credence for these beliefs in the minds of his audience and offers neither lesson nor condemnation. If his racialized frustrations stem from mainstream willingness to accept the basest stereotypes of Blackness, Monk is all too willing to embrace them as well.

Pointing out the arbitrariness of race or the ridiculousness of racialization alone does not beget the erasure of any racial hierarchy. For these reasons, satire is especially useful in dissecting and addressing issues of Blackness and racialization more broadly. Because Everett provides context both within and without the text, he is able to articulate his concerns around racialization and its impact on interior space and exterior physicality to confound our assumptions of a simplistic racial dyad. As a result, Everett demonstrates the foolishness of the readers of *My Pafology* and the harm both Monk's and their engagement with these tropes can cause to all involved. Blackness becomes phantasmic in Everett's writing and is sustained in the popular imagination through spectrality—what is assumed to exist. It is why Monk can adopt the persona of a folkloric hero who died in 1912 and be taken as authentic in the contemporary age—the tropes are unchanging and are merely adapted to their new time. It is the recurrent "trauma porn" found not only in *Push*—a text from which Everett clearly draws inspiration in creating Juanita Mae Jenkins's *We's Lives in da Ghetto*—that allows bleeding hearts to *tsk* at vivid and grotesque villains without feeling in any way responsible themselves. By addressing this difficult subject matter from a satirical angle, Everett creates a fictitious American public that is abhorrent enough to shock readers out of their own complacency and self-absolution, but familiar enough to simultaneously highlight audience culpability. This gesture creates a space for laughing to keep from dying that recognizes the transgressive possibilities of the Black interior.

My Pafology is indiscernible from the earnest and sincere, and this is why its portrayal of Blackness does nothing to undercut any sense of Black abjection, unlike, for example, the selling of Keith Obadike's "Blackness," which refuses Black objectification by satirically highlighting it. While both the Obadikes and Monk both tread in the absurd, the performance art skillfully makes the performative aspect overt—it is impossible to sell the abstraction of Blackness in literal terms, and so its place in a marketplace signals the satiric mode—whereas Monk's physical performance of Stagg R. Leigh reinforces the alleged reality of the narrative. As Stagg R. Leigh, the author of *My Pafology* is, on the one hand, initially an unknown and relishes in this performative anonymity. And if the author is unknown, how can the audience be sure of the authorial stance as required for the acceptance of satire? Neither the author's background nor the text itself offers any touchstones. On the other hand, the context he provides for Stagg R. Leigh is so *immediately* known in its abjection and lack of Black interior space that one primed by the miserable source material would no doubt assume the validity and reality of the author. Zora Neale Hurston is informative here. In her essay "What White Publishers Won't Print," Hurston explains about Black identity, "It is assumed that all non-Anglo-Saxons are uncomplicated stereotypes. Everybody knows all about them. They are lay figures mounted in the museum where all may take them in at a glance. They are made of bent wires without insides at all. So how could anybody write a book about the non-existent?" (118). Hurston's assessment is intriguing as it not only acknowledges the oversimplified understanding of the communal lives of people of color but also reminds us of the recurrence of the images—the lives of people of color are seen as structured in ways that lack nuance and individualization, so much so that the possibility of variation in experience, of kaleidoscopic Blackness, is often popularly viewed as preposterous.[4]

Everett demonstrates the clear understanding of racial absurdity necessary for effective contemporary satire. Race has *always* existed in the realm of the arbitrary and absurd, even as spectators assume racial essentialism or phenotypic specificity, and so conversations about race naturally offer the potential of satiric readings. These conversations open up the effective nature of laughing to keep from dying, the way the laughter—here the recognition of the fallacy of essentialized portrayals of Blackness, the ability to articulate that these portrayals are distinct from the authentic—may prevent Black people from being destroyed or consumed by the racial anxieties of others. Nevertheless, much popular understanding of race is connected to performativity—a person may *act* in concert with or against the racialized expectations in spite of or in tacit approval of his or her attributed race. By blurring the distinction, Everett bridges the gap between the real and the fictitious. This skillful blurring also explains why, both despite and because of the ridiculousness of his transracial presentation, viewers understand the satirization of racial essentialism and commodification in *Atlanta*, or Mendi and Keith Obadike's performance despite their straight delivery. This message is lost in Monk's emotionally driven articulation.

Monk presents no new trope to complicate the mainstream understanding of fearsome Blackness as commodity. Both he and his protagonist are simply raging, and while rage does have its purposes, as framed by Monk it provides nothing more than momentary and fleeting catharsis. Indeed, even their attempts at absurdism are mere rage, rather than satire or satirical critique. As Monk speaks to his publisher, this satiric ineffectuality is crystallized. His publisher asks, "'So what do you want me to do?' 'Send it out.' 'Straight or with some kind of qualification? Do you want me to tell them it's a parody?' 'Send it straight,' I said. 'If they can't see it's a parody, fuck them'" (132). Perhaps Monk's disdain would be reasonable had he given any indication that the work was parody. But it is important to reiterate here that the absurdity apparent to the audience of the satirical *Erasure* is not enough, because these are expressly not the same readers of *My Pafology*. This difference is particularly crucial as readers of *Erasure* are aware of Monk's frustration with the glut of literature focused on an oversimplified portrayal of Blackness, where the readers of *My Pafology* instead are the sincere consumers of that same literature.[5] Instead, for Monk, the joke is not his narrative—the joke is his reader. Certainly then, *My Pafology* written by Thelonious "Monk" Ellison could be coded as satire. This same text written by Stagg R. Leigh is at best unclear. Thus we engage in Everett's incisive metanarrative conception of racialization where *Erasure* is received as satire because it is a calculated depiction by an author who refuses simple stereotypes or performativity in favor of complicated characters existing in a recognizably racialized society, and where Everett intensifies the reality of Black stereotypes as both consumable and consuming, but Monk's *My Pafology* is not, as it does nothing to deconstruct ideas of racial essentialism.

Is Anyone Afraid of Post-Blackness?

So what is the answer to the question of how to survive the difficult and often painful racialization of the nation? Is it, as has often been argued, simply to move past *race*—usually meant to signal, at least in the popular realm, a move past *Blackness*? What would the post-Black look like, and how is it currently addressed in public imaginaries? Was Keith Obadike's selling of his own Blackness the ultimate post-Black gesture? It might be useful to think of the post-Black as possibly serving a function different from other ideologies of "the post"—the post-soul, postmodern, or even *post*-postmodern—and as associated with an idea of performative Blackness within a contemporary context. Paul Taylor defines the "post-black" as "blackness emancipated from its historical burdens and empowered by self-knowledge—the knowledge that race-thinking has helped create the world with which critical race theory and liberatory notions of blackness have to contend" (640). Indeed, Taylor's definition covers a great deal of ground in distinguishing the post-Black within the contemporary and potentially differentiating the *post*-Black from meaning the post-racial or the *anti*-Black in its focus on "self-knowledge" and a turn inward. Where the post-Black is really problematized, though, is in the popular realm, and this is important in thinking about racial essentialism and the mythology of the post-racial, and how the deconstruction of both might lead to individual and communal justice.

Perhaps nowhere in the mainstream has the post-Black been more colluded with Blackness as problematic than in Touré's *Who's Afraid of Post-Blackness* (2011). Although this work is not a satire in a traditional sense, Touré has a prominent background as a satirical writer[6] and engages his own satirical sensibilities throughout to point out what he views as the inherent absurdity of race, or more specifically, of Blackness in public realms. Here, Touré appears as self-appointed poster child for the post-Black, as he presents his own experiences and ideas in concert with interviews with other Black intellectuals and cultural figures to work out what post-Black might actually mean. Touré naturally provides the lens through which the text is read, and he makes no pretense toward objectivity. Ultimately, in the moments where his own negative experiences surrounding racial performance are centered, the post-Black inadvertently becomes a vehicle to air his racial grievances. This is very different from the frustration Everett or the Obadikes express in view of the simplistic portrayals of Blackness. Instead, Touré seems less interested in deconstructing these portrayals in terms of Black interior space or evaluating a society that reinforces these tropes and instead seems to express anger at individuals who subscribe to these beliefs in a limited Blackness. There is little social critique to be found here. As a result, while the interviews with scholars, activists, and artists are fascinating and provide useful insights on a *continuing* conversation about the post-Black, Touré's own voice and palpable anger occasionally overwhelms what is otherwise a nuanced conversation about Black identity in the twenty-first century.

Touré overtly dedicates his book "to everyone who was ever made to feel 'not Black enough.' Whatever that means," later going so far as to note, "a special thanks to the guy who long ago told me to my face, 'You ain't Black.' You started me down the path that would become this book" (243). Audre Lorde has noted that anger has its own usefulness, but it is difficult to view Touré's particular voicing of anger as much more than venting within the context of his book.[7] Indeed, in Touré's estimation, there is no revolutionary laughter to be found in this moment, even in retrospect. He is unable, or perhaps unwilling, to recognize the ridiculousness of the statement and found solace there. He continues by explaining, "There is no dogmatically narrow, authentic Blackness because the possibilities for Black identity are infinite. To say something or someone is not Black—or is inauthentically Black—is to sell Blackness short. To limit the potential of Blackness. To be a child of a lesser Blackness" (5). One is left to wonder who would pick up a book titled *Who's Afraid of Post-Blackness?* without already being inclined to imagine myriad possibilities for Blackness, without already knowing that "post-Blackness" at its best could be a frame for imagining kaleidoscopic Blackness and the opening up of Black interior space. This is to say, the title is a misdirection because Touré doesn't imagine what the post-Black is so much as focus on what the post-Black is not—an essentialist vision of Blackness he could not replicate and a communal Blackness from which he felt excluded. With echoes of Everett's Monk, the post-Black Touré describes ultimately feels synonymous with popular conceptions of a post-racial that places undue emphasis on race, rather than *racism,* as damaging. Throughout the book, he seems less interested in the widespread ramifications of racial essentialism and instead focuses on an inherently problematic post-Blackness that seems to discount valuable shared Black experiences. And so, Touré's rhetoric seems to imply that he needs to convince readers of something they are already ostensibly predisposed to believe. It is challenging to concisely articulate the problem with Touré's appropriation of the post-Black because it seems to be trapped somewhere in the lacuna of what he *is not* saying about Blackness. I am calling this appropriation because I think Touré is intentionally muddling his intent behind his use of the term. As his book continues, it becomes clear that he is the primary voice in the text who articulates such displeasure over representational Blackness outside the confines of even respectability politics. His use stands in clear conflict with other definitions of the post-Black, even within the book itself.

It may be that because, like Antwoine Smalls, Touré defines Blackness by negative experiences—indeed, Blackness seems here to be marked specifically by the intraracial trauma of being told that one cannot be Black enough, that Blackness here is defined *by other Black people* in such strict parameters that Touré himself could never achieve it—the post-Black here seems to inherently make the value judgment of Blackness as problematic and the post-Black as the *only* way to successfully survive Blackness. This lessens the significance of whiteness as privileged space or even as void, instead pathologizing Blackness intraracially, as if intraracial tension emerged from a vacuum. While this definition of the post-Black is imprecise, Touré's book has been so widespread and he has positioned himself as the spokesperson for a post-Black sensibility, that this understanding of the post-Black is, quite problematically, perhaps the most commonly known and accepted. In "'What Was *Is*': The Time and Space of Entanglement Erased by Post-Blackness" Margo Natalie Crawford explains, "Now 'post-black' (unlike the earlier murmurs) begins to sound like 'post-race' as public intellectuals such as Touré use their personal anecdotes about black exceptionalism to celebrate an Obama-inspired post-racial terror mood. Touré's title, *Who's Afraid of Post-Blackness?*, is disingenuous; 'post-black' often sounds comforting compared to the tension tied to 'Black'" (28). Indeed, in Touré's articulation, the post-Black signals the end of Black communal identity not because it signals any actual achievement of some mythological post-racial utopia but because Touré feels he has been denied membership and is eager to move "post-Black" to ease his own racial anxieties surrounding Blackness. He conflates post-Black with the popular articulation of post-racial; where he cannot use the term *post-racial* because it is fraught, he offers up the post-Black as a soothing alternative. Touré becomes a real-life Monk as he is unable to shake free of his desire to move *past* his own racial hang-ups in significant ways.

Later, Touré quotes the musician Santigold, who most succinctly and clearly states, "I'm Black and I'm making it, so it's Black music" (54). Her idea of Black identity is useful insofar as it sounds similar to the space opened up by kaleidoscopic Blackness, or the multiple ways of *being* Black. The linguistic sensibility of the post-Black means that when it is used carelessly or inconsistently, intentionally or otherwise, it indicates that it is moving away from a separate force of Blackness—here, post-Black leaves Blackness squarely behind. Because kaleidoscopic Blackness is rather ineffable and carries with it less intrinsic, socialized baggage—and gestures to our looking at Blackness from a number of perspectives and vantage points—it may not have these connotations.[8] In this sense, within the frame Touré provides, the search for justice that marks the contemporary moment, for example, is reduced from a communal sense to a very personalized, self-centered justice that works to absolve the speaker of racial anxieties or a racial inferiority complex.

Interestingly Touré only brings one person into conversation who raises the question of the titular term itself within the book. Professor Robert Farris Thompson wrote to Touré via email, "[I] am not big on 'post-Blackness' because to me Black culture is forever and therefore never 'post'" (215). This comment is so salient, and yet Touré relegates it to the end of the book in a section reserved specifically for interesting tidbits that fit nowhere else in the text. It is troubling that Touré did not see questioning the terminology itself in this way as relevant to a book on post-Blackness. His refusal to fully address or acknowledge Thompson's valid concern gives even greater credence to the worry that "post-black advocates fail to understand black abstraction, black improvisation, and, even, *black* post-blackness" (Crawford 22). There is something unseemly in Touré's use of the phrasing *post-Black* because, given the context provided within the book itself, it appears to mean that Blackness has ended or that it was a phase that *needs passing,* with all the connotations of the word *pass,* without fully addressing that there has never really been only one way to be Black, even as the twenty-first century overtly draws this idea to the forefront. Touré's book, published in 2011, feels almost anachronistic in its insistence. Moreover, he claims the belief that there are multiple ways to be Black while also reminding readers over and over of the times when he was called "not black enough." It reads like a satire about intraracial tension, under the guise of explaining post-Blackness, which for him means moving away from Blackness altogether. It feels troublingly like Touré's own traumatic experiences within Blackness have left him desirous of this shutdown to end his own concerns surrounding race and identity politics.

Perhaps some of the most precise definitions surrounding the potentiality of post-Blackness can be found in the collection of *The Methuen Drama Book of Post-Black Plays* (2013). The editors explain that "post-black" is specifically chosen "to emphasize the dichotomous ways in which these works incorporate but also diverge from what have become normative dramaturgical formations of black drama" (Elam and Jones xi). This definition is so useful because it does not rely on a specific sense of thematic unity. Here, the term "post-black" may signal one possible way to understand Blackness in a new context—indeed, even the term itself signals perhaps a multitude of ways to perform Blackness if the post is thought of as a move beyond without being an abandonment. The problem arises, of course, when the post-Black is conjured as a way to allay anxieties surrounding Blackness, as often happens. The distinction between what this term is meant to convey and how it is occasionally erroneously used—often to imply "post-race" with all of its negative connotations—is crucial.

Race and the Space for Play

In an interview with Anthony Stewart, Percival Everett remarked,

> I don't pretend to represent anyone but myself. Now, does that mean I don't think I can possibly be a decent role model for a kid someplace? Well, no. That idea is thrilling to me. But I would think that if I were a really good carpenter, I could be the same role model for that kid. But a carpenter doesn't go to work thinking he's representing anyone when he builds those cabinets. (303)

Everett, however, may be intentionally eliding the fact that a carpenter from a marginalized group should be aware that his or her carpentry serves as inspiration to an aspiring carpenter from that same group—further, that a carpenter who claims to build cabinets must build a structure that is identifiably cabinet-like to continue to be seen as a carpenter. And much is the same for authors—the stories they recount, even when they are specific to their own unique, personal experiences, must in some regard represent something identifiable to readers, where both communal and individual identities are validated. This identifiability is crucial in an interrogation of Blackness in the twenty-first century. When most effective, these texts do not attempt to argue for a monolithic Black community, nor do they believe the hype about abject Blackness. Instead, they embrace the plurality of Blackness and Black experience. As Gates argues in *Figures in Black*, "A text becomes 'blacker' . . . to the extent that it serves as an index of repudiation" (36), and so it is the refusal of an essentialist view of Blackness that matters in reframing Black futures and Black potential, rather than merely ridding oneself of Blackness—an impossible and undesirable suggestion.

The successful conventions of these contemporary texts and performances speak broadly to the conventions of the contemporary era, particularly a large-scale consideration (if not full condemnation) of the racialization inherent in the public sphere and a critique against the persistent reliance on racial essentialism and a system that feeds racial anxiety. When these features are undertaken well, they work in concert not only to problematize a certain perception of abject Blackness but also to indict both active participant and passive observer for its prevalence. Thinking through these critiques reminds us that race itself is not the problem; the problem is racism. In utilizing the satiric mode, these works address a particular and troubling desire to limit and confine Blackness to the static, easily identifiable, and quantifiable. They shine a light on the stifling of the Black interior and the ways that kaleidoscopic Blackness is often impeded. Twenty-first-century satires and engagements with satirical ways of looking at the public sphere reveal the myth of the post-racial by forcing the idea of "race" itself to the forefront and then heightening its tropes to reveal its hazy borders and remind us that race is, in fact, a socially constructed idea. This reality of the widespread devotion to race—and race as tantamount to racism and racialization—when underscored through satire asks audiences to double back in laughter at the absurdity of the concept. However, those works that offer no touchstones for historicity, no explanation of the social system that breeds racial anxiety, and offer no pushback against racialized assumptions, ultimately refuse the possibility of revolutionary laughter and reinforce ideas of Blackness as abject, as something to move past, in the mind of the audience, regardless of authorial intention.

Laughter does not change the fact even though race, in its definition as a social construct, does not substantively exist the *effects of racism* are real and tangible. Race matters because these are the spaces where our national and cultural consciousness is formed: laws are created and enacted in the public realm, images are disseminated throughout popular culture. However, laughter encourages our thinking about the contemporary era with intentionality—not to imply, as Robert Farris Thompson rightly worries, that this means leaving Blackness behind or, even worse, that there is something inherently negative about Blackness—thinking of this moment as creating a space for play in which the negative stereotypes of Blackness can be reclaimed or left behind, rather than emerging as a continuing and oppressive force. In the coming chapter, we move to the overtly comedic to consider performer intentionality and vulnerability in the presentation of Black public interiority and personal vulnerability on stage to create new articulations of Blackness and enact the reclamation of negative tropes. This emphasis on interiority and vulnerability offers the prospect of much pleasure within Black self-hood, but also the possibility of pain if the articulation is misconstrued. This satirical play is founded on notions of racial essentialism and takes form in the deliberate performance of racial expectations in an effort to reappropri-ate and repossess Black selfhood—a difficult dance where the satirist must admit to recognizing the negative tropes of Blackness and then engage the satiric mode to ironically *subvert* them, rather than simply accepting their existence or proving their validity. What follows reaffirms the need for clear, calculated, and focused satires and reminds us that even on the comedic stage the impulse to ridicule must avoid collateral damage and remain fixated on the target worthy of ridicule rather than on laughter alone. Because when it comes to satire, impact is always greater than intent.[9]

"When Keeping It Real Goes Wrong"

Vulnerability and Satiric Misfires

> Satire is the least commercially viable
> form of comedy. There really is a distaste
> for being preached at. People have a
> very low tolerance for it—newspaper
> audiences have a way higher tolerance
> for it than others.
>   But it's tough on TV.
> —Aaron McGruder

In W. Kamau Bell's comedic memoir, *The Awkward Thoughts of W. Kamau Bell,* he recounts the feedback given by his friend Martha Rynberg after an earlier stand-up routine. After considering some of Bell's less-progressive jokes—including the use of the word "bitch" as a part of the punch line—Rynberg remarked, "Well, you know you can't end racism and also make sexism worse" (168). Well, indeed. Bell, by his own admission, was initially resistant to accept his own potential misstep—after all, can a left-leaning member of a marginalized group contribute to the further marginalization of another group?—until stepping back and considering his own two-pronged approach to the satirical. Not only did he note that a satirical comment remaining focused on its specific target can be just as funny, or more, than a joke with an indiscriminate target, but an insistence on *punching up* might provide space for a greater impact on the intended target. He explains, "It's a very easy thing to do in comedy, to make fun of the person you hate—like blah blah blah Republicans—but then as a part of making fun of Republicans, suddenly it turns into jokes targeting disabled women at McDonald's. Suddenly you're making fun of people who have nothing to do with the original thing you're talking about, and it both demeans them and diffuses the point you were making" (173). Bell's vulnerability here is crucial—it is by revealing his own comedic mishaps that he is able to reframe for his readers what effective satire might look like and mean. Bell describes here a satiric *misfire,* common particularly in the world of stand-up, where jokes are often *rapid-fire.* When satirists forget to punch up or disregard their own various privileges, limited though they may be for many, what damage is done to the message? What happens when satire and the satirical are misconstrued or, to borrow a phrase from Dave Chappelle, what happens "when keeping it real goes wrong"?

I want to focus here on a few examples of satiric misfires by brilliant comedians to demonstrate the ways that even satiric geniuses can miss their mark[1]—they aren't beyond reproach, but neither do these moments in isolation *necessarily* lend themselves to a broad condemnation of the satirist in total. These are, just as described, significant *moments* that serve as reminders of the tricky nature of the satiric mode and the wide-reaching ramifications of satiric misfires. In these cases, the misfires can be broken down into three general categories of satiric confusion—the misreport of the contemporary realm; the misrepresentation of the past and its historicity; or a fundamental misreading of the satiric import by the audience themselves. All of these stifle the revolutionary potential of the laughter itself, instead ironically leading to a dangerous terrain where survival may be impossible. Satire is complicated because in its effort to reframe the rules of the social game, the purpose of the game itself may ultimately be lost. What I argue here is that avoiding these misfires necessitates that the satirists make themselves personally vulnerable by revealing their own biases, difficulty with the subject material, or even their own fallibility as thinkers on the subject being discussed. Are they a member of the group being targeted? Is their perspective limited or biased in some way? What are their own shortcomings in delivering their joke or making meaning through laughter? This engagement with vulnerability is not only a difficult prospect—in a world that imagines *just* jokes, this deliberate focus on meaning and significance has the potential to reduce widespread comedic appeal—but also a potentially dangerous one, depending on the audience.

Since the late 1990s, Chris Rock has refused to perform his controversial "Niggas versus Black People" stand-up bit, in which he raucously expressed his disgust with the behaviors and attitudes of the former as he spoke indirectly toward a politics of respectability. Similarly, nearly ten years later, Dave Chappelle walked away from a reported $55 million contract with Comedy

Central amid personal concerns that his jokes were missing their mark, and that the laughter inspired was occurring as his performances were viewed through a racist—in stark contrast to what he meant to provide, a racially conscious—lens. Chappelle later succinctly explained his rationale for leaving by saying, "I want to make sure that I am dancing and not shuffling" (qtd. in Robinson), indicating not only an understanding of his role as entertainer but a real desire to perform and an enjoyment of the performance, but only when it occurs on his own terms. This admission marks a departure from a traditional and oversimplified understanding of the satirist as a vessel for speaking cleverly framed truths about the social realm. Instead, as Chappelle constructed it at the time, the role of the satirist, if the satirist is to be effective, requires centering the *self* as societal representative, a highly vulnerable act in which the speaker becomes the target of the laughter and shares a hazy—or even indiscernible—border with the object of ridicule. The misfires experienced by both Rock and Chappelle occur, then, in part because vulnerability is avoided in favor of easy outward-looking joking. Rather than evoking laughing to keep from dying, where the articulation of Black selfhood creates space for new and autonomous ways of being, these jokes close off introspection and mask Black interior space, inadvertently reaffirming traditional limited portrayals of Black identity.

Satiric laughter is meant to highlight audience in-group status—the audience "gets the joke," and in being understood, the joker is proven to be objectively dissimilar to the object of ridicule, or at least found to have the potential for salvation. In "Exploring Niggerdom: Racial Inversion in Language Taboos," Richard J. Gray and Michael Putnam explain, "to laugh at someone, is to expect the individual to curb the behavior and operate in a way more in conformity with the rules established by our society. When someone shows the inability to curb a behavior, laughter reveals our disapproval" (19). Yet when the distinction between the joker and the joke, the satirist and the satire, is blurred, the laughter may be heard as acceptance rather than disapproval, or at least offer enough plausible deniability to be effectively misconstrued as acceptance by audiences who do not wish to understand the joke teller's meaning. This is a particular risk when in-group lines are hazy—in moments where the satirist is telling a joke *about* his own in-group in a realm where an out-group may claim ownership of the joke itself. The vulnerability of the satirists ideally reminds audiences that satire is defined by its stakes and by its clear focus, but this only matters insofar as the audience is willing to accept it as satire.

Herein lies the potential difficulty with performance and audience interpretation: if the satirical mode imagines the object of ridicule out to an absurd conclusion, and if racism and racialization already verge on the inherently absurd, the distinction between the reality and the satire may be indistinguishable. This can be an especially damning prospect if African American satirical performance is meant to subvert the mainstream acceptance of and propagation of the racial status quo—particularly for groups outside African American communities, it may be seen as commentary on what *is* rather than exaggeration used as active criticism. The performance then runs the risk not only of distorting meaning but also of inadvertently reifying stereotypes and undercutting the nuanced, autonomous selfhood with which these satirical ideologies are so concerned, causing severe psychic damage not only to the satirists but to the groups the satirist does not intend to target.

Vulnerable satiric performances, then, require an *affect* of disinterest—a line that must be negotiated skillfully, lest this appearance of disinterest overwhelm clear intentionality—that ultimately allows the comedian introspection and reflection, this opening up of Black interior space. Contemporary satirical texts, performances, and comedians emphasize the importance of conversations about race and representation even as they performatively eschew, in many cases, the significance of racial difference. They seem to imply that conversations about race are tiring and overwrought, even as they ironically engage with the very subject matter at length. For instance, in framing a *Chappelle's Show* sketch, Dave Chappelle cautions, "I hate to hit this point so hard, but remember: whenever we do these racial commentaries, it's all about the subtleties. We're all part of the same human family. Our differences are just cultural, that's it," before entering into a scene about the soporific qualities of barbecue ribs in Black communities. Chappelle's insistence on the inconsequence of race as culture belies a deeper truth—Chappelle offers no differentiation between culture and race in meaningful ways because he doesn't really distinguish between the two; without these "cultural" differences that Chappelle feigns are insignificant, he would have no racial propellant behind his jokes, no material, and no show. What is interesting is that Chappelle's denial of racial significance here is ultimately not post-Black, nor does it imagine post-raciality in any real sense. Instead, Chappelle's monologue works to provide his audiences with an introduction that immediately disallows reductive assumptions of racial essentialism by colluding race and culture as synonymous. Chappelle claims race is irrelevant while cleverly demonstrating through his joke telling that, in his estimation, we cannot truly distance ourselves from our own racial assumptions or the assumptions of others.

It would appear, then, that Chappelle trusts his audience to watch these performances with enough discernment to glean the true racial significance once he offers them his brief context as disclaimer—a point on which his comedy is contingent, and on which he later reneges and admits an initial misreading of his viewer. The belief in audience discernment and his later admission of error is the origin of Chappelle's vulnerability. It is why audiences continue to look back at his early material as the height of not only his comedic prowess but of his incisive, *subversive* cultural commentary. Compare this to his comedic ancestor, Richard Pryor. Unlike Chappelle, Pryor not only trusted his audience to understand his meaning but also actively stepped away from the comedic in moments where the meaning might be lost and where meaning took on more significance than the laughter—a model that Rock has emulated in recent years and a comedic risk that Chappelle, at least until his 2018 and 2019 specials, was unwilling to take. And it is for this reason that Chappelle's work after 2017 lacks not only the rigor and provocative observation of *Chappelle's Show* or his early stand-up specials, but also any sense of revolutionary laughter—this later laughter at the expense of the LGBTQ community and sexual assault survivors is only meant to save those who don't need saving. In this way, Chappelle's later comedy has suffered from his lack of vulnerability and his association with—and newly discovered comfort among—those in positions of power.

Although Richard Pryor actively heightened rather than feigned trivializing the significance of race in his material, he is perhaps the contemporary era's most direct forefather. Pryor merged man and myth and, unlike most legends, seems to have earned his reputation in both theory and practice. During an interview on *60 Minutes*, Dave Chappelle said of Richard Pryor passing the figurative comedic torch to him, "That's more pressure than $50 million. That's a lot of pressure. He was the best, man. For him to say that is, you know, that's something I don't even know if I'll attempt to live up to that" (Leung).[2] Richard Pryor informs the comedic persona of most Black comedians who emerged after him, and by their own admission in many cases. What is most striking about his persona and his performance as a comic is that he was consistently and unabashedly willing to make himself the target of the joke. His vulnerability was profound, yet it never relied on pathos alone; his stand-up was self-deprecating, but he was not a clown.

This vulnerability, coupled with his biographically inspired, pseudo-confessional stand-up, made audiences willing to listen to his jokes without jumping to conclusions—to patiently wait for the end of the joke before they assumed his meaning. This is a difficulty both Rock and Chappelle have experienced for reasons regarding the cult of celebrity surrounding comedy in the contemporary era—our desire for rapid-fire laughs often usurps the time and space a performer would use to set the parameters of the joke itself and lead us to its conclusion. Rock has generally eschewed vulnerability in his performances since the mid-1990s[3]—he is instead *Chris Rock,* the leather-clad rock star comic playing to enormous amphitheaters. With the exception of his semiautobiographical coming-of-age sitcom, *Everybody Hates Chris,* Rock himself is seldom the target of his own jokes. Conversely, Chappelle assumes the posture of the ne'er-do-well slacker with the heart of gold, playing to historic but frequently less ostentatious venues even as we recognize him to be perhaps the most in-demand comedian of the twenty-first century. Even their attire—Rock's ever-present glitz and shine, compared with Chappelle who, at his most formal live performances, puts a blazer or military-inspired jacket on over a T-shirt—positions them on opposite ends of the spectrum of celebrity. Unfortunately for Chappelle, this persona was more difficult to maintain once he was proclaimed by many to be the greatest comic mind of his generation and was offered the huge contract, seeming to prove this fact. Chappelle's initial vulnerability revealed the Black interior and articulates a desire for justice in its portrayal of a nuanced and kaleidoscopic Blackness that refuses reductive stereotypes. Yet in a society where the private lives of celebrities are considered fodder for media reports, Chappelle seemed unable to continue allowing himself this degree of vulnerability for myriad reasons that did not, at least until the 1980s, impact Pryor in the same way.

However, vulnerability is often by necessity extinguished in anticipation of broad public consumption of jokes outside an in-group communal sphere. In these spaces, vulnerability can be problematized, either read as insincere by audiences reluctant to see Black people as potentially vulnerable or, more troublingly, by a sloppy or miscalculated joke inadvertently lending itself to fodder for ad hominem attacks that implicate broader African American communities. For this reason some comedians work to decenter themselves from the joke itself and reimagine themselves as discrete *joke tellers,* mere vessels through which the joke is articulated as if the joke exists on a separate plane. Of course, doing so is rife with serious problems of its own.

Chris Rock and the Dangers of Misreporting the Present

Unlike Pryor or Chappelle, Chris Rock performs within the realm of stand-up comedy with a tenor similar to rock 'n' roll stardom. Rock got his start doing stand-up before briefly appearing as an ensemble player on *Saturday Night Live.* However, Rock is best known for his movie roles and, most significantly, his number of HBO specials like *Big Ass Jokes* (1994), *Bring the Pain* (1996), *Bigger and Blacker* (1999), and *Never Scared* (2004). For the purposes of this discussion on the risks and rewards of satiric vulnerability, his *Bring the Pain* merits closer examination. The special is groundbreaking and innovative and cemented Rock's place as one of the most brilliant comedic minds of his generation. However, the special isn't without its misfires. Rock performs his infamous "Niggas versus Black People" set, where he elucidates perceived differences between two groups within a mythologized Black community. He speak-shouts, in his characteristic frenetic intonation,

> Can't do shit without some ignorant-assed niggas fucking it up. Can't do nothing. Can't keep a disco open more than three weeks—"Grand opening! Grand closing!" Can't go to a movie the first week it comes out. You know why? 'Cause niggas are shooting at the screen. What kind of ignorant shit is that? "Hey, this is a good movie. It's so good, I gotta bust a cap in here." Hey, I love black people, but I hate niggas. I wish they'd let me join the Ku Klux Klan. I'd do a drive-by from here to Brooklyn.

The bit continues, ad nauseam. Rock delineates between worthless "niggas" and worthwhile "black people," situating himself and his primarily Black audience[4] within the latter group. Eddie Tafoya articulates the immediate impetus behind Rock's set and in-group efforts:

> First of all, by establishing an out-group, the dishonest and irresponsible people, he is implying that there is an in-group, one that is comprised of people who laugh and cheer at his proclamations, a move that not only makes the crowd like him more but solidifies the crowd as a single unit. Secondly, the distinction deracinates the epithet as Rock implies that what is at issue here is not one's race but one's behavior—not skin color, but personal choices. Finally, by calling out people on such shortcomings, he is also suggesting that anybody who lumps all black people together into one kind of group, culture, or value system is simply not seeing the whole picture. He pounds on this issue for seven minutes, saying, "A black man that's got two jobs, going to work every day, hates the nigga on welfare—'Nigga, get a job. I got two, you can't get one?'" (226)

Tafoya is correct, and the problems inherent in Rock's articulation extend beyond the stage itself. For one, the in-group cannot exist as Rock has established it. Farai Chideya incisively notes in *Cultureshock: Chris Rock's Bring the Pain* that "the joke was perfect for Washington, D.C., because these are the people who are being judged by the standard of 'are you a nigger?' when they're really trying to be, like, super-black." Within the context of this in-group of upwardly mobile African Americans, the joke creates a space for a nuanced articulation of Black interiority—a space in which the audience can resist the negative stereotypes attributed to them and say "I am not *that*," even where it means, problematically, disavowing other apparent group members by saying "and yet I recognize *that* exists and is not a myth." Rather than vulnerably admit his own fears of being misunderstood in negative terms rather than as the "super-black" figure with whom he identifies, Rock positions himself as so far from the stereotypical portrayal that he, too, is disgusted by the characters he describes. The move he makes is different from even problematizing the stereotypes or their prevalence. Instead, he seems to give the stereotypes legs and then separates himself from the stereotype, rather than admitting that the widespread belief in the stereotype renders him vulnerable as well. This is perhaps compounded by the fact that while the live audience is primarily African American, the HBO audience watching from the comfort of their homes is primarily *not*.[5] What this means, then, is that the home viewers witness an African American comic spouting "nigga" as a definitive, racially specific, if not outright racist slur, African American audiences laughing, imagining themselves by virtue of their own laughing response grouped in with an in-group that not only permits the usage but finds it necessary for the communication of difference.

Despite what Tafoya notes as Rock's efforts to argue that "not one's race but one's behavior—not skin color, but personal choices" are the characteristics that define "niggas," Rock's definition is still couched in language of coded and overt racial specificity for a home-viewing audience who may not recognize this subtlety. In particular, his proclaimed desire to join the Ku Klux Klan can be understood as nothing except, if not an outright connection between "black people" and "niggas," a collapsing of racial otherness and "niggas"—an overt even if unintentional misreporting of contemporary racialization. If the only people who can be "niggas," in Rock's ascertaining, end up being only "black people," then the claims to racial nuance inherent in the intended joke certainly miss their mark and provide resistant audiences interested in the humor of disparagement with ample fodder; this is especially damaging and damning in consideration of the ubiquity of questions regarding who is "allowed" to say "nigger" or "nigga," despite the number of African American scholars, theorists, and pundits who have offered guidance on this question. This is not the "punching up" or the speaking truth to power required of effective satirical output—he attempts to save one marginalized group through the further marginalization of another. Within the context of the mainstream, there is no justice to be found in this articulation, only a misreporting of racial identity politics even within the realm of a supposed post-racial ideology, allowing Rock to eschew vulnerability and protect himself. With an all-Black in-group, the joke may have landed as a humorous oversimplification, tough love, or even a demand for the acknowledgment of kaleidoscopic Blackness because the inherent vulnerability of the position may have been apparent; when the in-group and out-group are merged as they are for an HBO viewing audience, the frame for the joke itself cannot hold.

Rock is a charismatic orator whose cadence rises and falls like a preacher in a Black church—and indeed, his grandfather was a minister—and is every bit as compelling. His persuasiveness and rock star sensibility are part and parcel of the problem of misunderstanding within this joke. Rock is so dynamic that the distinction he makes was seen as not only his viewpoint but an extension of the viewpoint of *all respectable* Black people, as he describes the group—a conflation less likely within the in-group he seems to imagine. Unlike Pryor, whose heightened vulnerability gestured toward a communal articulation of the harm of racialization, the risk with Rock's articulation is that he becomes the exception that proves the rule—if Rock is disgusted by "niggas," then his racially mixed audience is justified in their distaste as well.

This sense of distaste overtly refuses any possibility of a vulnerable revelation; if there is any justice to be found, it is only for Rock as an individual, in his misreporting himself as separate from the rabble, but even this possibility is untenable in practice.[6] As a result, a routine that is inherently classist and racist in structure offers wide usage by individuals who not only do not understand the nuances Rock seeks to imply but also may be uninterested in even acknowledging the existence of those nuances while Rock actively protects himself by separating himself from this group. In a *60 Minutes* interview, Rock tells Ed Bradley that he has never done the joke since, "and I probably never will. 'Cause some people who were racist thought they had license to say nigger. So I'm done with that routine" (Leung). It is interesting here that Rock positions the use of the word *nigger* as something some people have a right to where others—those he defines as "racist"—do not, squarely situating himself in the former category. Yet even in this more calculated later articulation, Rock does not delineate the able from those who should not speak the word.

Certainly a thoughtful, "nonracist," contemporary audience member of any race should have been able to differentiate between his performative use of racist language and his lack of earnest endorsement of the ideas in practice, it seems to follow for Rock. But without his own vulnerability on display—his own concerns that these limited descriptors might be assigned to him and without naming them as a fabrication—the distinction is unclear. While Rock's joke could indeed highlight "that anybody who lumps all black people together into one kind of group, culture, or value system is simply not seeing the whole picture" (Tafoya 226), it still forces racial otherness onto an already marginalized group because Rock ultimately argues via this misreporting that some Black people *are*, in fact, "niggas" and thus may deserve the term and the related disparagement and violence, but that he and his specific in-group are not and should be separated from it. The joke operates not as any effort toward wide-reaching understanding or collective justice but instead as an attempt at present separation and self-preservation on the part of the teller. What audiences witness instead is a performance that, when stripped of its context, bears no dissimilarity from any argument about respectability politics at best, and from racist propaganda at worst.

This "Niggas versus Black People" set was not the last time the comedian controversially framed identity by way of misreporting. While there are many analyses of the aforementioned set that all point to the problematic nature of Rock's specific jokes, little has been made of its connection to the similar issues revived in his 2009 documentary, *Good Hair*. Chris Rock's documentary addresses the relationship that some African American women have with their hair, utilizing elements of satire to underscore the larger sociopolitical significance of these seemingly innocuous choices. Here Rock merges his role as comedian with his emergent role as social commentator. Perhaps Chris Rock deserves credit for having achieved what has often been described as the seemingly impossible. Through the production of this documentary, Rock ostensibly sought to open up a space where African American women could and would publicly comment on their own hair and cultural hair *issues*. This effort is full of promise and ultimately feels more successful compared to the earlier comedic set in large part because Black interior space—here, the vulnerability of Black womanhood in these conversations—is acknowledged. Black hair has often appeared to many as an exclusive club that outsiders never quite understood—a *secret* society. It hasn't been something Black women are traditionally encouraged to talk about, and certainly not to women who weren't Black, for a variety of reasons including those related to class, gender and sexuality, respectability, and Western ideals and standards of beauty. This documentary forces the issue of hair into the mainstream spotlight. Rock's editorial decisions in framing this narrative, however, are troubling.

Good Hair was dreamed up by Rock under the pretense of answering his daughter Lola's question as a young child, "Daddy, why don't I have good hair?" To this end, Rock traveled to Atlanta, Greensboro, Los Angeles, and India to understand and analyze the complicated relationship between many African American women and their hair. He interviewed a number of Black women—most of them famous from television and film—and allowed them the opportunity to divulge their hair history and musings as he consulted both "experts" and the opinionated masses. The film skillfully navigates the razor's edge (pun intended) between the problematic—a six-year-old girl sitting patiently and uncomfortably as a relaxer is painstakingly applied to her hair—and the humorous—stylist Derek J.'s simultaneous tantrums and dazzling glamour in the Bronner Brothers hair show in Atlanta. Yet, while the information in the documentary is undeniably compelling, there are more than a few troubling moments in the film. Many of these issues emerge from a clear lack of context that fosters an environment in which Rock misreports Black women's (apparently universal) motivations as shallowly striving toward whiteness as though this is fact, with little evidence besides his own interpretations of anecdotes. In the creation of this documentary, Rock was afforded the allowances that are only provided celebrities. He had money, fame, means and, as an African American man, presumed credibility on issues related to African American people—whether this credibility was deserved or not. And while *Good Hair* is consistently interesting, it never fully engages its purported purpose as an exploration of questions surrounding good hair within cultural experiences and, as a result, misses its implied aim of elucidating Black female selfhood, instead often going for predictable jokes at the expense of Black womanhood. What this signals is a failure to effectively meld the satiric mode with the documentary form as the film attempts to occupy the space of each at different moments throughout.

So then, if Rock doesn't specifically answer his young daughter's question of "why don't I have good hair?"—nor does the film engage the concept of the social implications of the *absurdity* of the politics of Black hair outside what Rock marks as Black communal interests—then it would seem that the related, wide-reaching concern for Rock should be "does good hair even exist and why should anyone watching care about it?" By never directly addressing the latter question and, even more specifically, by never rejecting the assumption of "good hair" or addressing the origins of the concepts, he unintentionally implies that "good hair" is not only a *real thing,* but that it's a valid concept and one that exists separate from socialization while simultaneously implying that Black women are shallow or foolish for subscribing so devotedly to it—once again, Rock imagines himself above the fray, as commentator who is absolved of the critique by critiquing others more marginalized than himself. In this way, his commentary *becomes* the satirical lens through which Black womanhood is viewed. Rock's interactions in the film indicate that not only does he believe this thinking is widespread in others, but he also demonstrates that he subscribes to the mythology of good hair. He runs his fingers through one woman's hair and swoons over its straightened texture, announcing to everyone present "I think I'ma marry you." The joke lands and the people present chuckle, but Rock negotiates the line between comic and documentarian unsteadily in a film meant to address the fraught territory of Black women and their appearance in the mainstream—Rock unintentionally demonstrates that he is as culpable for the perpetuation of the myth of good hair as the general public he is tacitly condemning, even as he is framed as the final word on the subject.[7] The tension between the seriousness of the subject and Rock's desire to inspire comedy is seen in a few moments throughout the film—Rock's jokes about Black women's desire for the hair of Indian women *to* Indian women or his running away from a giant "tumbling tumbleweave" a la Indiana Jones in *Raiders of the Lost Ark*. As far as forwarding his purported message, these comedic moments fall flat. The tone of the film is already so light, even in view of serious subject matter, that these overtly comedic moments seem to verge on farce and muddle the point. This can be the difficulty of melding two generic forms—the documentary and the comedy—in a way that allows them to maintain the sensibility of either. Rock's comedic desires naturally win out and the documentary nature of the film is lessened as a result. These comedic moments alongside Rock's own performed expertise on the subject—in this case, the wants and needs of Black women—contribute to a general lack of seriousness and nuance that ultimately reobjectifies Black women in a frame that denies them compassion.

The problem of a comedian creating a documentary on a serious subject can be the incongruence between content and context. Rock is tackling an important topic, but audiences still anticipate some infused humor because of the name attached to the film—this was, after all, his first real foray into the genre. So, unfortunately, the seriousness of the subject goes unheeded by viewers, and the history behind these ideas is unmentioned. Indeed, the film isn't merely ahistorical—it is *antihistorical*. It doesn't merely ignore history but actively removes the important and necessary historical origin from the context so that Rock can forward his beliefs without contestation. Nowhere in the film is slavery, miscegenation, or racism even mentioned, let alone discussed in earnest. In fact, the 1970s, a time when African American women in popular culture shunned chemical hair treatments and embraced Afros in large numbers, goes completely overlooked both in the filmic conversation and in the opening montage of Black women and their hair through the years—it begins in the 1920s or 1930s, completely disregards the 1970s, and moves to elaborate, highly-processed styles of the 1990s and early twenty-first century. The intentional elision of the body work of the Black Power movement and its literal articulation of the idea that Blackness, natural and unencumbered by Western ideals or conventions, is not only worthy of consideration but is unapologetically beautiful is a distracting lacuna that undermines the historical content and context of the film. Indeed, although the modern resurgence of the natural hair movement was not as prominent in

2009 as it has been later years, it was a growing movement that is conspicuously absent in his film.

Most disturbingly, audiences are never privy to the causality behind the idea of good hair. Leaving out historicity in a conversation about African American hair politics is tantamount to disregarding the backstory of a war. Rather than seeking to dismantle or even acknowledge the systems that foster an environment in which the idea of good hair can thrive, the absence of rationale renders any implied importance impotent. In fact, the shock footage of relaxers and the exorbitant prices of weaves appear as narcissistic rather than indicative of a racially oppressive system dating back to slavery and the value of Eurocentric features—indeed, Rock seems more interested in comedic effect than in the psychology behind these choices.

Rock consistently toes the line when it comes to tone—vacillating swiftly between embracing a satirical impulse in talking about hair as "important" and condescension as he addresses the significance of hair in some Black communities, which he sees as one monolithic community.[8] When asked why women would put themselves through what he himself frames as torture, he states flippantly and largely erroneously "to look white." The implication—that Black women, apropos of nothing, merely subscribe to a white standard of beauty—is both hurtful and harmful, and not one substantively reinforced by anyone he interviews in this documentary. Women are never asked *why* they have relaxers or weaves, or for their thoughts on the long-term ramifications. They aren't even asked about the historical significance of their autonomous hair choices. The film addresses the where and the how, but never goes any deeper than this surface level to ask the more impactful questions of why or when. There is no sense of Black selfhood—communal or individual—that can be established or reclaimed. Instead, the negative stereotypes of poor money management, shallowness, and unattainable Western beauty standards that are unfairly waged against women of color are reinforced.

Ultimately, the greatest misreporting is seen in the incongruence between the purported moral and the footage selected. Rock states in the end that he wants to teach his daughters, "the stuff on top of their heads is nowhere near as important as the stuff inside their heads." If so, he might have achieved an articulation of a just selfhood that held meaning for his daughters. Yet this idea is never textually implied and this assertion that gestures toward public Black interiority goes unresolved. He picks some of the most beautiful and powerful African American women in the public realm—Nia Long, Kerry Washington, Meagan Good, among others—and has them discuss their weaves while he chuckles at the cost and what he identifies as the frivolity of the subject, and then delves no further into these questions. One must wonder, then, whether his daughters are in fact his intended audience. The content of the film surely indicates that his daughter's question was a narrative conceit. Certainly, the language and general raunchiness indicate his daughters, who were elementary school–aged at the time, are not truly his target viewers. If the audience isn't immediately his daughters, then who is it? If it is African American women, then that intention is a bit muddled and unclear because, while African American women in some communities may be intrigued by a film that ostensibly centers their experiences, they ultimately have nothing new to learn from the film and are made out to be foolish. If the intended audience is white America, *Good Hair* doesn't provide any real insight except to display private hair choices, stripped of historicity.

What then is the goal of *Good Hair*? Ultimately, the film moves unsteadily toward addressing a mainstream audience by holding up a mirror to an African American cultural frame and then blaming the culture in a vacuum for what Rock views as its shortcomings, irresponsibly omitting the present issues around assimilation and popular standards of beauty. By never answering any significant questions and instead focusing on what he views as Black women being held captive by the trope of good hair without dismantling good hair as a fallacious construct in itself, the idea of Black culture as mere spectacle is reinforced and Rock emerges, once again, as wise and above the foolishness. This is a standard trope of these sorts of popular culture documentaries—I think of Bill Maher's straw-man attacks against religion throughout *Religulous,* a documentary that came out the year before Rock's—but here doubly marginalized Black women are targeted as fodder for the joke in mixed company. Rock uses the rhetoric of a still-damning new brand of politics of respectability where, unlike even in *Bring the Pain,* respectability means gesturing vaguely to his perception of an authentic performance of Blackness that is tangible and ultimately easily quantifiable, where respectability means exposing the vulnerability of other marginalized groups, here Black women, while eschewing one's own.

Misrepresenting the Past

Certainly Black women are in a vulnerable position both within and without the frame of respectability politics. E. Francis White writes, "To be positioned outside the 'protection' of womanhood was to be labeled unrespectable. Black feminists of the first wave understood the costs of this label to all black women. They did not miss the irony in the contrast between the fiction of black men's molestation of white women and the very real rape suffered by black women" (33). Indeed, the stakes of "respectability" are particularly high in this regard for Black women as they are at particular risk of a lack of respectability thought to signal their own abjection. This line is especially difficult to negotiate for African American women because the expected prerequisites for "respectability" are often those that are also not considered conventionally funny. Women are then damned if they do, and damned if they don't—they are either the boring prude or the grotesque clown. Of course, even this so-called protection emerges as a falsehood—there is no amount of respectability a Black woman can perform that would ultimately protect her from violent assumptions about her sex and sexuality. Black women have been denied the protection of membership in the cult of true womanhood, where (white, land-connected) women were seen as pious, pure, submissive, and domestic, and thereby worthy of a level of esteem and protection. Indeed, the overwhelming emphasis on enunciated sexual availability or sexual silence of Black women disallows such attributes—white women in the cult of true womanhood were sexualized insofar as they were seen as women in the traditional sense but never thought to be deriving any subversive sexual pleasure from their own femaleness. In this sense, Black female sexuality is often imagined on a binary—entirely present for the pleasure of others, or entirely absent in the caretaking of others.

Oftentimes, Black female comedians shirk an essentialized view of Black female sexuality by attempting to articulate ownership of their own sex lives, to varying degrees of success and clarity. In doing so, they simultaneously refuse both easily imagined tropes of the mammy and the Jezebel. The continued reliance on the imagined existence of mammy in contemporary society speaks once again to the power of mainstream cultural production to shape our understanding of both ourselves and of others. The Jezebel emerges in the national consciousness as the diametric opposition to the mammy—not only is she sexually available and sexually provoking, but she is sexually insatiable. Her sexuality is her defining characteristic—if she has children, their welfare is secondary to her desire to feed her own sexual appetite. As a result, both of these tropes gain significance only to the extent that they offer a disavowal of the other. If both of these tropes remain in steadfast existence, there is a dismissal of Black female dynamism at best, and the reification of white and male domination over that which is marked as racially and sexually different at worst. Ultimately, these tropes prescribe parameters in which these female comedians struggle to exist. They are seemingly misfit within the limited view of Black womanhood and, as such, audiences are often automatically resistant to their joke telling. As a result, the joke telling itself collapses the possibility of self-actualization and its potential justice-seeking in both personal and public realms.

Although women do push back against negative presumptions about female-driven comedy, there is often a great deal of resistance from audiences toward reconfiguring the existing schema. While these comedians, doubly marginalized (at minimum) at the intersection of race and gender, are not at as great a risk of refusing to punch up, jokes made by women are at an intensified risk of being reductively determined to be incompatible or grotesque. In an effort to avoid these critiques, many of these jokes are couched in history and historicity, to greater or lesser success. Of course, in situating the comedy in the history, in saying "we already know the story and can assume its meaning," there is a risk of misrepresenting the past to validate a present perspective, in which case both the comedy and message may be lost. One infamous case in point is the 1993 Friar's Roast in which Ted Danson, an actor and Whoopi Goldberg's paramour at the time, appeared in blackface and performed a grotesque caricature of Blackness. The couple met while guests on Arsenio Hall's late-night talk show, becoming friends and later engaging in a romantic relationship—the affair led to Danson's separation from his wife at the time in one of the most expensive Hollywood divorces, allegedly costing Danson $30 million in the settlement. When Danson came to the stage in full blackface attire, the mostly-celebrity audience was notoriously scandalized and disgusted. Roger Ebert wrote,

> Friar's roasts, which are never taped for telecast, are traditionally raucous and obscene. But the specter of a white man in blackface repeatedly using the word "nigger" and other strongly coded words seemed to cross a line that was sensed by most of the people in the room. The event demonstrated that the painful history of black-white relations in America is still too sensitive to be joked about crudely. Goldberg, whose real name is Caren [sic] Johnson, has used her entire career to try to break down racial stereotyping, and in encouraging Danson's approach she may have thought it would play as satire. But, as stand-up comics say when their material isn't working, he was dying up there.

Here the idea of laughing to keep from dying takes on a new form—when even the *audience* isn't laughing, there is nothing *except* (comedic) death. Is it, then, that blackface in the twentieth and twenty-first century is always over the line? Perhaps. Even as we may want to leave open the possibility that *anything* can be made funny, this territory may be too worn and too fraught and, as aforementioned, too frequently stripped of context to be effective, or any nuanced meaning refused in favor of an oversimplification. This is the ultimate example of the audience not being in on the joke when the joke is treated in such a cavalier manner. Still, even if blackface could be flawlessly performed as satire, the troubling and exaggerated hallmarks that made it a historical space for "humor" remain—it is difficult to exaggerate the already exaggerated blackface performance to *contemporary* comedic effect.

It is unsurprisingly a struggle to think of a recent use of blackface that has been effective at making contemporary meaning.[9] However, in this particular usage the implications, intentional or not, are far more problematic. For one, Danson's white masculine body in blackface does not, on the surface at least, work to subvert a current understanding of racial performativity or offer any real vulnerability in the articulation of the joke. Instead, it speaks most directly to a national understanding of how blackface works to reinforce a racial hierarchy where white men appropriate and misunderstand Blackness, dehumanizing Black people and rearticulating white superiority. Danson's performance highlights this historical intention and inadvertently reaffirms the racialization of Black people and of Black women more specifically. His jokes surrounding his sex life with Goldberg, her genitalia, and rife with the use of the word "nigger," do no real work to shift the status quo or to highlight anything useful surrounding the ludicrousness of race or racism; the joke merely misrepresents past sexual and psychological abuses by white men on Black women as containing possible realms of consensuality and pleasure. The performance certainly isn't antiracist. It isn't even merely *not* racist. Blackface is in no way subversive in the abstract—it cannot be engaged with subtlety or nuance because it cannot exist outside an overt historical frame. As a result, it must be enacted as a clear and focused satire where the target is known to all—if this is even possible—or it only emerges as reification of the racist trope.

What autonomy is offered Goldberg, in this situation, where she is still the performative target? Even if she wrote the jokes, as she claims, how can audiences understand these words as her words when waged at her by Danson? Of course, the gendered aspect of this performance—a white man in blackface riffing on the appearance and sexuality of a Black woman—is particularly problematic, especially within the lens of historicity. Neither Goldberg nor Danson provided any framing outside of what audience members brought with them, and so audiences can only interpret the material given the existing parameters of racism and taboo. Danson and Goldberg may have evoked for audiences through this performance the specific historical context of white male slave owners sexually and physically abusing Black slave women and the false claims of Black female sexual willingness and readiness—they were the wrong performers at the wrong time, and no misrepresentation of past contexts could shift this natural reception.

In Whoopi Goldberg's autobiographical *Book,* she references the fallout, writing,

> When you go to see *Rosewood,* and Jon Voight says *nigger,* he's got an attitude when he says it. He says it negatively, because that's the character he's playing, that's the way it was written, but no one goes out and strings up Jon Voight because of it. We get that he's just reading his lines, that he's just acting. We don't hold him to it.
>
> But the people held me to mine. Man, did they string me up and hold me to it, and I still don't get why. The material I wrote was funny, 'cause I tend to write funny stuff, 'cause I'm a funny person. And the person who was reading my lines, who happened to be white, performed the material as I wrote it. He was a white man, made up in black face, performing material written for the occasion by a black woman. It was no different than if I had gotten up on that platform and said the words myself. It was a piece written about me, by me, that I put into the mouth of a character. (187)

To her point, there may have been a difference in audience interpretation of the violence implicit through Danson's articulation versus the material as self-deprecating or told through "the mouth of a character." Yet her comparison to Jon Voight's character in *Rosewood* is disingenuous and, ultimately, a misdirection. What Goldberg seems to purposefully ignore here is the question of framing. The difference in Voight using racial slurs in *Rosewood* versus Danson in blackface at a roast is that Voight is playing a historicized character in a historical piece. He is framed as despicable and meant to be despised not only by modern audiences but even by all sympathetic figures within the film. Danson's role as minstrel is unclear, particularly as his jokes are directed at the real physical person of Goldberg and are told as Ted Danson in blackface—where audiences expect the appearance of *a person* and not *a character*—and not some discrete other persona given the frame and context of a celebrity roast.

Ultimately, much of this failure may be attached to a vague idea of likeability and relatability—if this were a movie, the audience might not like a character but understand the need for the character and appreciate the character's significance within the frame of the plot; in the case of a live roast, the audience did not like or relate to the *actors*. A roast is constructed to rib and ridicule the honoree to loving effect, but what can be assumed about the joke teller and the target when these harsh and raunchy jokes are made about an African American woman by a white man in blackface? What is the ultimate takeaway? Laughter is normally offered as a tacit agreement or acknowledgment that what is being said is said intentionally with the aim of some affective state. Yet, within the presentation of blackface, this sense of relatability has shifted so completely over time—in the nineteenth and early twentieth centuries, the performer and his performance might be "likeable" in direct or subversive frames; in the contemporary era, any performative capacity for likeability is instead usurped by the grotesqueness of the performance. Instead, it is a muddled and mottled hodgepodge of offensive images and stereotypes that exposes the historic vulnerabilities of Black womanhood without the *gotcha* at the end that holds the listener culpable. It doesn't miss its target because there *is* no target. A risqué premise does not a good joke make. By the same token, if Goldberg had performed the material herself, it still may have been unsuccessful because of her historical misrepresentations. She argues that the material was funny, yet the audience was uncomfortable and the initial titters of polite laughter stopped. Even if her material was funny, it missed the primary goals of satirical comedy as it seemed to make people neither laugh *nor* think in the ways she claims to have intended.

Leslie Jones encountered similar controversy surrounding impact and intent during her early sets on *Saturday Night Live*'s "Weekend Update" news segment. Let me be explicit and clear: while no one is above criticism for the execution of a joke and its content, Jones deserved *none* of the vitriol and violent threats waged against her. These threats and responses had a particular racialized and gendered component that had nothing to do with the content of her comedy. Additionally, it is important to note that Jones's performances on *Saturday Night Live* have been, in most cases since then, hilarious and inspired; she has done wonders to infuse the flagging show with insightful critique and contemporary appeal. Her jokes and the blowback, when taken in tandem, indicate the special risks for Black female comedians in being vulnerable and reveal the inherent anti-Black and antiwoman misogynoir of many broad mainstream viewing publics. For these reasons, it is interesting to consider not only the failure of an early joke alongside Jones's response to the criticism she received. Most notorious was a set performed May 3, 2014, on *Saturday Night Live*'s "Weekend Update." In it, Jones bemoans being single—traditional fodder for stand-up comedians. She uses Lupita Nyong'o's appearance on the cover of *People* magazine's most beautiful list as an entry point for a conversation on Black beauty standards. She begins by explaining, "The way we view black beauty has changed. Look at me! See, I'm single right now. But back in the slave days? I would've *never* been single. I'm six feet tall and I'm strong, Colin. *Strong!*" Host Colin Jost, a white former *Harvard Lampoon* president, looks both amused and uncomfortable, which is part of their schtick, but when coupled with the hesitant laughter of the audience, it seems to absolve Jost of his participation in what is later to come. Jones continues imagining a number of contemporary popular figures and athletes she would have birthed, finally calling herself the "number one slave draft pick."

From an artistic standpoint, the inherent meaning in the joke cannot be understood in the context of *SNL*. The metaphor of slavery and the NBA, while apt in a certain regard, here is either executed with too much nuance for audiences to understand[10] or its articulation is inchoate—there is ultimately no evidence that Jones herself is consciously making the connection between slavery and the role of African American men in the NBA, so the awkward comparison is particularly disturbing in what it may unintentionally conjure for viewers by misrepresenting forced breeding in slavery with problematic presentism as *being in a relationship*. Substantively, her joke makes no interventions by way of a more complicated understanding of Black womanhood or even the legacy of a chattel slave system. The joke is introduced as one engaging traditional comedic material—that Jones is single and lonely[11]—and it never shifts from this intention but just bizarrely centers slavery as its affirmative context. There's no sense of shame waged at the national history of slavery, nor at the slave owner briefly mentioned. She focuses the jokes inward by positioning her largesse as laughable and implying that she thereby cannot find a man to date. This is a clear effort toward laughing to keep from dying, where audience laughter should signal sympathy and support. However, it misses its mark because the general audience of *SNL* is so different from Jones's past audience and thus cannot (or will not) read the cues she offers. Instead of making a rightful criticism of the unattainable Western standard of beauty or a social commentary on the rising numbers of single Black women in the nation, she instead seems to explain that she would have been "better off" in a slave system. All of these misfires may have appeared as self-deprecation or social commentary in Jones's more familiar comedic settings—the stand-up stage in front of primarily Black audiences—but in the context of her new environment at *SNL*, her meaning is muddled.

Jones's articulation misrepresents historical rape as a convoluted "love life," and forced breeding as "having a man" for a predominantly white mainstream audience—a wholly horrifying convergence. Audiences feel entirely uncomfortable and perhaps rightly so—and indeed she gets less of the laughter traditionally expected from these "Weekend Update" segments—but this discomfort is not translated into any sense of culpability. After all, what lesson is there to be learned here? What is Jones attempting to demonstrate to this late-night audience? The use of Nyong'o as her framework is particularly unsettling, as Nyong'o has been hailed for a beauty that, in many ways, refuses the stereotypical portrayal of Black beauty in Hollywood. While certainly petite and lithe, as most movie starlets are, Nyong'o's skin is a dark chocolate and her hair was, at the time, closely cropped and tightly coiled. Her most famous role at the time was that of Patsey, a slave, in *12 Years a Slave*. Focusing her complaint around Nyong'o is peculiar, especially where there are other celebrities who are perhaps more worthy of her ire. For this particular audience, if her joke had been focused on size discrimination, it might have been a compelling social commentary. Using Nyong'o as juxtaposition within a commentary on slavery is troubling and confusing. It lessens the impact of her valid criticism of beauty standards within the frame of Blackness. Moreover, since Nyong'o has come to prominence by portraying a slave—one whom audiences witness bearing the brutality and trauma of the dehumanizing system—Jones's jokes' reliance on Nyong'o's physicality as the premise is quite problematic as well.

The following day, she took to Twitter to respond to social media criticism—and, more specifically, Black Twitter[12] criticism. At the time, Twitter only allowed posts, or tweets, of 140 characters or fewer, and so Jones tweeted in rapid succession to create a comprehensive whole. She wrote, in part,

What part of this joke that wasn't true? I would have been used for breeding straight up. That's my reality. And it saddens me that BLACK PEOPLE bitch and moan about the most stupid shit. I'm a comic it is my job to take things and make them funny. To make you think. Especially the painful things. Why are y'all so mad. This joke was written from the pain that one night I realized that Black men don't really fuck with me and why am I single. And that in slave days I would have always had a man cause of breeding. If anybody should be offended is white folks cause it's what they did. Y'all so busy trying to be self righteous you miss what the joke really is. Very sad I have to defend myself to black people. Now I'm betting if Chris Rock or Dave Chappelle did that joke or jay z or Kanye put in a rap they would be called brilliant. Cause they all do this type of material. Just cause it came from a strong black woman who ain't afraid to be real y'all mad. So here is my announcement black folks, you won't stop me and Im gonna go even harder and deeper now. Cause it's a shame that we kill each other instead of support each other. This exactly why black people are where we are now cause we too fucking sensitive and instead of make lemonade out of lemons we just suck the sour juice from the lemons. Wake up. I wouldn't be able to do a joke like that if I didn't know my history or proud of where I came from and who I am. (original spelling preserved)

Jones later apologized, writing, "sorry had a moment, can't when over the haters i am not the jackass whisperer. that is all . . ." Jones's response offers much to unpack. She focuses the blame for her comedic misfires on a number of targets—sexism, intraracism, hypersensitivity, and a lack of historical consideration. It is worth considering Jones's grievances as she lists them here. Her anger is justified. She is entirely correct that male comedians get away with more than female comedians as a whole. Their comedy is allowed to be more provocative, raunchy, or downright offensive. As aforementioned, women are assumed to be inherently less funny than their male counterparts, and even in the twenty-first century, there is a tacit sexist expectation of the speech and behavior of women as necessarily needing to be respectable—the impetus remains on women to encourage and structure right behaviors and politesse in society. Further, her astute acknowledgment of the racialized sexism—the misogynoir she had already experienced and would continue to experience in the coming months and years—should remind viewers that some of the critiques thrown at her had less to do with a failed joke and more to do with a Black woman taking a huge comedic risk (failed or otherwise). Here the vulnerability of Black women, as we've seen in *Good Hair* and elsewhere, often creates spaces for further criticism due to misogynoir, rather than a more nuanced understanding. This is the "damned if you do, damned if you don't" nature of Black womanhood in public spheres.

Certainly, each of the men Jones named have discussed slavery or Black beauty standards to some degree, and even have reinforced problematic or inappropriate images of Black female sexuality. However, none of the men she has named made a joke that implies any Black woman would be better off as a slave, and certainly not without rendering whiteness the object of ridicule. Jones did so with seeming flippancy, *in mixed company*, in front of an audience that may be eager to hear for their own absolution that slavery wasn't really *all bad*—which opened her to criticism that not only was the joke problematic but the venue itself inappropriate. Similar to Rock's trouble with the set in *Bring the Pain*, the meaning of a joke changes as the knowing in-group is diluted within a broader public space. The men named, when they have engaged in comedy surrounding slavery, usually do so to undercut the system of slavery through a juxtaposition of the fears surrounding Black masculinity against the confines of the slave system, as in when Dave Chappelle creates an imaginary blooper reel for *Roots* in which he feigns attacking the actor playing the slave master and laughing as he tells the other African American actors, "See, I told y'all he was scared of me!" Here Chappelle misrepresents history by playing up the idea of autonomy—and, problematically, seeming again unable to imagine a slave who is not a male figure—yet this is a *reclaiming* of negative tropes of Blackness. Jones, instead, shirks a reimagining of the slave system in the vein of autonomy and instead, through her joke, inadvertently recommits herself to the physical and sexual control that slavery required.

This is another moment where audience becomes a primary factor. Jones was speaking on *Saturday Night Live* on NBC, rather than, for example, a theater full of people who paid to see her perform and knew what to expect. On her former stand-up stage with a primarily Black audience already familiar with her irreverence, it is possible to imagine the crowd understanding her implicit meaning, but this is a primarily white and middle-class audience, and this was her first occasion on "Weekend Update"—this audience wasn't prepared for the material and had no idea what to expect from this new performer. To this same point, Jones's newness did show as she stumbled over much of her material, making a difficult piece perhaps clunkier and thus seemingly easier to debunk or discount. Jones was also, quite famously, hired to *Saturday Night Live* in the midst of claims that the show did a poor job of representing Black people—prior to Jones's arrival, the show had very few Black writers and only three Black cast members in Kenan Thompson, Jay Pharoah, and the newly added Sasheer Zamata,[13] and three was its highest number ever. If Jones was brought on, at least in part, to represent an undervalued or underacknowledged "Black perspective," this was quite a troubling introduction for people who had no context for this perspective by their own admission.

Perhaps even more troubling, though, are her claims of intraracial tension as the reason behind her maligned reception. Jones asserts that African Americans are unsupportive and that they have no cause for alarm, while white Americans should be the injured party. Yet Jones never addresses white people in her set, save a casual mention of "master" as a rhetorical afterthought. Her target *is* Blackness. Why would white audiences be offended, when they are not the subject of the comedy, particularly as "massa" emerges here as saving her from loneliness in front of this predominantly white audience? Any possible offense of white people is not merely lodged in the past but *missing* as she rhetorically distances herself from the criticism. Her complaints about Blackness and dating while Black—both experienced and assumed—while positioned in the past are meant to frame her very present existence. It is not at all, as Jones claims, an issue of hypersensitivity. Instead, the problem extends from the implication that the traumas of slavery had silver linings for a group of people who, even by Jones's own explication, still suffer from posttraumatic slave syndrome. While Jones is personally vulnerable in revealing her own loneliness, she avoids the perhaps more impactful vulnerability of historicity in favor of a misrepresentation of the reality of slavery and the lasting impact on Black bodies, and this is ultimately why the set was viewed unevenly—even the oversimplified understanding of slavery in the national consciousness usually presumes that it contributed to a negative understanding of Blackness today.

Since this controversy, Jones has revised her comedic persona in thoughtful and engaging ways that highlight her new, broader public role. On September 27, 2014, Jones returned to "Weekend Update," continuing to address dating woes. Her complaints surrounding contemporary dating are more subtle than in their previous incarnation, even while Jones seems to continue in the vein of racial specificity—this is now less a critique of even Black men broadly and speaks instead to an experiential criticism. Jones returned to specific, personal conversations about her physicality on Weekend Update on March 7, 2015, but now to largely different effect. She bemoans, "And none of y'all scared of me, at all. I used to be able to scare the hell out of a white girl in L.A. Just walk up to 'em, give 'em my best Compton stare. [stares angrily] Not out here. You white bitches are strong." Now she is setting up a more nuanced and engaging trajectory about what it means to be Black and female. Even while her own physicality bears the brunt of the joke, she speaks more subtly to how racial understanding may be shifting in the twenty-first century. Jones retains her vulnerability without ultimately misrepresenting the past, or the present. The initial controversy seems then to have impacted her in a significant way—she didn't back down, but she is now more intentional. She is not softening herself, but the way she associates herself in this joke to white womanhood within the space of a nuanced Black interior in pursuit of joke telling is intriguing and encouraging.

Perhaps even more compelling is a recurring joke on *Saturday Night Live* in which Jones has a relationship with a white, younger, male cast member, Kyle Mooney. Here the joke is not at Jones's expense—none of the traditional trappings of laughing *at* her are present. Instead the jokes are mostly at Mooney's expense. He is soft-spoken, nebbish, awkward, and seemingly filled with youthful inexperience. The relationship elicits laughter because it is unexpected that either party would be interested in the other—the odd couple component they evoke—not because of any inherent devaluing the relationship itself, or of either party. In fact, asides from other cast members in these sketches indicate happiness for both Jones and Mooney, who are presented as *vulnerable* loners within the *SNL* hierarchy. To this end, Jones is not forced to subscribe in her joke telling to an essentialist view of Black womanhood. She is instead able to luxuriate in the space of autonomous self-definition and demonstrate an acute understanding of the potential for equity within her comedic sphere. This is a different sort of vulnerability, and one that is often more effective—not just the revelation of racialization but an opening of Black interior space. In this sense, Jones may have been able to articulate a sense of selfhood, and to great professional and comedic payoff—her audience is laughing heartily with her.

However, for Black women, vulnerability has clear risks even outside the realm of comedy and satire. Jones experienced immense and vulgar backlash regarding both her role on *Saturday Night Live* and, later, in the 2016 female-cast remake of *Ghostbusters*. While the entire cast was targeted because male fans of the original mainstream success and current classic disparaged the idea of women in the film, the vitriol Jones herself experienced was unparalleled—her phone was hacked, nude photos were posted, and she was compared to Harambe, a Cincinnati Zoo gorilla who was famously killed after a three-year-old child got into his enclosure. Jones's experiences with misogynoir and the psychic violence tacit to this framing demonstrate the undue demands on Black women in the framing of their comedic persona and rip claims of a post-racial era asunder. Thus we see that there is, perhaps, no way that Jones could have structured herself, no calculated opening of Black interior space, that would have prevented the limited imaginations of a racist audience from viewing her through a sexist, racist, easily conjured trope—misogynoir is everywhere. The framing may also be inconsequential when the expectations of racialized performance are so readily available in the public imagination, even within a supposedly post-racial context. Here, it seems that the issue is not necessarily one of a need for racial uplift or even racial neutrality but instead the avoidance of racial self-denigration, particularly in mixed company, where personal opinion of the racialized speaker is often taken as representative of a monolithic race, especially when that opinion can be construed as negative. Yet what Jones's case demonstrates is that even this intentionality may not be enough.

Dave Chappelle and Audience Misreading

Dave Chappelle's comedy was initially marked by his seeming satiric intentionality. In his acclaimed series, *Chappelle's Show*, he satirizes the concept of Blackness as a monolith by imagining race as a space of simultaneous meaningfulness and meaninglessness. Jelani Cobb considers the differences in how Rock and Chappelle address issues of race by wisely pairing Rock with subversive cartoonist and screenwriter Aaron McGruder[14] and Chappelle with Richard Pryor. Cobb recalls Rock's infamous aforementioned set, explaining,

Rock's and McGruder's humor are driven in large part by intraracial anger. Rock's famous "Black People vs. Niggers" bit centers on an alleged civil war pitting the hard-working, respectable members of the race against the kinds of black people that the old folks refer to as "trifling." For Pryor and Chappelle, though, those kinds of divisions were not possible, or even desirable. (252)

Indeed, for Chappelle, racial lines are drawn solidly even while he acknowledges their performative nature. While Chappelle may hark, in one sketch, to a racial draft—mimicking the NBA draft, where racial delegations choose new celebrity members of their race based not on phenotype but instead based on their perceived racial ambiguity or fluidity as paired with their racialized performance—this set underscores the monolithic and absorbing nature of race and racialization and then criticizes it as ridiculous. Rather than viewing racial groups as striated from within or even differentiated in significant ways, Chappelle's focus is on race as understood by the gazer, not the object of the gaze. By imagining monolithic race out to an absurd and impossible conclusion, Chappelle sought to highlight the ridiculousness of racialization.

His jokes on *Chappelle's Show*—fueled simultaneously by debauchery and intense social inquiry—were so immediately hilarious that some audiences misread his meaning, perhaps unwilling to peer beneath this surface level to the connection to more complicated interior space. Chappelle's deep engagement with political and social issues is hidden underneath a veil of uninterested slacker comedy. Chappelle was born in Washington, D.C., to two professors. His mother, in addition to being a professor, was also a minister. Perhaps owing in part to his parentage, his humor is couched in the political, social, and performative. Rick DesRochers argues that "Chappelle works to confront racism by exposing its arbitrary and capricious nature, born of willful ignorance and ingrained hatred from America's resistance to dealing with its legacy of slavery and its complex relationship with immigration and colonization" (122). However, more than the arbitrariness of *racism,* Chappelle is concerned with *the mechanisms of racial identification* and how these foster racism in his own articulation for the need for justice through satire. The distinction here is subtle, but critical. Chappelle seems to argue that the expectation of a simplistic performance of race itself is to be satirized and problematized. Whether it be a white family named Niggar who feel no sting when their last name is used or Black people who perform race in ludicrous and ultimately self-harming ways, Chappelle is not only conscious of the lived experiences of racialized people but attempts to bring this racialization to the forefront by implying that it is a slippery slope that ultimately results in the harm of the object. In that latter sketch, aptly titled "When Keeping It Real Goes Wrong," Chappelle highlights a Blackness that fervently announces itself through stereotype. Traditionally, the phrase "keeping it real" in African American vernacular is meant as an intraracial attempt to prove or reinforce Blackness in presumptive ways. To "keep it real" is to perform behavior that seems to refuse assimilation and heighten Blackness. It is couched in a somewhat playful understanding of fears surrounding Blackness—toughness, confrontation, and speech without a filter or having what is termed in popular parlance "no chill"—and Chappelle leans into this idea. Here, the actors react to perceived slights with violence and threats, to comedic effect. Ultimately, the perpetrator is victorious, and the individual who "kept it real" is severely punished—a statement on the unsustainability of a refusal to assimilate.

To write these sketches off as mere slapstick would be erroneous. This is Chappelle's leitmotif, the idea that race is performed and that the performance matters as much as or more than phenotypic appearance. Chappelle's stand-up and his comedic persona are defined by his openness and his belief that his audience follows his train of thought. Where Richard Pryor made himself vulnerable—he is all too willing to be the butt of his own joke—Chappelle follows suit, but extends this vulnerability to a too-trusting view of his audience. Pryor worked to guide his audience to the conclusion. Chappelle trusts that his audience can handle the responsibility of his merger between laughter and serious social commentary. He is ultimately, in his own estimation, proved wrong.

Chappelle's trouble here, at least before 2017, seems to emerge more in his sketch comedy than in his stand-up.[15] Faedra Chatard Carpenter rightly notes,

> Chappelle comes from a stand-up comedy background in which the audience, like that of any live performance, is relatively stationary and engaged. Contemporary television viewing, on the other hand, offers audience members the opportunity to tune in and tune out on a moment's notice. Despite the fact that *Chappelle's Show* was consciously structured to incorporate moments of reflection and commentary from Chappelle, there was no way to ensure that audience members—with their remotes in hand—would linger long enough to allow their readings of the skits to be properly contextualized. (191)

Indeed, even as Chappelle performs stand-up for larger, televised crowds, the setup for his jokes is lengthy and precise. Unlike Rock, whose rapid-fire delivery prohibits greater elaboration, Chappelle works to explain the significance of the joke in ways that leave little room for misperception. This framing is much more difficult in sketch comedy. Although Chappelle introduces each sketch with a pithy statement on its construction or meaning, he is allotted very little time to do so or even to revisit the sketch upon completion. The burden of understanding is on the audience, the majority of whom are watching—perhaps distractedly, and certainly not with the attentiveness of a live audience—from their homes late at night; they are prone to misreading by visually and aurally skimming his content rather than scrutinizing it.

The moment this trust is most clearly shaken is in season three and Chappelle's infamous "Racial Pixies" sketch. More than solely addressing the specific moment in the sketch that triggered Chappelle's departure, it is important and necessary to expand on these analyses to consider the three other scenes in the sketch *and* the way that the sketch in total treads on Chappelle's own comfortable and well-worn territory from previous stand-up performances. "Racial Pixies," although usually discussed in reference to minstrel performance, is actually a four-pronged sketch—the Black pixie is first, followed by a "Hispanic" pixie, an "Asian" pixie, and (finally) a white pixie. When the sketch begins, Chappelle himself is dressed in full blackface attire as a Zip Coon minstrel—he wears a red jacket and black pants, black greasepaint on his face, overarticulated lips, and a constant, seemingly simple, foolish grin. The pixie encourages Chappelle to request the chicken over the fish on a flight, specifically to succumb to stereotypes surrounding Blackness, as Chappelle looks on at the pixie, disturbed and saddened by this suggestion of performativity. As Chappelle tells the behind-the-scenes story, while he was dressed as the minstrel pixie, he was made uncomfortable by the laughter of a white stagehand, hastening his leave from the show—this is the laughter that, when wielded inappropriately, leads to social death.

When the sketch proper is closely examined, it has the potential to work well as a commentary on racial performativity and the insidious ways that racism impacts the understanding of and articulation of an authentic self. However, in practice, the message was lost. Indeed, "Though outrageous, the skit was clearly a multileveled exploration of racism. It was a smart piece that reflected upon minstrelsy's echoes. . . . But apparently, for a contemporary African American performer, standing in front of a white audience (even a handful of crew and cast members) is not easily reconciled with performing buffoonish comedy in blackface" (Taylor and Austen 2). However, due to the feigned aloofness of slacker comedy, Chappelle was contextually unable to break that fourth wall to the extent necessary for his vulnerability to be seen as sincere or to make his purpose unequivocal.

What makes the significance of context and audience awareness even more acute here is that this moment was not the first time Chappelle addressed issues of food consumption and Black performativity. In his 2000 stand-up special, *Killin' Them Softly*, he recounts a time he went to a restaurant in the South and the waiter assumed, based on his race, that he wanted chicken (which he did). Chappelle notes, "All these years I thought I liked chicken because it's delicious. Turns out, I'm genetically predisposed to liking chicken!" He later goes on to explain that the incident made him concerned about eating chicken in public from that moment on, fearful that white onlookers would view it as spectacle, remarking among themselves, "Look at him: he loves it! Just like it said in the encyclopedia! Look how happy he looks!" This set was met with laughter and clear, apparent understanding of Chappelle's larger point. Here is where communal and individual justice may emerge, where Chappelle is able to well articulate the quotidian impact of racism and racialization on himself as well as on broader Black collectives while never undercutting the humor inherent in the delivery. His vulnerable admission that he now fears eating certain foods in public—a seemingly ridiculous behavior to fear, but one that limits his ability to act with autonomy—is because of the very real and tangible stress of racial performance. In this way the humor doesn't undercut the message but instead reframes it for popular dissemination. Likewise, Chappelle mentions in his 2004 stand up, *For What It's Worth*, "just because I eat chicken and watermelon, they think there's something wrong with me. Listen: if you don't like chicken and watermelon, something is wrong with *you*. . . . The only reason these things are an issue is because nobody knows what white people eat. You've been very good about keeping that shit a secret among yourselves!"[16] In juxtaposition with his response to the racial pixies sketch, these jokes beg three questions—what is the difference? What remained unaccomplished in his first articulations of this idea that merited a revisiting that led to misunderstanding? And why did Chappelle find one set to appropriately engage in a discourse surrounding racism and one to have a potential devastating effect?

There are two possible reasons for the intensity of what Chappelle interpreted as a misreading. The first is that this analysis of racism, when viewed in context with the other racial stereotypes as presented, began to verge on a performance of anti-Blackness rather than a critique of these stereotypes in total. This sketch, when viewed in its entirety, reinforces his initial inclination. While the other pixies, all played by Chappelle, speak to racial stereotypes, their significance is not as readily felt nor conjured as the Black pixie. The "Hispanic" pixie is actually meant to be Mexican, speaking to actor and Chappelle's friend, Guillermo Diaz. Dressed as a stereotypical matador with castanets, a mustache, and sombrero, he encourages Diaz to buy leopard skin seat covers in a thick, Californian-Mexican accent. The "Asian" pixie pushes a man to respond to an introduction to television personality Lala with "Rah-rah." At his refusal, the pixie commits seppuku before strangely sliding into Lala's cleavage to die—Chappelle's comedy does often veer toward traditional juvenile sight and sound gags. The white pixie tries to teach a man how to speak to his Black friends through incorrectly applied rap lyrics before commenting on his preference for flat backsides. Later, the white pixie reassures a different white man, seemingly humbled while at a urinal next to a Black man, that he runs the world.

All of these performances are problematic in their reliance on stereotypes without sufficient context—Chappelle is right to worry that the laughter may be at the object, rather than the broad subject of the racist imaginary being skewered. These pixies are meant to highlight the ways that racism shames the object of racialization into arbitrary "right behaviors" to the detriment of personal choice. Yet the shift from the first three pixies to the white pixie renders this possibility unlikely as it is performed. Where the comedy is derived in the other three by demonstrating that seemingly innocuous behaviors can cause psychic harm to racialized people—food choices, fashion statements, the phonetic *l- r* merger as examples here—the white pixie encourages his man to engage in racist stereotypes of Blackness in an effort to be Black before discussing his desire for a flat-bottomed woman and stiff, erratic dance moves. Whiteness here is literally *defined by* its association with anti-Blackness—the sketch only makes sense in view of white fears surrounding Blackness and what Blackness represents. Even while the latter gestures speak to clear stereotypes of whiteness, these stereotypes do not hold the same weight as those of the Black, "Hispanic," or "Asian" pixie—a point driven home in the final scene in which the pixie reminds the man of the continuation of white supremacy.

Indeed, in the DVD commentary by cocreator Neal Brennan and performers Donnell Rawlings and the late Charlie Murphy, they express confusion over what the white pixie could have done—which is precisely the problem. There are no substantive stereotypes that serve to prove the inferiority or inhumanity of whiteness. There is no real sense of equity in comparing the racialization of whiteness to that of marginalized people. This is further illuminated by Brennan's statement, "I'm so sick of talking about this shit. I'm so sick of thinking about this shit." Even as Rawlings and Murphy bemoan Chappelle's decision to leave, their silence seems to indicate a tacit refusal to cosign Brennan's statement. It would appear that only Brennan, the lone white man featured in the commentary, is afforded the luxury of being sick of the issues.

The second possibility is that the scope of the show grew so large so quickly that it soon became unwieldy for Chappelle—as an intentionally unflashy and somewhat reclusive celebrity, Chappelle now had bona fide superstar status and the paycheck and public expectations to go along with it. Unlike Rock's, Chappelle's stand-up comedy always had a clear autobiographical bent—while Rock spoke harshly against public figures and society at large, in his early stand-up Chappelle placed himself front and center of the critique as the everyman who both participates in and is affected by the peculiarities of social structure, his individual experiences standing in for communal identities. Even his criticisms, which are waged against society, are directed at Chappelle himself as a member of society. He never implies that he is above reproach—if he verges on the blameless in one sketch, the next centers him as a target of ridicule.[17] However, once heaps of adoration were thrown upon the man, it became more difficult to convince the audience that Chappelle— Dave, the affable everyman—was just like them and they, likewise, should be critically considering their role in the society around them. Indeed, this must have proven quite disillusioning, as Chappelle's collaborators plainly articulate in the DVD commentary their disinterest in responsible humor. This attitude from Brennan, in particular, is disturbing. In his uneven first one-hour stand-up special, 2014's peculiarly named *Women and Black Dudes*, Brennan positions himself as a white guy who "gets" race and—in large part because of his highly publicized friendship with Chappelle[18]—is able to speak on issues of race frankly. Moreover, this cavalier attitude surrounding comedy seems to disregard the fact that the name of the show is *Chappelle's*. The burden of responsibility weighs heavily on Chappelle's shoulders and it is one the other men do not have to bear. This flippancy stems from the fact that he knows, perhaps unconsciously even, that he will not be taken to task for his performance in any substantive or lasting way outside of how it might frame Chappelle's own responsibility.

Despite the protestations of his cohorts,[19] Chappelle made it clear from the show's inception that he felt an obvious social and political responsibility. Even in his choice of musical artists to frame the sketches, he chose from among the most conscious and politically inclined musicians—Mos Def, Talib Kweli, The Roots, Erykah Badu—to be featured throughout. Additionally, the willingness of his comedic colleagues to jettison responsibility lies in stark contrast to the show's role as satire. If satires operate as social critique, then there is a level of social responsibility for the satirist that remains implicit. This humor is not abstract, and no matter how many childish jokes Chappelle makes about body parts or bodily functions, he cannot negate what he clearly feels to be his social responsibility. Indeed, Chappelle felt this sense of discomfort so acutely that he left the realm of comedy for more than ten years. That his cowriters and coperformers are willing to overlook what, for Chappelle, is the show's impulse, is not only troubling on its face but speaks directly to a possible impetus for Chappelle's departure—audience (un)willingness to understand the nuances of racial performance may overwhelm the performance itself. Ultimately, there is a great and damaging difference in articulating racial stereotypes as Chappelle the man or even the persona, versus having them performed by an identifiable minstrel—even in a "post-racial" society, the specter of these racialized performances looms too large, no matter Chappelle's efforts to subvert them, particularly for a too casual, home-viewing cable audience. It is absolutely as Jelani Cobb notes: "The moral of the story is clear: Chappelle's character lives in a catch-22 where anything he does fulfills some trait on an infinite checklist of stereotypes. It is a riff on the racial gymnastics required to negotiate the most routine of daily scenarios. Or it is a hilarious bit about a jigaboo dancing on an airplane. Depending upon who you're talking to" (251). Indeed, there is a significant difference between a space of productive vulnerability and a space in which your vulnerability is exploited in the aim of the absolution of others.

The public and private burden of racism—the fear of saying the wrong thing from a position of power—was so weighty that Dave Chappelle decided for a full ten years that he could ultimately no longer engage in comedy on a broad public platform. Even in his absence, he remained hailed as one of the greatest comic minds of his generation. Yet his initial unwillingness to participate in comedy in this same way may have stemmed from the burden of not only racism, but of racial *mis*understanding. In the past few years, he has ventured back into the comedic spotlight with a few performances, which have been noteworthy for problematic reasons—ranging from audience members demanding he perform old material from *Chappelle's Show* to throwing a banana peel at him in the middle of his routine in New Mexico to Chappelle's own grotesque jokes in 2017 and 2019 doused in transphobic and sexist rhetoric.[20] Similarly, while Chris Rock remains in the comedic realm, his material has shifted to have a much more overt and dynamic political thrust. Even his 2018 Netflix special, *Tambourine*, shifts substantially away from overt comedy as Rock situates himself as a near cautionary tale as he discusses his failed marriage, his relationship with his daughters, and gender dynamics more broadly. While he does fall back on the same assertions about differences between women and men we've already heard from him, Rock is subdued and more introspective than we've witnessed in early comedic routines. While the vulnerability perhaps does not serve to heighten the comedy, the message itself is made clear. Indeed, since the fallout from the "Niggas versus Black People" set, Rock has reinvented himself as a touchstone for African American social and political insights. Now the comedy seems secondary to the message. Indeed, recent interviews with Rock have shifted away from asking the funny man about his jokes and instead toward asking his opinions on social events, perhaps indicating Rock's own understanding of the limitation of satiric comedy in the contemporary moment. He has become a trusted commentator—and in the past few years he has begun to fully embrace a new role as unanticipated mouthpiece for what is popularly described as *the* Black community and seems to fully accept the responsibility therein.

When facing her initial controversy, Leslie Jones opined that "just 'cause it came from a strong black woman who ain't afraid to be real y'all mad." Her assertion—again tinged with questions surrounding the effectiveness of "keeping it real" in the mainstream—is worth further interrogation and points to the double burden that women of color face not only in the comedic realm, particularly in non-Black publics. Nevertheless, it is critical to consider the ways that, in many cases, when male comedians fail, their failure is all their own; when Black women fail, their failures have ramifications regarding widespread notions of race and gender simultaneously. What the controversies surrounding Jones and these other performers may highlight is that the framing, in concert with audience awareness, is necessary because the expectations of racialized, or racialized and gendered, performance are so readily available in the public imagination. There is no possibility of a nuanced selfhood without the clear parameters that push back against racial expectations in identifiable ways—and this fact gets to the heart of the complicated nature of satire.

Here, it seems that the issue is not necessarily one of a need for simplistic racial uplift but instead a more nuanced and accurate portrayal of racialization. It is a refusal to reaffirm stereotypes as they exist through racial self-denigration, particularly in mixed company, where the personal opinion of the racialized speaker is often taken as representative of a monolithic and marginalized race, especially when that opinion is the same old degradation through misrecognition, misreading, or misrepresentation. W. Kamau Bell explains in his *Awkward Thoughts*, "Some jokes are like a shotgun blast, where a bunch of pellets come out and hit whoever's in the area. That's the point at which I decided, to use a clumsy analogy, to be very target-focused" (173). Indeed, the failure to focus satiric joke telling on a particular target and the real-world ramifications of this failure necessitate new ways of thinking about satire and satiric impulse—and perhaps even suggest that, in the context of a *post*-post-racial twenty-first century that the parameters of satire themselves may not hold. I continue examining the expanding parameters of twenty-first-century satire as connected to the refusal of both a post-racial mythology and a subscription to racial essentialism by contemporary artists. When these writers and performers begin to move away from overt satires, this too is a deliberate choice and the shift signals a different sort of social commentary that heightens the *Blackness* of Black interior space but also refuses to allow racism preeminence—here Blackness on its own terms, outside a white gaze, is critical. In the case of some of the aforementioned misfires here, the refusal of the satirist to acknowledge the social significance of the satirical joke and to instead claim the refuge of mere "joke telling" does not diminish the impact of the joke itself—indeed, the disavowal of meaning only reifies to careful listeners that jokes cannot emerge in a vacuum and are founded on social expectations and presumptions. However, some satirists move away from overt satires not as a disavowal of social commentary but instead to demonstrate that traditional notions of satirical methodology need to be complicated to continue to hold meaning in an increasingly absurd, self-satirizing world.

"How Long Has This Been Goin' On, This *Thang*?"

Centering Race in the Twenty-First Century

> One of the best things about being black is that,
> barring some key exceptions, it's not a volunteer
> position. You can't just wish on a dark star and
> become black. It's not paid either. It's more like a
> long internship with a chance of advancement.
>
> —Kevin Young

While Jordan Peele's horror film, *Get Out* (2017), and Issa Rae's comedy series, *Insecure* (premiered in 2016), may seem strange bedfellows generically, both engage and then stretch beyond the bounds of the satiric mode to disrupt our expectations of genre and reframe an understanding of Black identity as focused on the Black interior free from the implications that Blackness is inherently fraught. These works center Blackness and the Black private sphere and, in doing so, refuse traditional notions of Blackness as abject. In imagining Black centrality, they refuse the anticipated privileging of the white gaze. They reject preeminent contemporary ideologies of the post-racial as a safe space for identity formation or the post-Black as a required sphere for fruitful identity performance. These works instead demonstrate the insufficiency of these frames not only because the frames do not acknowledge the new forms that racism takes but also because the frames lack the capaciousness necessary even to imagine a nuanced Black identity that is informed by race but *not* crushed under the weight of racism. These works refuse the necessity of *post-*

raciality or *post*-Blackness and instead articulate a self-assured understanding of race and identity that lessens the reach of racism—they acknowledge that racism is real and unavoidable but also provide the fictive kinships of the homosocial relationship and sanctuary from the always otherwise present specter of racial discrimination and trauma. The Black friendships depicted here offer the strength and self-certainty necessary to refuse racial essentialism and are connected to a twenty-first-century desire to establish spaces for authentically and autonomously expressing Black selfhood. It is a sense of selfhood derived from supportive Black friendships that may also open up possibilities for laughing to keep from dying, where communal laughter or communal understanding and kinship may ward off what would otherwise be a psychic—or, especially in the case of horror, *physical*—death.

The satirical mode and what lies beyond its borders here are especially effective in articulating a sense of ennui with a post-racial or post-Black impulse because the frustration and cynicism[1] of the twenty-first century do not necessitate strict didacticism at the narrative's end. Instead, is it possible to imagine that the satiric writer or performer, "like a prophetic Christ railing at the Pharisees, also denounces the time and the times, also reveals and uncovers the doubleness of action; but unlike Christ, the satirist possesses no certain promise, his fulminations are very much 'in' time" (Seidel 20–21)? Despite the inherent ambiguity forwarded in these accounts, these narratives anticipate a continued social trajectory of race and racialization from myriad intersectional vantage points. Additionally, in reaffirming the dichotomous nature of race as marked both by meaningfulness and meaninglessness, these works refuse devotion to discrete modes of performance and articulation and push the boundaries of conventional generic form. In doing so, they significantly reveal not only the insufficiency of the post-racial *and* racial essentialism but also the inadequacy of traditional frames to contain the nuances of contemporary Black identity. In the case of *Insecure,* this revelation emerges as a reimagining of the nature and expectations of comedy that is both Black and female, in which the endgame is not the romantic relationship but the steadfast, homosocial, female friendship. For Jordan Peele, this means acknowledging the limits of the comedic itself to articulate the experience of Blackness in the twenty-first century by merging satire in overt ways with the realm of horror. Both of these works engage and distort a satiric frame to disrupt our traditional expectations of generic form and, resultantly, undercut our traditional notions of Blackness and Black performative identity.

Of course, a connection between satire and horror, and the catharsis they both ostensibly inspire, is nothing new. On *Key and Peele,* Jordan Peele, along with collaborator Keegan-Michael Key, created a sketch entitled "White

Zombies." In it, two Black men (played by Key and Peele) find themselves survivors of an apocalyptic zombie suburban wasteland. After their leader (played by white actor Kevin Sorbo, formerly of the television show *Hercules*) is attacked and killed by a zombie swarm, the two men fearfully make their way through the living dead. As they attempt to stealthily weave through the mob, they notice that the zombies first ignore them and then respond with overt, racist performativity—shirking in terror from the men, locking car doors, zombie parents pulling zombie children away from the men. Although this moment is meant overtly to inspire laughter in a way that the frightening *Get Out* is not, it also serves to destabilize the idea of the apocalyptic or the dystopic as somehow post-racial. Here is the inherent catch-22 in our awareness of racism in the twenty-first century—it hastens consideration of racism as a permanent structure of American society, and simultaneously tacitly requires our active work toward displacing it. We know that racism is *permanent,* and yet our antiracist desires compel us to fight for its end. In this way, by utilizing zombies, *Key and Peele* refute the common notion that racism will eventually die out—here we see the *living* dead harboring these same racist inclinations.

In 2015 Jessica Baker Kee noted, "the main cinematic barometer of cultural anxiety—the horror film—has for the most part avoided explicitly addressing imagery of historical violence against Black men" (47). Horror films as a genre do seem reluctant to engage with overt issues of race and, given the prevalence of Black characters dying first in horror movies, the films often do not engage with race in meaningful ways. The genre is noted for structuring dilemmas such that, as Kee explains, "the underlying threat of horror is the breakdown of the exclusionary matrix itself and the loosening significations ascribed to various identities. The horror genre promises repulsive yet seductive encounters within the semiotic realm of affects circulating between bodies, and finally to affective encounters with the ultimate figure of abjection: the corpse" (49). Indeed, we are "seduced" by this narrative of the American Everyman who, traditionally, happens to be not only male, but cisgender, straight, and white, and who, thanks to his wit and cleverness, is found deserving of survival as compared to a motley crew of cohorts ultimately rendered abject. And so, even when these films engage race, they offer enough plausible deniability to refuse interest in race—even when race is salient, these remain, we are told, films that offer no racial commentary.

Take the case of *Night of the Living Dead* (1968), for instance, arguably the most famous classic example of a mainstream horror film where overt racial anxieties take hold. Our Black male protagonist survives the zombie apocalypse and outlives his compatriots only to be shot dead after a gathering police posse "mistakes" him for a zombie. Despite this seeming racialization, director George A. Romero denies any intentional racial commentary. The film may be interpreted racially, but that's not inherent to the film, he implies. Instead, it's the social situation in which the film emerges that lends itself to our erroneous reading because the social realm merely overwhelms our imagination. We want to accept Romero's articulated assertion because it's easier and more comfortable to believe that the film offers escapism with no racialized significance in a larger context—the film exists uncorrupted, even if we read it through our particular cultural lens. In this sense, we would refuse our own culpability by distancing ourselves from the real-life applicability. If we'd all do the morally right thing in the zombie apocalypse—if racism, sexism, and other forms of prejudice no longer existed and we could move *beyond* these frames—perhaps then we don't have to confront the ways we do the *wrong* thing in our actual lives and actual lived experiences.

Still, this denial is, of course, difficult to accept on its face, because there is no cultural production that exists in a vacuum, independent of its contemporary social realm, despite the protestations of Romero and other auteurs. Racism is conjured in American horror movies because these movies take place within the realm of an American possibility, even when there is no explicit commentary being offered. It is difficult to imagine *Night of the Living Dead* appearing at the height of the civil rights movement without the perception of this racial specificity emerging. It is even more difficult to imagine a film emerging through an American cultural lens and viewed through the same lens that exists without real or implied racial meaning. Indeed, even if no racial commentary were intended, it seems unlikely for the filmmakers not to anticipate the film being read in this light. It is interesting, then, to consider the context in which *Night* erupted and the ways it creates space for satirical revisitations of the horror genre as a possible zone for intentional racialized commentary. Romero and John Russo initially wrote the film as a "horror comedy" about aliens, which seems to already blur the line between what inspires the potential catharsis of fear and what inspires laughter. Eventually, the film evolved with zombies at its forefront, shifting it away from what Romero worried would be seen as too directly inspired by Richard Matheson's *I Am Legend*. What is thought-provoking here, though, is Romero's assertion that his understanding of Matheson's film did not stem from a sense of terror but instead a sense of impending revolution: "I thought *I Am Legend* was about revolution. I said if you're going to do something about revolution, you should start at the beginning. I mean, Richard starts his book with one man left; everybody in the world has become a vampire. I said we got to start at the beginning and tweak it up a little bit" (McConnell). If a revolution implies not only the ending of a thing—residual impacts aside in the revolutionary imagination—but the beginning of a *new* thing, then what might it be about a sense of revolution, then, that could be inherently significant or even possible within the horror genre? And is there a point at which the frame of comedy, or even "horror comedy," might lack the capaciousness necessary to evoke effective revolutionary action? Is this, ultimately, where revolutionary laughter might lead?

Revolutionary laughter at its best opens up space for autonomous identity formation, but when that possibility is foreclosed, perhaps it leads to a sort of horrific realization. After all, there is certainly a horror to be found in a post-racial mythos. Kee's aforementioned reading of the horror genre as understating Blackness and Black masculinity is an apt reminder of the function of fear as a supposed equalizer. Here, horror serves to acknowledge that the *real* monsters are people, or human nature, and holds viewers complicit within that frame. The nastiness of the individuals in the film is usually distorted to melodramatic effect, and so they lose their humanness even as the film attempts to make assertions about humanity. For instance, in *The Walking Dead*—both the graphic novel series and the television series—although the real action begins in Atlanta, the presence of systemic racism is now fundamentally nonexistent. Even the most outright racist character, Merle, is initially depicted as foolish and almost cartoonishly villainous, horribly out of step with his changing world until he demonstrates personal growth and is able to become martyred—having learned, perhaps, that race "doesn't matter," or matters less at least in the face of the zombie apocalypse. Perhaps even more tellingly, in the face of this dystopic reality, not only does racism not exist but *all cultural output* seems to be erased. Particularly in the case of *The Walking Dead,* there are no relics of cultural production or even remembrances of anything that would signal a larger human connection or the particularities of regional or social experiences or identity writ large. These erasures seem to imply, then, that it takes the emergence of the literal subhuman and the destruction of not only a formalized social sphere but of society more broadly for the marginalized to be recognized as human. For racism to end, it is implied in this view, *everything* must end. In this sense, racism seems quite acutely attached to the functioning of traditional society, and when society as an abstract no longer exists, racism dissolves in the presence of the *real* threats of zombies and individual selfishness or hubris. Still, it is difficult to discount the implicit significance of race in *The Walking Dead* when characters of color often die sacrificial deaths having never been fully developed as individuals (as in the case of the perhaps aptly named T-Dog, who appeared as a static trope of "the Black male character in an ensemble cast about whom we learn nothing") or are elevated to near-saint status only to be served a gruesome death, having been betrayed by some villain (as in the separate and horrifying deaths of Noah and Glenn). Indeed, this strange expectation of having *nothing* to do with race but *everything* to do with race is so rote for the genre that when Robin Means Coleman wrote in 2011, "Thus far, the twenty-first century is providing a fairly clear answer about its next move: the horror genre is not reaching for the new; instead it is digging back through past horror catalogues to present old horror warmed over" (198), it was difficult to imagine what a fresh approach might even look like.

Racial Panic

It is because of this expectation of the mundane in horror film that the popular emergence of 2017's *Get Out* was not only unexpected but also felt in many ways like a revolution unto itself. The film is one of the first mainstream endeavors to intentionally center race and racism itself within the lens of horror, and admit to doing so. Through a utilization of both the conventions of the horror film and the readily conjured images and rhetorical posturing of racism within collective national memory, Peele imagines a return to the overt racial terror of the past in the present. Peele's background is that of satirical comedian on sketch comedies *Mad TV* and *Key and Peele,* and so his utilization of consummate horror reminds audiences that satire is not always that which is necessarily funny; instead, it heightens the existing absurdity within the mundane—it underscores the difference between comedy and humor through the use of the ironic and the absurd. The use of horror in this context demonstrates that the stakes of the post-Obama era may necessitate a more direct articulation of the trauma and potential catharsis associated with horror as an affective mode—it is the horror of systemic racism made literal. In this way, a return to overt racial abjection, objectification, and essentialism requires that utilization of a generic form that makes the fearful feelings of marginalization more readily sensed and acknowledged by broader audiences. Ultimately, *Get Out* demonstrates new possible directions for African American satiric performance as a shift away from the humorous political and social commentary of *Chappelle's Show, Key and Peele,* and others toward critique that more overtly centers revealing racism as its goal in opposition to a twenty-first-century mythology of the post-racial.

Get Out focuses on Chris, a young Black photographer, going away for the weekend for the first time to meet the family of his white girlfriend, Rose. When Rose admits she hasn't informed her family of their interraciality, it gives the protagonist pause, though he ultimately discounts his own disquiet.

Although Rose's lack of racial awareness is meant to make audiences uneasy, neither viewers nor Chris himself can anticipate the impending trauma of the narrative arc, as anticipated micro-aggressions give way to full-on assault and scientific racism underscored by the possibilities of science fiction technology—hypnosis and brain transplantation. Chris learns soon enough that his apprehensions were well founded and that the Armitage family and friends want him—literally his body—in an effort to appropriate his corporeality for the physical accoutrements they assume it will provide and for the sake of their own eternality. He discovers that Rose and her family have been stealing Black people, particularly Black men, to allow their wealthy friends to bid on these Black bodies, using bingo cards in a silent auction horrifyingly evocative of the antebellum selling of slaves. The mother, Missy Armitage, hypnotizes these victims into the unwilling retreat of "the sunken place"—a place of mental paralysis in which they are trapped, subdued, and effectively marginalized. Dean Armitage, the father, then performs brain transplants, allowing the white bidder to take over the youthful Black body. Although *Get Out* is couched soundly in the realms of science fiction and psychological horror, it has been almost universally praised for its incisive depiction of race relations, compounding appropriation, and fears surrounding suspected micro-aggressions. What is especially interesting in *Get Out* is that the villainous Armitage family presents themselves as typical "limousine liberals"—wealthy, left-leaning, highly educated bleeding hearts who performatively harbor no racist feelings while simultaneously having no significant relationships with members of any marginalized group. Although audience members cringe at the reductive and oblivious conversations surrounding racialized others, the effusive liberalism performed by the white antagonists must be read not as a ploy to coax victims into a false sense of security but instead as demonstrating their sincere understanding of themselves through a binary, mainstream assessment of racism. It is this distinction that is most revolutionary and similarly has the greatest repercussions.

The Armitage family, by popular contemporary definition, is expressly "not racist"—they voted for Barack Obama, they use no overt racist language, they are well aware of the problematic racial symbolism involved in their own lives and consciously and carefully seek to explain it away. Indeed, they even seem to have none of the expected fears of miscegenation, particularly in regard to the historically disparaged white woman/Black man pairing, expressing no discomfort with their daughter's relationship and allowing the unmarried couple to share a bedroom in their sprawling and secluded lakeside home. Even more, they have none of the easy identifiers of racist characters with which film audiences are already familiar—they are highly educated, they lack southern drawls, and they seem to have no connection to any southern geographic space of origin. It is these distinctions—that they cannot be easily written off as racis, uneducated, or ignorant—that truly inspires terror and indicts viewers. If racism isn't simply driven by a lack of knowledge or education, then from where does it come? These are quite simply *good* and *enlightened* white people. Their physical commodification of Black bodies, they argue, has nothing whatsoever to do with race but is mere happenstance. However, as created by Peele, this disconnect is a particularly insidious form of racism that dwells in the space of plausible deniability. It demonstrates that "non-racist" white Americans also conceptualize Blackness within the frame of a racialized society so that, ultimately, despite their protestations, they still find Black people more easily and readily commodified than other groups—they're not choosing Black victims because Black people are inherently inferior, or even necessarily physically superior, although Peele's writing doesn't foreclose that possibility. Dean Armitage, for instance, makes mention that his father raced and was bested by Jesse Owens and "almost got over it," but that significance throughout the film is, I would argue, intentionally underdeveloped. While Dean Armitage's father embodies the groundskeeper and does in this sense seem interested in Black bodies as a vehicle for physical prowess, the rest of the Armitage family seems more interested in Black bodies as viable objects for their experimentation.

Similarly, Chris is noted for his "eye" as a photographer, and the first Black man who is taken in the film's cold open, Dre/"Logan," is a noted jazz musician, as briefly evidenced by an online search that occurs later. His connection to an older, lusty white woman, coupled with the comments directed at Chris about expectations of Black male sexual potency, is certainly provocative, but this probability is never fully addressed. Instead, more explicitly, there is a direct correlation to the systemic disavowal of Black life throughout the movie—here Black lives unequivocally do *not* matter to people in positions of power—that facilitates the completion of these crimes. Despite Dre's quantifiable musical exceptionality, he is still ultimately embodied, it would seem, for his stereotypically assumed sexual prowess (although perhaps connected to assumptions about virility and jazz related to ideas of Black masculine performance).

When Chris's best friend, Rod, reports his concerns to police, that the Armitage family is stealing Black men to turn them into sex slaves—an assessment that serves as comic relief but is ultimately not too far off—the primary officer, a Black woman, brings in other officers to laugh at Rod, dismiss him, *and then never investigate his claims further.* Here the limits of laughter and of laughing are on display—this laughter leads to death. While it may be understandable that they disregard a missing adult over the course of a single day, what is more troubling is that they disregard Rod's photographic proof that another long-missing Black man is found residing in this same community. Thus Peele disabuses us of the notion that racism exists on a binary of "racist" and "non-racist," instead arguing that more nuanced thinking will be lifesaving. Peele seems to note that even "non-racists" benefit from systemic racism and, to this end, draws a clear distinction between "non-racist" and the "anti-racist" actions that specifically operate to disrupt racism in all its forms. In this sense, the specifics of why African Americans are targeted are irrelevant, be they assumed physical prowess, the lack of concern of people in positions of power, or any other possibility. Ultimately, the result is the same—the commodification of Black bodies and the abuse and violence enacted against Black people. As a result, *Get Out* demonstrates that the status quo is, in and of itself, a way to reinscribe racism in its assertion that neutrality in the face of active evil is enough.

In *Faces at the Bottom of the Well* Derrick Bell explains, "We are now, as were our forebears when they were brought to the New World, objects of barter for those who, while profiting from our existence, deny our humanity" (10–11). It is this denial of humanity, consistent and unrelenting, that allows *Get Out* to make its most critical intervention as it rearticulates the parameters for social justice. Here, Peele plays in the interstice that compels him to ask, "how can someone view another group of human beings as *less* human and *not* be racist?" The answer is that when the rest of the world *also* views that group as less than, then the Armitage family are the beneficiaries of the racist social system while attempting to deny a position as creators or proponents. It reinforces not only a racial hierarchy but a hierarchy of racism. Indeed, when Rose hears the tacitly racist comments waged at Chris by her parents' friends, questions regarding his sexual potency and assertions that Blackness is "in fashion" once again, she scoffs in disgust—*she*, of course, is *not* a racist. *She* knows these racist comments are worthy of scorn. *She* knows better than to harbor these feelings consciously, or at least better than to articulate them publicly. And so, even as she engages in the practice of luring young Black people to their deaths, she indicates that to her mind, like the aforementioned claim many horror movies make at the outset, even when it's about race, it's not really *about* race.

While the entire Armitage family, their friends, and society more broadly are held accountable and indicted for the racist system, it is the daughter, Rose Armitage, the protagonist's girlfriend on which the didacticism of this narrative rests. The character is played by Allison Williams, best known for her role on the *HBO* series *Girls* as Marnie Matthews. Ultimately, much of what Williams intentionally does with Marnie that makes the character so performatively grating is what makes Rose feel so innocuous, seemingly innocent, and the perfect purveyor of the terror the film makes manifest. Jordan Crucchiola wrote for *Vulture*,

> A casting choice this obvious shouldn't feel so inspired, and yet by putting Williams in the part of Rose—a character whose intentions constantly keep the audience guessing—Peele uses her image as a stand-in for the dangers of white complacency. In mainstream media, Williams's type of whiteness represents safety, security, and comfort. But in the context of a horror movie, it's exactly what makes us feel most safe that puts us in mortal danger.

Indeed, part of what makes Williams's portrayal of Rose so initially appealing is this sense of unassuming *beige* she exudes that lulls viewers into a false sense of security. Williams is quite beautiful, to be sure, but much of her appeal as both Marnie and Rose stems from her aesthetic situatedness as "all-American," with all the racially problematic connotations of that descriptor, to such an extent that her beauty is taken as a casual given—Marnie's array of yoga pants and lattes and Rose's riding pants, Benetton sweaters, and milk all stem from ideas of all-American innocuous innocence in the twenty-first century. No one would use the words "exotic," "modern," or "unique" to describe the appearance of these characters—terms that emerge as twenty-first-century dog whistles used to describe the few women of color accepted as mainstream beauties or the racially ambiguous but primarily white-presenting women so on trend in advertising campaigns. In real life, Williams's father is Brian Williams, the broadcast television journalist— a profession that not only values but traditionally necessitates a sense of American ambiguity devoid of identifiable otherness or accent—and by grace of genetics her appearance strikingly matches his own brand of inoffensive, comforting, and noncontroversial attractiveness.

Williams and the characters she plays become the personification of the cult of true (white) womanhood. It is for this reason that, even upon the devastating reveal where he discovers Rose's box filled with photos of her past victims, both Chris and the viewing audience desire the continued suspension of disbelief in Rose's participation. Sure, her family may be slowly revealing themselves as the monsters that they are, but the audience retains hope that Rose is the exception. That she is, in fact, not simply the bait but the *perpetrator*—a willing and active participant and offender—throws overarching misconceptions surrounding gender, race, and racism into stark relief. It compels audience members to acknowledge the beautiful packaging of white supremacy. Rose's willingness to uphold the quotidian expectations of white supremacy, and audience willingness to excuse her and absolve her of her guilt even when confronted with concrete evidence, not only prompts us to remember the existence of white supremacy but its persistence and our social complicity in it.

It is for this reason that Chris's inability to ultimately kill Rose should be unsurprising. It is an unambiguous reminder of the insidious nature of social expectations regarding white female innocence and lack of culpability even in the face of evidence to the contrary. Her probable death[2] is, literally, left out of Chris's hands. Certainly, this is symbolically resonant because it parallels his own mother's death in his childhood and his lingering feelings of guilt and helplessness, underscoring the continued mental and emotional paralysis that allowed his mind to be so fully infiltrated by Missy Armitage, the family matriarch. Yet, perhaps more importantly, this moment serves to reify his humanity over hers in important ways. Here we see when Rose whispers that she loves Chris that it stifles his ability to kill her because he is reminded that he did once love her—it is ultimately irrelevant whether or not her feelings were feigned; what matters is that she is the irredeemable monster, not him. In fact, even if her love claim at the end resembles the truth in any way, her inability and lack of desire to remain steadfast against her family is indicative of the ways that we are all ultimately beholden to the white supremacist mindset of this country. Indeed, Kendra James explains rightly that,

> The thought that white people may see you as no more than a body for use or a culture from which you can pick and choose what you like while discarding the rest *and* those who invented it? The idea that a white woman you see as your potential friend or ally will eventually prove to be looking out for her own best interests over yours or the greater good? These are concepts that the people of color watching this film are intimately familiar with.

It is James's assertion that these interests could fly in the face of the greater good that is particularly compelling. Indeed, what Peele makes strange is the nature of whiteness itself, through the idea that white supremacy is, in fact, not in the service of the common good and that it may ultimately hurt our common good.

The Armitage family is hopeless. Viewers are not meant to understand their participation in the dehumanization of Blackness and Black people as somehow signaling their own victimization. There is no pitying treatment of these perpetrators, and audiences hate them in the end. And yet, simultaneously, they are such a familiar, all-American nuclear familial ideal that they are almost innocuous in their excessive villainy. As a result, the criminality that we find horrifying and would normally call unbelievable becomes a plausible extension of reality. In this way it is the familiar, all-American system that allows the Armitage family to thrive that is culpable—the Armitage family exists as the conspirators. This conspiratorial sense naturally begins to include the viewers for their willingness to excuse Rose. Again, Peele seems to note, it is not only the active participation in a racist system but the refusal to agitate or acknowledge the reality of the situation with discernment once we see it that is also worth condemnation. If, as Marilyn Corsianos argues, "in order to strive towards a just society, people must strive towards a just world where there are certain freedoms guaranteed and where *everyone constantly interrogates one another's actions in order to ensure less inequalities*" (11, emphasis added), it follows that a lack of interrogation begets an unjust and unequal world. *Get Out* is founded on the premise that our socialization matters because it determines our relationship to social justice realms—that a performative lack of public racist rhetoric does not undercut tacit participation in a racist system. That it is Chris's best friend, Rod, who drives up and saves the day—Black brotherhood emerging as deus ex machina at just the right moment—underscores the colloquial paradigm where "justice" can only be found in the sphere of "just us." This point, for Peele, cannot be overemphasized. He reifies this idea by having Rod appear at the end in a "TSA Vehicle," as his nearing flashing lights signal to audiences that police are approaching and theater audiences register audible relief at the realization that it is *not* the police, who would certainly presume Chris to be the aggressor.[3] The stakes for Black people in this system are overtly reinforced in this moment, while Peele allows audiences the reward of catharsis when Chris's life is suddenly spared. Yet despite this respite, the moment gives us pause. When Rod and Chris ride off into the proverbial sunset together—Black men who *do*, in fact, survive the trauma of the racist horror—there is no sense of lasting catharsis or relief. After all, where might the men now go that offers a reprieve, particularly in the wake of white bodies strewn about as remnants of his self-defense? Dre's screams at the Armitage house of *get out* may be rightly conjured here in the moment where the only possible response is *I can't*. There is no permanent reprieve. The film ultimately advocates for an active response *against* racist social structures and beseeches us to seek justice in this capacity, while still reasserting that there may be no escape. It is the traumatic quandary of racism—our simultaneous acknowledgment of what Derrick Bell describes as "the permanence of racism" and our discontent with a racist status quo.

Peele utilizes this satire-infused horror genre as a form of social justice-seeking to assess contemporary racism and address Black interiority in view of the precariousness of Blackness and Black life in a post-Obama era. In pursuit of this goal, the film offers an interesting possible reading of Black assimilation into white culture. The merging of a white mindset into a phenotypically Black body—made unbearably literal through the surgical transplants performed by Dean Armitage—is, ultimately, what assimilation requires. Journalist April Ryan explains assimilation further in her book *At Mama's Knee: Mothers and Race in Black and White,* writing, "My mind screams 'identity' for the word, *assimilation.* But it also begs the question, assimilation without the loss of identity or the strengthening of who you are? Or is it really about a melding of people?" (99). What *Get Out* imagines is that there can be no melding *without* this painful loss of identity—"the sunken place" resists simple categorization as marginalization or even broad oppression, because it is ultimately the stifling of autonomous Black interiority. It is a space of both the physical act of being rendered invisible and hypervisible while denied selfhood. There is only one sense of the self that can be strengthened; the other is, quite naturally, sacrificed or repressed. This potential is an interesting reimagining of what assimilation might look like if evaluated with a sympathetic understanding of its effect on the Black body—what we witness here is the imagery of the *Oreo,* who is in this case literally Black on the outside and white on the inside. The space of the Black interior becomes, literally, repressed. Kevin Young explains, "There's a long-standing American tradition of whites donning blackface, or redface, or any other colored mask they pretend is a face. Those who wear blackface reduce blackness to skin in order not to be white. The implication of course is that black people are just miscolored or extra-dark white people" (101–2). What *Get Out* does that is especially provocative, then, is shift our understanding of assimilationists as unwilling blackface performers by rearticulating them as actual white people in Black bodies.

This reimagining is particularly compelling, because so often the question of assimilation is construed in terms that suggest a willing rejection of personal cultural trappings or attachments for some tangible benefit. Here, Peele offers that this conflict isn't even an autonomous choice but is something forced on Black bodies and against which the Black mind struggles. This sense of tension and struggle emerges throughout the film as the stolen Dre mentally breaks free from his "Logan" persona momentarily in an attempt to save Chris during the Armitage party by screaming "Get out!" and pushing him, and as Georgina responds with a single tear signaling her trauma and dejection even as she reassures Chris of the kindness of the Armitage family. In an interview for *At Mama's Knee* unrelated to the film, April Ryan asked actress Erika Alexander, interestingly, the same actress who portrayed the dismissive officer in *Get Out,* what assimilation meant to her. She described it by saying, "Annihilation. Dilution. To fit into. Or, more optimistically and in the spirit of a modern-day slang, a new-age, brain-drained mashup! Assimilation is the filtered absence of what originally makes you, you. You become 'curated'" (99). Alexander seems to anticipate Peele's fears of annihilation a few years before the movie was produced. If assimilation is an absence, a corrupted Black interior space, then the frightening sunken place in which the Black mind is entreated to reside is a devastating retreat into the void, breeding unsatisfying mobility within the frame of the mainstream. It highlights the cohesive nature of assimilation and appropriation and the ways in which they work to essentialize and ignore the lived experiences of objectified bodies. Indeed, this curation, evident in Rose's own museum-like room filled with images of Black bodies stolen and undone, ultimately argues that the appropriation of culture is a mismatch of body and mind, of real belonging and entitled appropriation. These assimilated figures we meet are unable to interact comfortably or casually within the white spheres where they reside or when they come into contact again with unassimilated Blackness. It is an untenable mental state.

Post-Racial Racism

Nevertheless, in examinations of assimilation and of race and racial meaning, oftentimes whiteness is conspicuously left out of the conversation. The silence surrounding whiteness indicates, either tacitly or explicitly, that race is intended to be synonymous with nonwhiteness—only people of color are racialized; whiteness is the absence of race and white people are simply people. This problematic interpretation leads to an understanding of race itself as inherently negative. If people of color—marginalized populations—are the only people who have a race, then it is race itself that is the cause of the attendant traumas beget by this hierarchy. This oversimplification is rampant throughout American social understanding and works to absolve society of its calculated reification of race as a presumably visual indicator of low status and place or placelessness. It is for this reason that whiteness as racialization is particularly relevant to contemporary satire. Considering the active nature of whiteness provides insights into the traditionally overlooked position of whiteness within the frame of "race." The contemporary moment manifests in this perspective; by refusing the near-ghettoization of "the racial," a frame opens up for conversations where the social-constructedness of race—rather than only ultimately melodramatic portrayals of race as curse of the abject and the sphere of quantifiable difference—can be addressed.

These considerations surrounding the unequal treatment of race have always existed in the minds and conversations of people of color. This reality, however, has not been addressed as explicitly in the public sphere until relatively recently; bell hooks notes that,

> Usually, white students respond with naïve amazement that black people critically assess white people from a standpoint where "whiteness" is the privileged signifier. Their amazement that black people watch white people with a critical "ethnographic" gaze, is itself an expression of racism. Often their rage erupts because they believe that all ways of looking that highlight difference subvert the liberal conviction that it is the assertion of universal subjectivity (we are all just people) that will make racism disappear. They have a deep emotional investment in the myth of "sameness" even as their actions reflect the primacy of whiteness as a sign informing who they are and how they think. (167–68)

This white rage, as hooks identifies it, exemplifies why a more complicated understanding of both Blackness *and* whiteness matters. This new perspective necessarily disrupts the traditional paradigm. In doing so, it allows new conversations about race to emerge that may offer productive possibilities through the tension. The satirical mode creates space for conversations that alter the forms social justice might take by complicating notions of the centrality of race and, thereby, our naturalized understandings of the self and the other. What is most important here is that thinking about whiteness as race actually and ironically decenters whiteness from its traditional position in the narrative. By placing the expectation of unraced whiteness under erasure, a space for a close analysis of race in America opens that refuses whiteness and white people as normed within the racial hierarchy.

Returning once again to Derrick Bell's *Faces at the Bottom of the Well: The Permanence of Racism,* it is this sense of eternality that is most affecting. Originally published in 1992, Bell's collection of essays imagines contemporary race relations through an allegorical lens. Bell, the first tenured African American law professor at Harvard University and an originator of critical race theory, uses narrative form to conceptualize the continued significance of race from the historical past up through the present. If, as Moon Kie-Jung argues, "matters of racism are not and have never been simple matters. They were not contemporaneously more transparent in the past, before the Civil Rights Movement, and they are not consistently less powerful now" (16), Bell's rearticulation forces readers to consider the immediacy of a racist status quo and its constant need of reification for its own survival. In this way, while it may be a disservice to discount the gains of the 1960s and 1970s, it is also necessary to acknowledge the inherent concentricity of the past and present. By offering *The Permanence of Racism* as a subtitle, Bell alerts readers immediately that this is not a reimagining of racism or even a prediction of its return. This is, literally, an overt recognition of racism as a permanent fixture within the American social realm—and, indeed, within our understanding of American selves and selfhood. Bell's assertion is simultaneously prescient and right on time.

Perhaps the most famous of the stories in *Faces* is "The Space Traders," a science fiction tale in which aliens come to the United States in the year 2000—the near future, from its 1992 original publication date—and ask to take all African Americans with them in exchange for new knowledge and unlimited resources for the non-Black citizens left behind. The catch is, of course, that the extraterrestrial visitors will not explain what their plans are for African Americans, nor are they ever revealed. The nation decides to vote, the results are unsurprising, and off African Americans are sent in shackles to a new intergalactic world. The narrative has echoes of Rod Serling's *Twilight Zone*, most specifically episodes like "To Serve Man" and "The Monsters are Due on Maple Street," in which the enemy is not only the potentially monstrous nonhuman but even more acutely a sense of careless human selfishness and self-interest in the face of widespread fear. Yet even more notably, it anticipates Peele's Afropessimism by signaling not only the objectification and marginalization of Black bodies but the literal *minority* status of African Americans that renders Black bodies subjectable to harm.

What "Space Traders" does in seeming anticipation of *Get Out* is not only render ideas surrounding Black exceptionalism fallacious but demonstrate the ways in which they can ultimately frame these "Black exceptions" as targets for their own demise. The protagonist, Professor Gleason Golightly, neatly fulfills tropes of contemporary Black exceptionalism—he is a well-educated, self-interested conservative mouthpiece—his subscription to respectability politics ultimately still renders his very real racial anxieties void to his white compatriots. He explains, "It is a mark of just how far out of the mainstream black people are that this proposition is given any serious consideration" (167). Indeed, that the nation ultimately, unsurprisingly, votes to permit the space traders to hold all African Americans captive—and, similarly, reneges on its promise to keep Golightly protected during the exchange—is emblematic of the limitations of respectability to save the Black body from psychic or literal harm. "Space Traders," like *Get Out*, demonstrates the limits of liberal white allyship by framing this allyship in terms of self-righteous egotism. By placing this narrative in the context of a not-so-distant future and ending with the imagery of slavery—the story closes with the sight of chained Black bodies forced onto a spaceship waiting at a former slave port—Bell demonstrates the ways that the position of Black people within the national frame has changed while it simultaneously remains the same, even as the position of Black people to power within the nation has shifted and become more denaturalized than ever before. Bell rightly explains that "Indeed, the racism that made slavery feasible is far from dead in the last decade of twentieth-century America; and the civil rights gains, so hard won, are being steadily eroded" (3). What Bell, like Peele, reminds us is that our passivity cannot protect any of us from racism, and it certainly cannot free us from it either. In this way, not only does Bell offer the necessary pushback that disabuses readers of the notion that the legacy of slavery is less significantly felt in a contemporary time, but he also demonstrates that individual Black exceptionalism offers no real reprieve from the systemic horror and trauma of modern-day racism.

On ending *Faces* with the overt cynicism of "Space Traders," Bell writes, "By concluding the book on this dire note, I hope to emphasize the necessity of moving beyond the comforting belief that time and the generosity of its people will eventually solve America's racial problem" (13). The myth of contemporary generosity is problematic not only because it is fallacious but because it offers a comforting distraction couched in ideas of human moralistic evolution. If we assume that what happened *then* could not happen *now,* then we indicate either tacitly or explicitly that hoping for a change through vague, passive optimism is enough. This thinking renders protest unnecessary and contributes to a frame in which "social justice warrior" becomes a slur and is disconnected from the real need for articulated selfhood as a form of justice. It not only undermines our sense of what justice is, but also the obligation to seek justice in all of its forms, where seeking justice might, at least in moments, signal revolution.

Regular Black People Living Life

Contemporary efforts toward articulating both individual and communal selfhood through satire not only emerge through the utilization of tropes of the horror genre but more broadly through the intentional recentering of the focus of comedic narratives. As Peele likewise undertook in *Get Out,* there is meaning in the move to allow Blackness—both as overtly racialized and as representative visualization—to move in from the margins. In this way, the tension between simultaneous hypervisibility and invisibility of Blackness rendered in the white gaze is lessened and, instead, Blackness can be naturalized within the previously limited scope of Americanness. Nowhere, perhaps, is this centering more necessary than for African American female comedians, where the requirement of representation can feel overwhelming. These performers and writers experience the presumed double bind of race and gender. Rebecca Krefting writes,

> For women comics, performing gender neutral has historically proven successful; audiences would rather not be reminded that this is a woman's point of view, making it harder for male audience members to identify. Women, on the other hand, are trained to identify with men early on and to see male struggle as human struggle. But for comics of color, performing race neutral can (though not always) yield the opposite result. (215)

Krefting's articulation here inadvertently seems to address race and gender as discrete entities, and does not overtly take into direct account the experiences of female comics of color. However, when expanded to examine these possible intersections, her argument takes hold in new ways. If we can imagine that these groups are often set aside as nonrepresentative of a core comic demographic, women of color in particular are at a larger risk of having their texts and performances to be assumed too niche to succeed, or having their performances assumed to be inherently unrelatable for large swaths of the population.

There has resultantly been an undue burden to present material in a way that seems somehow recognizable to racial and gender expectations and also easily identified through essentialist ideas. Consequently, the most prevalent portrayals of women of color are often so shallow and surface level as to no longer resemble identifiable human beings and instead emerge as race and gender personified. The push to be recognized as discernibly *human* has, in many cases, forced writers and performers to consider the politics of respectability and either embrace them in an effort to prove their own inherent goodness and value or aggressively and performatively shirk them to prove their personhood outside reductive modes of behavior. Neither choice allows for the nuance of actual lived experience. Roxane Gay rightly wonders, "Respectability politics suggest that there's a way for us to all be model (read: like white) citizens. We can always be better, but will we ever be ideal? Do we even want to be ideal, or is there a way for us to become more comfortably human?" (259). Indeed, respectability politics are predicated on proscribing behavior to the extent that there is no possibility of the comfortably human. Gay is correct to note that respectability politics presume model citizenship, and for Black people, respectability may not even just mean "like white." Instead, it requires conformity to ever-shifting and always unattainable rules of behavior to which white citizens are never uniformly held.

What might it look like when a female comedian, then, shirks respectability in favor of the dynamic nuances of Black female selfhood in the twenty-first century, stripped clean of the expectations handed down by misogynoir? One possibility might be Issa Rae's HBO series *Insecure*. The show, loosely based on Rae's web series, *The Misadventures of Awkward Black Girl*, centers on Rae's character, Issa Dee, her best friend since their undergraduate years at UCLA, Molly, and Issa's long-time boyfriend (and, later, ex-boyfriend), Lawrence. The show chronicles their respective work-life balances and shows the women working to define themselves personally and professionally in Los Angeles. By homing in on the experiences of millennial Black women—Afromillennials[4]—within the constructs of a post-racial era, *Insecure* demonstrates the simultaneity of racial meaningfulness and meaninglessness—this is a show that is clearly about the dynamics of race and gender without essentializing either. The show offers a useful counterpoint to *Get Out* because, although clearly not an entry in the horror genre, *Insecure* likewise shifts from traditional comedic performances of Black selfhood and relationships, underpinning the narrative with evocative dramatic content. Certainly, then, if comedy accepts the rules of the society in which it emerges and satire works to subvert these rules, *Insecure* contains the possibility of satirical readings—indeed, how else might we understand a performance that seems so casually uninterested in questions of the white gaze? In *Insecure,* Rae embarks on a new generic convention in pursuit of a nuanced portrayal of Blackness. The show depicts what she has described as "regular black people living life" by refusing the respectability politics that render Black bodies admirable while also refusing the reductive lens that renders Black bodies abject. In particular, *Insecure* demonstrates that race and gender are inextricable from identity but need not be the only facets of identity examined within the Black interior.

The shifting relationship between the protagonist, Issa, and Lawrence is compelling in its universal relatability. In season one, Issa and Lawrence have been together for years and the mundane details of life together are beginning to wear thin. Couple this with Lawrence's continued unemployment—he was laid off from a position in the tech field and refuses to look for any work that doesn't fit his very specific ideal—and the relationship has long since lost its luster. And yet Issa is reluctant to leave Lawrence because he's "a good guy." Even without demonstrating, at least early on, any sense of motivation, let alone a compelling personality, audiences are primed to sympathize with Lawrence because he seems kind (or, at least, *not* unkind), is handsome and clean-cut, has an admittedly great smile, and is described as intelligent. And, of course, people tend to root for the incumbent unless given a compelling reason to feel otherwise. Yet once again, there is an emphasis on the traditional assumptions of respectability politics within the frame of Blackness, but *Insecure* works to distort and refuse these expectations. Instead, Issa and Lawrence both grapple with their own shortcomings, and her frustration with him is palpable. In some ways, *Insecure* refuses traditional satirical frames. The primary romantic struggle is more nuanced than traditional sitcom spheres that so frequently depict shrewish women harping at fun-loving, childlike men. Issa's concerns surrounding Lawrence are valid and have real-world ramifications in terms of their ability to build a future together—it's not simply that Lawrence is aimless and that she holds this continuing personality trait in contempt; indeed, Lawrence does have personal and professional aims (albeit somewhat unrealistic and unfocused), and his present apathy in their relationship is explicitly a change from the beginning of their time together that actively presents a barrier to their intimacy and their successful growth together.

Because Lawrence is "a good guy," Issa's sense of ennui further departs from expectations of gender roles in depictions of Black relationships. Issa is dissatisfied, but this doesn't emerge as the shrill boyfriend-girlfriend fighting frequently depicted on sitcoms in the 1990s with characters of all races. She loves Lawrence and has offered support, but it doesn't manifest as the "ride or die" and "hold you down" expectations of sustaining Black womanhood. Nor does her frustration manifest through Lawrence cheating on her or turning cruel in some tangible, obvious way. So frequently, cultural production involving Black women, and even progressive productions, ultimately seems to settle on the idea that Black women should be grateful for the attention of men. This trope is so intrinsic to our understanding of Black womanhood that it creates a paradigm in which Leslie Jones makes a joke about "having a man" through the forced breeding of chattel slavery and then defends it by arguing that the joke is mere commentary on her Black, female, single status.[5] Clearly, the two aren't synonymous, but both speak to expectations that Black women should accept whatever romantic options are most readily available within their time and space. Ultimately, *Insecure* offers a satirical reading by demonstrating its own awareness of the expectation that it should conform to satirical tropes and then its resisting of those same tropes. Instead, through Issa Rae's depiction, *Insecure* centers Black female desire and desirability by interrogating the "good guy" trope and questioning whether "goodness" is merely the absence of malice, and if that should be enough to maintain a relationship.

Although the contentious #TeamIssa–#TeamLawrence debate that ended season one was compelling, it is less interesting than other relationships depicted. Ultimately, in the fallout of a relationship gone sour—fictional or otherwise—both sides usually find themselves to be wronged in some ways and, therein, equally justified in whatever vengeance is enacted. In this particular consideration of a satirical reading of *Insecure*, I am less concerned about the relationship between Issa and Lawrence and more interested in her relationship with her best friend, Molly, which is the true love story of the series. That Lawrence and Issa's relationship exists as a mere red herring for the intentionality of the series demonstrates a satirical reimagining of the (companionate) love as a story line unto itself. Issa and Molly are structured as the narrative heartbeat, and this "will they / won't they" dynamic reinvented as homosocial tension ultimately drives the action of the show and is the primary happy ending for which we are compelled and retrained to cheer. It is the bond between Issa and Molly that informs the primary love story of *Insecure*—similar to the bond between Chris and Rod in *Get Out*—where the heterosexual relationship between Issa and Lawrence distracts from a much more compelling narrative about the resilient love between the platonic friends.[6]

In this way, it is the nuanced relationship between these two women that forms the crux of the show and explains why the series was such a runaway hit. It is not just a portrayal of Black female friendships, which is significant in its own right. *Insecure* expands on existing schema by placing Black female friendships at its center and refusing any oversimplified tropes of Black femininity—this is a show about Black womanhood and Black women, but it denies racism its predictable primacy as a frame for understanding the nuances of race. In this sense, the program is a throwback to other fictionalized Black friendships from past sitcoms, such as the women of *A Different World*, *Living Single*, and *Girlfriends*—women who were defined by their Blackness, though their Blackness was never an overdetermining or even the primary factor of their friendship. These women are friends because they're Black, but not *only* friends because they're the *only* Black women in their universe. The distinction here is critical. This does not mean that race is unacknowledged or that the characters exist in some post-racial mythological universe. Instead, *Insecure* depicts the reality of many Black female friendships—a shared common language and cultural experiences that exist both within and without the white gaze. This structuring, coupled with *Insecure*'s specific commitment to modes of homosociality in which the female friend group is highlighted irrespective of male friendship or romantic interest, is in itself revolutionary as it centers Black womanhood without any implication that it needs a white frame in which to exist. It acknowledges the racism Black women expect as quotidian without centering white perpetrators through an undue focus on the racism itself or an attempt to teach the racist the error of his or her ways.

In fact, even when existing in predominantly white spaces, *Insecure* works to decenter the preeminence of the white gaze. In one such episode, Issa and her friends, Molly, Kelli, and Tiffany—all Black women—head to Coachella to watch Beyoncé headline the festival. Coachella is rather infamously known as a place in which young, white socialites and children of the wealthy flock to watch musical performances and engage in a multiday celebration of excess. However, the *Insecure* episode never addresses the presumed white centrality of Coachella, instead focusing on the core friend group and their participation in events attended by and centered on other people of color. This is particularly profound when we consider that Beyoncé herself was the first Black woman to *ever* headline Coachella, and her performance has now become the definitive Coachella performance—heralded as Beychella by many on social media. This Coachella episode reminds viewers that not only do Black people exist in seemingly white spaces, but that these spaces aren't necessarily marked by trauma or otherness within the context of communal identity and group support. And this remains true despite the fact that, of course, hilarity ensues, and the group is unable to actually see Beyoncé's performance in person.

In this way, *Insecure* opens up new potentialities for communal justice by allowing these Black female-centered narratives to exist outside the parameters of white understanding. Rae herself addresses the significance of this centering in her satirical memoir, explaining,

> I felt surrounded by the mainstream media's negative images of black women. This was all prior to the promising Shonda Rhimes takeover of Thursday nights, so as the negative portrayal of women in reality television broadened its boundaries, I grew angry, resentful, and impatient. How hard is it to portray a three-dimensional woman of color on television or in film? I'm surrounded by them. They're my friends. I talk to them every day. How come Hollywood won't acknowledge us? Are we a joke to them? (45)

What Rae does here so successfully is to underscore the frustrations of the limited views of Black womanhood as presented in the mainstream, when presented at all. Rae created a space for the reality of the "black best friend" that largely hasn't existed in nonessentialized ways or beyond a mere trope by reinscribing what it means for the Black best friend to actually *have* a Black best friend. This flips what author and pop culture critic Helena Andrews humorously describes in her memoir *Bitch Is the New Black* (2010) as the typical Black experience; instead of being *the Black friend* in the group, now the group is fully Black.

As such, on *Insecure*, when a clueless white coworker asks Issa to define "on fleek" for her, Issa's response that she doesn't know what the phrase means, followed immediately by clandestine eye rolling and her voiceover admitting, "I *know* what that shit means," shifts away from a tradition that would center this moment and unpack it into a "very special episode" about race and racism. Instead, Issa quickly points out the ludicrousness of the request and her unwillingness to fuel racially specific assumptions about her knowledge and experience, even when those assumptions are correct. She then retreats to the comfort of her peer group and they *never address this racialized moment*. Instead, they discuss the issues—love, work, and other aspirations—that ultimately do matter to them in critical ways. Race is one aspect of the show, but racism is not meant to be the defining characteristic for viewers and it is not the defining characteristic for these players, either. Instead, the show uses the satiric realm to undercut and reframe our expectations of love, of race, and of the traditional narrative endgame to potentially heighten the intersectional identities of women of color in the twenty-first century.

This "on fleek" moment recalls contemporary recollections of racism in the frame of Afromillennial world-weariness. For example, in Andrews's *Bitch Is the New Black,* she relies on her own very personal experiences without making them explicit moments for psychoanalysis. She recalls her sixth-grade teacher asking whether she minded the use of the word *nigger* during a read-aloud. Andrews nervously permitted the use of the word—was it even a real choice, given the age and power dynamics?—and vividly paints the moment,

> Then the main character goes, "S-see what they called us."
>   Then Mrs. Paul with all her ancient oratory skills goes, (*evil redneck old teacher voice*) "That's what you are" (*normal nonracist voice*) "she said coldly" (*racist voice*) "Now go sit down."
>   Sixty-six tiny eyeballs stuck to the back of my head for the rest of the hour. (49)

Andrews recounts these moments of humiliation as tied to interracial experiences. The adolescent self is thrown into question during a critical period of flickering self-actualization. This remembrance demonstrates what can be termed "unthinking racism." That her sixth-grade teacher couldn't immediately recognize *without asking* the impact of the vocalization of the word on a preteen—the only student of color in the class—speaks to a careless dehumanization of Black bodies. Indeed, it is important to frame this notion in the context of bodies and embodiment because the Black mind and Black interior are ultimately ignored, reduced, and discarded. Instead, in these moments, the dehumanization occurs in the callous treatment of Black *people* as empty vessels of Black skin, unworthy of empathy. For this reason, the teacher could place Andrews in a situation of false choosing without considering her humanity. Her classmates' stares attempt to reframe Andrews as a stand-in for Blackness—even the physicality of the word *nigger*—without her consent or ability to choose her own performance. Although Andrews infuses the moment with humor in her retelling, by differentiating between her teacher's "evil redneck old teacher voice" and "normal nonracist voice," the moment still resonates as one of adolescent racial understanding and confusion simultaneously. Even though Andrews's experience here isn't one of being called nigger directly, readers are shown that the word itself is impactful even in the imaginary and certainly because of its constant potential. Yet this moment isn't presented as an overdetermining factor in Andrews's self-development; she uses this moment to refocus her understanding of herself both within and without the frame of racialization, expecting these interracial moments and taking solace in intraracial experience.

Later racially charged moments would be less casually waged by the perpetrator. Andrews explains that now when white people argue that she isn't *really* Black, she anticipates these moments and has comedic, essentialist proof at the ready. In her inner monologue, she explains, "'First of all, I'm from Compton. I have a cousin on death row. I went to public school for a friggin' entire year. You don't know my life!' And my ghetto resume went on from there" (145). Her instant inclination is to provide her accuser with those features of stereotypical Blackness that are most readily conjured and easily commodified, indicating her knowledge of their reliance on black essentialism as racial validation. Importantly, however, she doesn't do this. "'Emily, I'm black.' That's as far as I got," she writes. "Because, really, she was a good friend of mine. A friend I allowed to ask me mildly racist questions because, really, who the hell else is going to answer them for her?" (212). Although she offers excuses for her friend's ignorance, by naming herself as Black and offering no other qualifiers, she implies that there is something about Blackness that is readily visible and intangible—she essentializes herself by ironically eschewing traditional frames of Black essentialist notions. Andrews ultimately throws her friend's understanding of Blackness into distress.

In *Insecure*, women reside in the nuances of race and gender—even within the realm of "protagonist and sidekick" they are not easily described but are admirable in their dynamism. When Issa and Molly fight and drift apart for a number of episodes, the tension hurts viewers not because it signals some sort of comment on the pettiness of Black women or the instability of Black female friendships writ large, but instead because it is recognizable. It is recognizable *because* neither of them are the strong Black woman archetype, neither are they the mammy or the Jezebel. They are significant additions to what Black women already know exists within the realm of their own personal experiences, now on full display in the public—and even their flaws are treated with simultaneous honesty and care. Their faults aren't meant to represent some sort of naturalized abjection. Neither of them is right or wrong; they exist, flaws and all. Roxane Gay echoed the annoyance of many marginalized groups when she wrote, "I'm tired of feeling like I should be grateful when popular culture deigns to acknowledge the experiences of people who are not white, middle class or wealthy, and heterosexual. I'm tired of the extremes" (253). Rae creates a realm where the reality of Black interior space, where Black womanhood, awkwardness, insecurities and all, might be more roundly reflected.

In her satirical memoir *The Misadventures of Awkward Black Girl*, Rae explains the necessity of her critically acclaimed web series of the same name, writing, "*Girls, New Girl, 2 Broke Girls.* What do they all have in common? The universal gender classification, 'girl' is white. In all three of these successful series, a default girl (or two) is implied and she is white. That is the norm and that is what is acceptable. Anything else is niche" (46). Rae's assertion is startling in its plainness and keen precision. Black characters are often punch lines rather than people—they are used as verbs and adjectives to enrich the white characters who are centered and highlighted in these narratives; their own human experiences are thinly depicted, marginalized, and discounted. Much of this essentialization may stem from the lack of diverse representation within the writers' room of traditional sitcoms and popular media accounts. For this reason, Rae's intentional construction of a diverse writers' room and depiction of nuanced Black womanhood is particularly resonant for contemporary audiences.

Perhaps her active embracing of Black sisterhood begins to explain why Issa Rae and *Insecure* have been so immensely successful. By creating a dynamic in-group of Black womanhood, Rae is able to refuse any essentialist notions of black femininity—she is not required to extend her experiences, or the experiences of her characters, as representative of all Black women. By depicting a close and recognizably fraught friendship between two Black women that converges and diverges in interesting ways, Rae ultimately proves to audiences that Black womanhood contains multitudes that must be acknowledged if it is to be understood comprehensively. In this way, interestingly, Issa Rae is able to demonstrate the dynamism of Black womanhood by framing the articulation of her self-identity. And even as we praise Rae for her satiric innovations, we must also consider that she stands on the shoulders of Whoopi Goldberg and Leslie Jones, and she has been able to learn from their successes and misfires. It is also important to acknowledge the generational difference in Goldberg (born 1955), Jones (born 1967), and Rae (born 1985). Neither Goldberg nor Jones were raised with a prevalence of media examples, the aforementioned *Living Single, Girlfriends,* and the like, that gestured to the centering of multiple Black women or Black female friendships without racial essentialism. Goldberg, problematic as some of her portrayals and joke telling may have been, *was* the centered, pioneering Black female comedian of her generation. Her Oda Mae Brown in *Ghost* and Deloris Van Cartier / Sister Mary Clarence in both *Sister Act* films could have been reductive racial stereotypes, and perhaps in some moments they were. Yet what Goldberg was able to achieve in these roles was a comedic sensibility that, while often rendering her the punch line, allowed her the space to exceed limited identity expectations and to articulate herself in her own terms—and often make her would-be oppressors the punch line as well. Jones similarly exists within this generational divide of expectations of Black female comedic output. While Rae's viewpoint is perhaps more nuanced, it is built on the legacies of those who came before her, those women who tried with varying degrees of success to disabuse audiences of the notion that Black womanhood could only look like one thing.

In work created by Afromillennials like Jordan Peele and Issa Rae, there is a tangible sense of frustration, occurring simultaneously with trauma. Afromillennials experience the trauma of racism and racialization—specifically under exponential rates of incarceration coupled with police brutality and police killings. However, due to the prominence of successful African American "exceptionals," most notably encapsulated in the presidency of Barack Obama, Afromillennials are often portrayed (like millennials more broadly) by media pundits as whiny and unappreciative of the work put in and gains made by earlier generations. Derek Conrad Murray is right to note "the frustrations of young African American artists (the post-civil rights generation) around notions of identity and belongingness that they perceived to be stifling, reductive, and exclusionary" (5). Indeed, for some Afromillennials, there may be a sense that at least the civil rights movement benefited from precise and easily identified goals. Now, the struggle continues but is accused of being fractured and hazy—any presumed or projected dispute or in-fighting of the Black Lives Matter movement used as apparent proof of their disorganization, rather than being read correctly as an indicator of the multifaceted stakes of the movement itself. Indeed, all movements have suffered from (and benefited from) the disagreements of their group members, and this dispersed leadership model in particular strengthens BLM as the inability to locate one individual leader or figurehead makes the movement more difficult to tear asunder.

Richard Dyer explains, "There is no more powerful position than that of being 'just' human. The claim to power is the claim to speak for the commonality of humanity. Raced people can't do that—they can only speak for their race. But non-raced people can, for they do not represent the interests of a race" (2). These new possibilities for satire and comedy in the twenty-first century acknowledge Dyer's argument and then approach a solution from a different angle. Instead of attempting to create cultural production that refuses racial specificity and thereby becomes "just" human, these performers instead demonstrate their own humanity *within* a racialization of their own choosing—it is an overt articulation where race is not problematized, and racism rightly is. In this way, race becomes one of *many* salient qualities that may frame a sense of actualization. In *Get Out,* Chris is expressly terrorized within the vicinity of racists but experiences no racialized trauma in other facets of his life. Indeed, his Blackness is framed as a comforting retreat in contrast to "the sunken place." His home is decorated with black and white photographs of Black children, a Black pregnant belly, and Black people, images of kaleidoscopic Blackness that offer the sanctuary of Black life and Black joy. Likewise, Issa Rae creates a show that works in conscious consideration of race without allowing racism to take primacy, thereby undercutting an idea of race itself as a social ill. Justice is attained through a selfhood that recognizes race without reducing black experiences to a narrow portrayal within the scope of racism. The reality of racism is addressed, but it is not the *only* significant experience in the personal lives of Black people. This is a difference that matters so much because it encourages justice through the creation of worlds that eschew the post-*racial* mythology in favor of a post-*racist* society, while acknowledging that post-racism may, likewise, be unattainable and also undesirable.

The twenty-first century ushered in, for some, a desire for a post-racial mythology as proof that race is less significant now than in years past. Although in recent years this idea of "less significant" loses much of its savor in view of the continuing upheaval in the United States surrounding race-based police brutality, border building, and legislation, the post-racial was always untenable and a frankly undesirable schema. The preceding satires and satirical readings remind us that there is nothing inherently problematic about race itself. Instead, the impulse is toward depicting a substantial degree of self-actualization and self-identification within and without racialization that refuses racist ideologies. The satiric in both fictional and lived experience opens up this space for an articulation of an identity that includes racial specificity but isn't predicated on racial essentialism as necessary for selfhood. And our selfhood, both individual and communal, is founded on the recognition of racism as a permanent feature of society and our simultaneous desire to fight systemic racism and refuse the prescriptions of racist ideologies. It is through the persistence of this refusal in all spheres of existence—in the reality of Black life and in its depiction in the popular realm—that we open up space for the revelation of kaleidoscopic Blackness.

CONCLUSION

Black Futurity and the Future
of African American Satire

What is self-analysis? What is the
direction toward unknown totality?
—Fred Moten

The role of the comedian is to tell jokes and, to that end, to be received as comedy, the jokes have to be *funny*. But funny is itself predicated on social constructs and expectations. It requires the comedian's acceptance of the social realm as it exists—the humor is derived from a person's ability to conform, or not, to social expectations. African American satire, including those nontraditional satires that urge our satirical reading, extends this role through the subversion of expectations; where comedy rearticulates the rules as they exist, satire refuses the rules and calls out their incompatibility within the lives of the marginalized. Satire imagines new spheres of possibility in which both physical and psychic Black life might be permitted to not only survive but to thrive. Dave Chappelle has emerged as a perhaps unexpected microcosm of the potentials of satire and its inherent drawbacks. On November 12, 2016, he returned to television with an appearance as a host of *Saturday Night Live*. This moment marked a return to the comedic stage after the ten years following *Chappelle's Show*, during which time, although he performed the occasional stand-up set and appeared in a small role in Spike Lee's film *Chi-Raq*, he was generally absent from the public realm. Chappelle's return was all the more noteworthy because it collided with the contemporary political sphere in unanticipated ways—he was the first host after Donald Trump's presidential win.

The absurdity of the 2016 election offers a useful context for Chappelle's return. Whether or not it served as actual catalyst for his reappearance, the potential not only for comedic fodder but also for critical and sustained satirical commentary seemed limitless. Even more significantly than the expectation of entertainment, an eager public positioned Chappelle as (perhaps unwilling) superhero, while audiences waited for him to hold Trump's feet to the fire and fix what had been seemingly broken. Unsurprisingly, of course, much of his commentary directly addressed the political sphere in an attempt to rearticulate what Chappelle has consistently articulated—the simultaneous meaningfulness and meaninglessness of racial identity that refuses a simplistic notion of the post-racial—through the tangibility of the election and national dis-ease.

Chappelle began with an eleven-minute opening monologue—two or three times the length of most opening monologues for the show—during which he spoke directly to the audience about the election and recent, racially charged events. He spoke about a party he had recently attended at the White House under Barack Obama, filled with a number of Black celebrities and, conspicuously, white actor Bradley Cooper. Chappelle explained,

> I saw all those black faces, and Bradley, and I saw how happy everybody was—these people who had been historically disenfranchised. And it made me feel hopeful. And it made me feel proud to be an American. And it made me very happy about the prospects of our country. So in that spirit, I'm wishing Donald Trump luck. And I'm gonna give him a chance. And we, the historically disenfranchised, demand that he give us one, too.

While this optimistic turn might have allayed some immediate fears, Chappelle elides the significant differences between the "hope" espoused by the previous administration and the narrowly defined return to "greatness" that many of the formerly hopeful fear. This feeling of hopefulness—and the BET-sponsored[1] party he attended—could only exist in the final year of a two-term president who need not worry any longer about political perception of future governing aims. The party itself, ultimately, does not signal the direction of the nation, nor can it reduce concerns about a future stripped of a sense of place and Black futurity.

What Chappelle does, ultimately, by saying he's going to "give him a chance" is to imagine for the general American public that these same communal engagements with joyful self-making are possible, when they have been clearly marked as prologue by a new administration harking back to an imagined "great" past nation that, in this articulation, exists *only in opposition to the present,* a present that was the cause for Chappelle's optimism itself. Chappelle's assertion that "we . . . demand that he give us one, too" is ultimately incompatible with the very sense of optimistic futurity that he espouses. But even as Chappelle gestures to the possibilities of futurity, he makes a necessary connection to historicity and the position of African Americans as "historically disenfranchised."

I want to end by thinking about Chappelle's uneven return to comedy and to his satirical engagement with the political sphere in this contested moment because it reflects a sort of potential and potential problem in satiric futures—the possible successes and failures of African American satire as it continues moving into the twenty-first century. His articulation of "the historically disenfranchised" here is particularly evocative as it forms a continued trajectory where Blackness is decentered from power. Whenever the historical is conjured, it reminds us that there is no liberation for Black people anywhere in the nation's past—that the *present* moment provides the most freedom, and even this is insufficient. By framing African Americans as *historically* disenfranchised, signaling a turn away from historicity, and then imagining that the *historically* disenfranchised have the privilege of choice to "give him a chance," Chappelle centers his critical address of Blackness in national spheres of choosing without explaining how this autonomy might occur. There is no joke to be found here, no revolutionary laughter to guide the way—he's attempting to articulate an idea that there is the *fix* he's been required to offer without knowing what that fix is in reality. Here, Blackness is summoned to allay the harm done to Black people by outside pressures. This is not a moment that opens space to reassert or reframe Black identity. Instead, Blackness is called upon to allay the culpability of an audience who may rightly deserve blame.

This moment is different from Richard Pryor's ending of "Bicentennial Nigger," where Pryor implicates an empowered public for historical sins. Chappelle offers no indictment and instead eases the guilt of those in power and with privilege by putting the burden of unfounded optimism on the marginalized. His assessment in practice does a disservice to a more impactful connection between the past and the present, between the present and Black futures. It offers him plausible deniability in his oration while dislocating and obscuring the actual meaning of historical disenfranchisement—this sense of not *just* slavery but also post-slavery subjugation and the continuation of anti-Blackness—for his audience. In this way, he maintains the necessary comedic veil while proposing hazy historicity to indict *history itself,* rather than his actual audience—as if history is something that just *happened,* without winners or losers, human victimizers and victims, and without weight in the present. So much of this sense of justice-seeking relies on getting the audience to laugh and then revealing one's true meaning while they are still invested in their own enjoyment and less likely to resist. Correlation is not necessarily causation, but timing is significant here—Chappelle turned down a $55 million contract from Comedy Central amid anxieties about being compared to Richard Pryor, and then returned to a broad national stage while being expected to make sense of the election of Donald Trump. It should perhaps then be unsurprising that his return has been somewhat uneven as he is thrust back into a role he has demonstrated is uncomfortable for him.

Initially, it could be argued that much of this disconnect might have to do with the fact that he is a guest in the space of *SNL* and may not be operating in a wholly autonomous manner—this is expressly not *Chappelle's Show*[2] and so he doesn't have the same audience or sense of freedom as he once did, and he also may not feel he has the same degree of responsibility. As a result, Chappelle's stint lacked much of the incendiary possibilities anticipated by those excited for his return, as well as the incisive critique for which *Chappelle's Show* was noted—he later apologized for saying he would give Trump a chance, telling his audience at a live performance, "I fucked up. Sorry." A few months later, he won his first Emmy for the monologue. However, much of Chappelle's later work after this initial return indicates that it was not a lack of autonomy that prevented his subversive comedy but a lack of interest in the punching up moves or in giving voice to the marginalized that once characterized his comedy.

What if it is *only* through audience acknowledgment of satirical intent that jokes can be acknowledged as effectual satire? After all, one of the surest ways to have a satire rejected is through audience inability or unwillingness to accept the material as satirical, which often comes from a lack of coding by the author, stemming from an erroneous belief that satire is a simple mode—one in which the only requirement is irreverence. Nothing could be further from reality. As Michael Seidel argues, "Satire is 'easy' because its subjects are so tantalizingly manifest, but it is difficult because its strategies are so deceivingly imitative of what it purports to attack. To put it another way, satire is easy because the satirist's impulse is to fight dirty, but it is difficult because the satirist's design is to play it smart" (10). Satire is not merely an attack on social ills or human evilness. It must be structured skillfully and with a specific target in mind not only for the precision of the satiric mode itself but also for the audience to understand the purpose of the satire. For this reason, the impetus for reading a text or performance as satire is often based on our knowledge of the author or performer, extratextual framing, or signposts in the text itself—this is why Chappelle's initial reappearance was met somewhat unevenly as he unsteadily evaluated the changing sociopolitical climate after his return from hiatus. Perhaps, though, satire need not always be extratextually identified—we may not need knowledge of the author or the author's motivations per se, but the satire itself must clearly demarcate the satiric mode throughout by adding an absurdist or identifiably preposterous element to the aspect of society being examined or criticized. It must refuse to play by the accepted rules of the game. Chappelle lingers in this absurdist tradition but hesitates to fully indict his audience for their complicity and complacence in ignoring history. It is only when enacted and recollected with precision that slavery becomes an impactful subject for satire—a frame that Frederick Douglass imagines but in which, of course, given the stakes of his own antebellum historical moment, he is unable to engage fully.

Chappelle returns to more effective and direct political commentary during the "Election Night" sketch. In this act, Chappelle plays the sole Black man watching the election returns with a group of white friends. While his friends prematurely celebrate Hillary Clinton's seemingly certain victory, Chappelle's character calmly cautions them that "it might be a historic night, but don't forget—it's a big country." As the election continues to veer toward a Trump victory, his compatriots grasp at straws to maintain their fleeting hope, explaining that certain states are "where the racists live," saying, "Black people vote late," and toasting "To Latinos!" with faith that these two groups will vote overwhelmingly Democratic and that this presumption will sway the election. To this last point, Chappelle's response, "Word? I guess that the Latinos didn't hear about your toast," reframes the narrative by placing the listener as the object of ridicule and reminds audiences that superficial gestures of solidarity—offered primarily in moments where the marginalized are needed for some benefit of those accustomed to traditional majority status—are useless. In this moment the critical satirical impulse is at its most acute, as it targets those with the power—in this case the potentially disadvantaged white liberal voting populace—demonstrating perhaps the subtle irony of the communal outrage of a group who has perhaps never before experienced these same feelings of disenchantment with the political system, mediated by a member of a marginalized group who has. In this same way, it addresses the complaint that white liberal voters looked to blame other racial demographics for not voting in large enough percentages rather than blaming white voters for their own tepid voting practices.

Significantly, halfway through the sketch, Chris Rock appears and he and Chappelle embrace; Chappelle then moves to stand behind the couch with

Rock while the other players remain at the front of the stage. This understated shift offers a visual cue that Rock and Chappelle are positioned as equals within both the realms of comedy and the attendant commentary, separate from the other characters both in status and ideology. In this sense, Rock's presence offers a physical voucher for Chappelle's commentary—Rock, who has hosted the Oscars and appeared in more mainstream performances, and was a cast member of the show himself from 1990 to 1993, is able to further legitimize Chappelle for audiences who are not as familiar with him as a late-night fixture. Additionally, the couch indicates a clear separation between the two men and the other actors in the scene—they will be "keeping it real" and speaking from their own particular perspective, both bracing themselves and being barricaded from the audience by the white actors present. It is at this moment, when Rock enters, that the commentary evolves from passive response to more active, as if there is now strength in numbers and Chappelle as such should not fear that he may be written off as a lone pessimist; it's an unspoken sense that this is how Black people talk, rather than how Black people talk in the presence of white people—it opens up that space of Black interiority in the public realm and alerts audiences to the varying spheres of Black identity.

The sketch holds promise and seems to signal contemporary concerns with historicity and the limits of white allyship, as Rock and Chappelle's articulation now shifts to direct critiques of both history and current events. This move is rhetorically significant, and overtly asserts that the present condition of Blackness in the United States may only be understood through acknowledgment of historical frames and continued institutionalized marginalization. It is why requests that Black people "get over" slavery feel instinctively hollow and untethered—the experience of slavery isn't one of mere history or past lives; it's never actually *past*. It informs the positionality of Black people to this day. In fact, it is the denial of the continued centrality of slavery that allows widespread refusals of complicity. By ignoring the histories of slavery and refusing the systemic and continuing disenfranchisement of Blackness, Black people are able to more easily be marginalized and widespread systemic oppression is ignored in place of a mythology of pathological, inherent failure. Rock directly addresses women, noting, "Yeah, I don't get you ladies. The country is 55 percent women. I mean, if the country were 55 percent black, we'd have *tons* of black presidents. I mean, Flavor Flav would be president!" Although the treatment of women[3] is particularly problematic, as women here seems to mean "white women" since African American women voted overwhelmingly for Hillary Clinton, this assertion at least does well to refocus the possible blame on whiteness rather than Blackness. Audience laughter indicates audience acceptance of this possibility as well, as there is no laughter at the assertion that there would be "tons of black presidents," but instead at the mention of Flavor Flav as president. Audiences seem to accept the essentialization of voting where Black people vote for *any* Black person and find the comedy in the seemingly absurd statement that Black people would vote for rapper and reality star Flavor Flav.[4] Not only does this statement ignore Black women as *women*—and Black women as a group that voted at the highest overall percentage for Clinton at 94 percent—but it also reduces Black voting practices to a sense of racial allegiance, and elides the fact that the "Black vote" is a recent phenomenon, and one from which Shirley Chisholm,[5] for instance, was unable to benefit.

Likewise, when their white colleagues remark with shock that they think the nation may, in fact, be a racist one, Chappelle responds with faux surprise, "Oh my God. You know, I think my great-grandfather told me something about that. But he was like . . . a slave or something. I dunno . . ." Similarly, when a cast member announces, "This is the most shameful thing America has ever done!" Chappelle and Rock burst into unrestrained, raucous laughter as the scene closes—they offer no words and their revolutionary laughter serves as response. I call this laughter revolutionary because it lingers in the pain the men cannot speak and opens up space where the men can wordlessly reveal their identity and reality—this is, once again, the sense of laughing to keep from *dying,* extending beyond the traditional laughing to keep from crying (and, indeed, silence to keep from dying) notable in the African American comedic tradition. Through this laughter the men refuse the national amnesia surrounding slavery and other racist national atrocities—a revolutionary act in itself!—and remind audiences that there *is* a clear historical precedent for current events, one that is so readily conjured they need not even name it for the absurdity of ignoring it to be realized.

In fact, slavery once again offers an interesting and necessary reference point for racial commentary because of its ubiquity within the national consciousness—because of the public refusal to address slavery in substantive ways, the imagery of slavery and the slave becomes a shorthand for the atrocities of an undefined past. When evoked in the way Chappelle does here, he offers two options for audiences—they can either acknowledge the trajectory from slavery to the election or view the contemporary era comparatively and absolve themselves of wrongdoing via relativity. By closing with their own laughter, Chappelle and Rock signal their understanding of this connectedness—this is laughter as its own potential revolution. In doing so, they engage in a particularly productive satirical effort in which audiences are indicted for their participation in the aspects of society that are being satirized, but their guilt is not implied to have emerged from a vacuum—this is Chappelle's most successful engagement on *Saturday Night Live* and makes for the most effective satire. Instead, the audience is satirized with the society while remaining redeemable participants of the society because of the inherent optimism connected to their sense of futurity and distance from the past. Unfortunately, much of the interpretation of this scene relies on audience understanding and awareness. This trust is unstable—audience desire to understand must at least equal the desire to laugh. As Rock and Chappelle undertake the joke, as two comedians who have historically engaged in political commentary, they offer an additional signpost by which to guide audiences—now, they are white America's Black friends. Although Chappelle's joking offers a potential of revolutionary laughter, it relies on audience willingness to tap into its understanding of slavery as both knowable and known. As Chappelle focuses instead on vague evocations that only reaffirm slavery as an *unknowable* notion, audiences who are eager to resist the significance of slavery in a presumably post-racial context may inherently ignore the implied significance in his articulation. Chappelle seems to feel the pull of the image of the slave as contextualization, but resists implicating himself in its evocation.

In 2017 Dave Chappelle completed a $60 million contract with Netflix for three stand-up comedy specials (he ended up creating four). Similar to the somewhat uneven reception topped by critical acclaim we witnessed in his Emmy-winning *SNL* turn, Chappelle won his first-ever Grammy for Best Comedy Album in 2018 for his first two specials, *Age of Spin* and *Deep in the Heart of Texas,* and his second in 2019 for the latter two specials, *Equanimity* and *The Bird Revelation,* even as he received rightful public criticism about his comedic carelessness and the psychic violence his rhetoric waged against marginalized groups—particularly women and LGBTQ people. The mainstream and public nature of Netflix and, resultantly, of these specials reminds us that it is the public sphere where we are most vulnerable and where questions of communal identity are most acutely felt. Throughout both of these specials, arguably not his *funniest* stand-up specials nor his most politically or socially thoughtful, but certainly his greatest effort toward mainstream *accessibility,* he clings unapologetically to carelessly transphobic, homophobic, and sexist rhetoric that was becoming dated when he left and now seems an anachronistic horror upon his return. Where is the punching up? Where is he speaking truth to power? In fact, where is the truth?

Chappelle doubled down on this new approach to stand up in *Sticks and Stones,* his 2019 Netflix comedy special. The response was similar to previous Netflix specials, split between accolades and criticism, although this time the response skewed slightly more negative, at least in terms of social media—a number of comprehensive posts and criticism about Chappelle's responsibility within the realm of history, with the pushback to these articles decrying supposed cancel culture and the inability of the public to recognize his comedy as "just a joke." What's interesting here is that in this special, a general rehash of some of his more prominent refusals of sympathy from the previous specials, the funniest moments revolve around when Chappelle gently ribs someone whose cell phone goes off during the set. We see glimmers of the focus of the old Chappelle here as he tells the person to answer without a hint of malice while also not missing the opportunity to make fun of the situation and the possible call in question. Here, Chappelle has no problem teasing someone who he thinks might ruin his set. And maybe it's this particular ease that marks part of the continuing issue with his comedy. Because Chappelle has been refigured as a sociopolitical and comedic superhero, all the world's a stage and he can no longer tell the difference between a real threat and an imaginary one. When it comes to what—or who—he thinks might ruin his set, everything is fair game. The audience member whose phone rings is an individual threat; a marginalized group whose existence he imagines might likewise interrupt his set is a bigger one. Even though the man with the ringing phone is a literal threat to the performance—he threatens to halt the performance itself with his very presence—Chappelle treats this moment with casual amusement, with recognition that there is no harm intended. The jokes are not specific to the man or attacks on his personhood. But when it comes to the theoretical idea of other targets—women, LGBTQ communities—Chappelle is no holds barred. Not only is his tone in the jokes themselves vastly different, but the potential trauma they create is likewise unequal. It could be then that this lack of distinction between real and imagined threats creates a scenario in which he feels not only justified but vindicated in waging a rhetorical attack, a claim that is specious at best and seems to disregard his own privilege not only as one of the most popular comedians in the nation, but as one of the most sought-after sociopolitical commentators, whether he likes it or not. It may also then be that Chappelle is leaning into the argument of his current supporters that his comedy is "just jokes." This shift from public responsibility is difficult to reconcile not only because prior to his departure, Chappelle indicated at every level his belief that these are not *just* jokes—indeed, his initial departure from comedy was in view of his concerns that his jokes were misinterpreted and enacting harm. Not only this, but as his platform was built on his ability to reconcile the comedic and the sociopolitically progressive, his deep consideration of the cause and effects of the social realm, his refusal now to think of impact outside of that which immediately impacts himself is incredibly disheartening. This is not the platform on which he established his career. And, as a result, the sudden shift is particularly troubling and seems careless—and, in moments, intentionally hurtful—in a way that was never previously attributed to Chappelle.

The disjointed response to Chappelle's return, the critical acclaim coupled with more public backlash than he ever experienced prior to his retreat from *Chappelle's Show*, ultimately signals that the line between satire and comedy has grown more distinct in recent years. These awards—for *comedy* rather than *satire*—make plain the difference between playing by the rules and subverting them. If Chappelle's jokes are meant only to inspire laughter, then perhaps he has accomplished that goal, regardless of how many people he offends in that aim. If he seeks to create effectual satire, if he wants to *disrupt* traditional structures of power and be *subversive,* then he has to respond to the zeitgeist and the laughter he inspires must be the lifesaving, revolutionary laughter the cultural moment necessitates—as in *Get Out,* the traditional comedic frame may not be able to hold and a new form must fit the function.

For this reason, it is important to remember that we've perhaps ascribed to Chappelle more power than he ever indicated than he wanted, especially after his decade-long absence on the heels of personal trauma surrounding satiric misfires. He now structures himself, to extend W. Kamau Bell's metaphor, like a comedian who was once hurt by the blowback of a satiric shotgun blast and refuses to allow himself the personal or communal vulnerability to get hurt again. This, of course, does not excuse the grotesque and harmful nature of this comedy but perhaps does explain some of his resistance to apologize or engage in focused, thoughtful satirical humor. Indeed, when we think about *Chappelle's Show* we often think in hindsight about the politically charged satirical moments and sketches, and often forget that those moments were punctuated by easy sight gags and fart jokes throughout. He has always engaged the satiric and the broadly comedic. Yet even the juvenile jokes did not resort to targeting large swaths of people without power, and certainly not without indicting a system that continues to oppress these groups. As a result, it's not only that this impulse feels rather unsatisfying in this particular political moment where the absurdity of the world seems to merit more than *just* jokes, but it feels out of step with Chappelle's most famous routines.

So, what now in a moment where we need satire to explain the self-satirizing sociopolitical? If satire is founded on some level on the element of surprise, on shifting our expectations, how can satirists today respond to our expectations about the unexpected? Satire is never merely about eliciting the biggest laugh—even jokes aren't simply *jokes* but offer broader social context and meaning. For this reason, satire in the twenty-first century must continue to contort itself and take innovative new forms. As society itself becomes more absurd, more inherently self-satirizing, a sketch comedy show doesn't have quite the savor it once did if its target is unclear—not only in the case of Chappelle's stint on *SNL,* a show whose viewpoint can perhaps be best described as ferociously the path of least resistance, but also in his own self-authored comedic and satiric interventions. What we are witnessing in the twenty-first century is the critical expansion of the parameters of satire because when quotidian lived experiences verge on the absurd, the frame of satire itself may not hold. After all, how can satire subvert the rules of the game when life itself seems to do so?

In a 2004 interview with Rone Shavers, Percival Everett explained, "I'm making fun of satire as well as satirizing social policies. I mean, I shouldn't even say this, but I write about satire." The idea of making fun of satire, and that satire itself is worth greater satiric consideration, speaks to Everett's authorial attempts at working through processes of autonomous re-memory, refusing limiting expectations and tropes, and it further explains why the texts and performance discussed throughout *Laughing to Keep from Dying,* while not all traditionally satires, are all still engulfed by the satiric mode. These authors and performers do not build toward a singular argument about Black identity but instead demonstrate the ways that kaleidoscopic Blackness considers and makes space for varied portrayals of Blackness and Black interior space. The twenty-first century requires our satirists to offer productive ways to express autonomous Black identity—whatever that Black identity may be. Sidonie Smith and Julia Watson explain, "How people remember, what they remember, and who does the remembering are historically specific. A culture's understanding of memory at a particular moment of its history shapes the life narrator's process of remembering" (23). It might be for this reason that so much of African American cultural expression emerges within the satiric mode—it is a genre based around processes of witnessing and remembering. The treatment of genre as porous allows these authors and performers the opportunity to represent their communities while simultaneously speaking to their own personal experiences. The storyteller is in power in satirical storytelling, and is thus able to construct the story in ways that hold both personal and communal significance. In this way, these writers and performers in satirical and genre-defying recollections and imaginings may be ultimately able to bolster themselves by writing their communities into historical and contemporary existence by defining themselves *for* themselves, rather than merely in flowing with or in opposition to expectations of a white norm.

That Black people are funny is frequently taken as a given, and the observation is just as often not afforded the rigorous investigation reserved for other groups, nor is its contemporary articulation often given the space it deserves for critical analysis. It's as if the humor of Black people is taken as so naturalistic and assumed that it is thereby not a real space for inquiry. James Baldwin writes,

> Ancient maps of the world—when the world was flat—inform us, concerning that void where America was waiting to be discovered, HERE BE DRAGONS. Dragons may not have been here then, but they are certainly here now, breathing fire, belching smoke; or, to be less literary and Biblical about it, attempting to intimidate the mores, morals, and morality of this particular and peculiar time and place. (816)

It is these same dragons that work, consciously and not, to continue to box in Blackness. As such, when it comes to the articulation of a Black identity, the personal is always political. The choosing is perhaps even more significant than the choice itself. It stands to reason, then, that the personal is likewise usually performative when carried out in the public sphere. As the intended satirical audience, we have no choice but to laugh at the target who is beguiled not only by what they actually see but by what they *expect* to see. As in the past, proper performance of racial identity has sometimes overwhelmed articulations of communal Blackness and individual Black selfhood. The search for a racial identity that is authentic to both the group and the individual, the public and the private, has been challenging at best and an impossible undertaking at worst. These contemporary texts encourage play within these expectations and, most importantly, autonomy in both their acceptance and refusal.

Baratunde Thurston explains in his satirical self-help book *How to Be Black,* "It is an inextricable fact of blackness that one will at some point be referred to as 'too black' or 'not black enough' by white people, black people, and others. I've yet to meet the Negro who is 'juuuuuust right' to everyone" (42). It would appear that the decision to employ the satirical allows the speaker to criticize the harsh realities of racism, or the limitations of racialization, even indicting their readers at times, without appearing moralistic or too close to the subject matter to be unbiased. This seems a peculiar requirement for Black authors writing about race, but perhaps this serves as an indication of the ludicrous demands wrapped up in the wake of the failures of the post-racial mythology. As a result, their utilization of humor creates a veil of seeming critical distance, where laughing retrospective allows them the benefit of surreptitiously indicting their target without their appearing overly didactic. It's a fine line and can be difficult to discern—it is why Chappelle's monologue, particularly in hindsight, seems to miss its mark, while the "Election Night" sketch feels not only funny but vital.

Laughing to Keep from Dying: African American Satire in the Twenty-First Century, written a mere two decades into the twenty-first century, is a project naturally concerned with futurity. And yet, the twenty-first century brings with it uncharted territory, rendering the future effectiveness of contemporary frames difficult to image and perhaps foolish to predict. Even prior to Trump's actual win, the rhetoric surrounding the possible first female president, herself a former first lady, running against a wealthy former reality television star, by its very nature blurred the line between the real and the imaginary—a satire writ large and played out with stunning implications regardless of the victor. It is because of this seeming indecipherability between reality and the satirical that a nuanced and carefully articulated satire, finely trained on its target, is more necessary than ever. This shouldn't mute the effectiveness of the element of surprise inherent to satirical invention, but its fulfillment requires thoughtful consideration of the harm that can be done to marginalized people who are at risk when used as mere cannon fodder for broad targets and individual self-saving. As these satirical endeavors become more and more necessary and widespread in view of a self-satirizing society, the responsibility of the satirist to invent a counternarrative that eschews the status quo and allows space for justice grows more immediate and more intense. And it is our responsibility as audiences to continue to demand this intentionality from our satirists. It might be this revolutionary laughter that keeps us from dying after all.

NOTES

Introduction

1. This is an unsatisfying and recurrent claim intended to reduce the potential impact of comedy and the satiric mode.

2. This is the African American tradition of repetition with a difference, having features of what Cheryl Wall calls "worrying the line," what Henry Louis Gates refers to as "signifyin(g)," a revisiting and revising of that which is already known. Gates explains further that "signifyin(g) is so fundamentally black, that is, it is such a familiar rhetorical practice, that one encounters the great resistance of inertia when writing about it. By inertia I am thinking here of the difficulty of rendering the implications of a concept that is so shared in one's culture as to have long ago become second nature to its users" (64).

3. Gene Andrew Jarrett explains the difficulty in articulating a collective Black experience, by writing that "editing an African American anthology in a postracial era entails counterbalancing the idea that its readers might be 'hungry for texts about themselves' against the idea that they might also be awaiting their own disarticulation from the straightjacket of racial authenticity and representation in African American political history" (163).

4. For this reason, within this book I intentionally discuss performances and texts that emerged prior to November 2016 in conversation with the perceived promises and failures of the post-racial. In chapter 4 and the conclusion, I shift deliberately to texts that originated or rose to prominence after the election of Donald Trump and the apparent dismantling of the mythos.

5. Indeed, Donald Trump has fueled much of this sentiment, by providing white supremacists with platforms (as in the case of former White House chief strategist

Steve Bannon), by refusing to decry hate groups (as in his unwillingness to outright condemn the KKK), and by his active embracing of alt-right figures and rhetoric.

6. While chronology may not be the supreme factor, since there were artists communicating this dissatisfaction with the limitations of expected African American cultural expression before the twenty-first century and there are surely those who subscribe to a more traditional portrayal of blackness contemporarily or who have other literary or artistic aims entirely, it is helpful to consider an identifiable point on the continuum of African American literature and culture to interrogate the ways satire has evolved with the *changing same* of Black citizenship in the United States.

7. Jourdon Anderson's recently repopularized letter to his former master is addressed in chapter 1.

8. I think here particularly of her rhetorical posture that requires its listener to respond resoundingly in favor with Truth and reckon with the incompatibility of the slave system with notions of "true" womanhood without Truth's own explicit condemnation.

9. Resistance not only emerges with non-Black readers but may also occur with Black readers who may desire to perform a "that would never be me" denial of the ancestral trauma and lingering impact of slavery in the contemporary world.

10. This trope is made literal in Colson Whitehead's *Apex Hides the Hurt*.

11. In the contemporary moment, Spike Lee's *Bamboozled* unveils the risks of this misconstrual when the subversive is received as sincere, and the damage it may do to the audience, the broader social sphere, and the joke tellers themselves.

12. The Bahamian-born Williams and his partner, George Walker, billed themselves as "Two Real Coons" beginning in 1896, and performed in blackface on stage and screen. In *Coloring Whiteness: Acts of Critique in Black Performance*, Faedra Chatard Carpenter describes Williams's role by saying, "Bert Williams was one of the first comedians to introduce the notion of *black comedy for black audiences*. White audiences could laugh without knowing that they were being criticized for their misperceptions and bigotry" (108, emphasis added). Indeed, it would seem that the use of blackface was integral to this goal for black audiences. The use of blackface *by* Black performers allowed them not only to acquire gainful employment in the few roles afforded to them but also to imagine race and racialization out to an absurd conclusion.

13. Given the present-day unreliability of reports of Black violence or initial attacks waged by Black people as justification for the subsequent murder of Black men and women, I am unconvinced that Wright actually had a gun on stage or that he fired into the crowd with wild abandon. While this may be the case, it sounds so similar to the retroactive excuses that popularize these accounts today that it gives me pause.

14. The pair arrived to freedom in Philadelphia on Christmas Day and, after being pursued by and eluding bounty hunters for two years, relocated to England, where they remained until returning to the United States—and the South—in 1890. The story of the Crafts seems unbelievable enough to be relegated to the realm of fic-

tion, and the Crafts's cunning blurs the line between satirical imaginings and lived experience into self-satirization.

15. "Tar brush" is a derogatory phrase used to identify and degrade individuals of African descent.

16. What is especially interesting is that White makes the act of choosing his own racial identity explicit. He says, "I consider myself a colored man," flouting the one-drop rule, any sense of inherent Blackness, or any idea that blackness is something to avoid or disavow. Instead, even writing in the early twentieth century, White sees race as having a fluid potential and blackness as desirable. White's understanding of himself as colored is particularly significant, given his characterization by the *New York Times* in his 1955 obituary:

> Only five-thirty-seconds of his ancestry was Negro. His skin was fair, his hair blond, his eyes blue and his features Caucasian. He could easily have joined the 12,000 Negroes who pass the color-line and disappear into the white majority every year in this country. But he deliberately sacrificed his comfort to publicize himself as a Negro and to devote his entire adult life to completing the emancipation of his people.

While the articulation of 5/32 Blackness verges on the nonsensical, the *Times* here is seeking to quantify and qualify the terms under which a man could look white but remain Black. There is no sense here that 5/32 is too minute a quantity to matter, even in the 1950s. Indeed, it expressly does matter, for White, to be sure, but also apparently for the *Times*'s expected readership. For this reason, the unreliability of visualization is critical to these representations and highlights the instability and absurdity of racial assumptions—when race is tied directly to phenotype, it leads to self-satirization where seeing is *not* always believing and racial assumptions take hold.

17. Here Pryor's willingness to make himself vulnerable—alongside his bravery in doing and then undoing comedy—underscores the lasting impact of slavery on the black bodies of slave descendants in the United States and forces audiences, who without critical examination listened to everything that came before on the album, to consider the implications of their own laughter and their own culpability. Yet it also establishes his own selfhood as he frames this narrative as resistance to claims that slavery exists merely "in the past."

Chapter 1. "The Storm, the Whirlwind, and the Earthquake"

1. These neo-slave narratives take the generic conventions, in many cases, of slave narratives but were, importantly, written by people who were never enslaved. These forms share similarities with neo-slave narratives, yet they are usually more explicit in their acknowledgment of a contemporary historical context, winking at the reader in this overlapping of the past and the present.

2. I address the commodification of Black bodies more fully in chapter 4 in consideration of the film *Get Out* (2017).

3. Baartman's remains were not returned to Africa to be buried until 2002.

4. We witness a similar disruption of expected catharsis at the end of *Get Out*, discussed in chapter 4.

5. Whether or not this is meant to stake Tarantino's claim to the song "Strange Fruit" is unclear.

Chapter 2. "Race Is Just a Made-Up Thing"

1. This offers a possible inversion of Chris Rock's "Niggas versus Black People" bit, discussed at length in chapter 3.

2. This is not meant to imply, of course, that biraciality precludes Blackness, or that biracial individuals may not also identify as Black. However, Miz Rain's phenotypic presentation in the book is so significant in Precious's evolving understanding of Blackness and Black possibility that the casting of Paula Patton indicates a significant erasure—if not of Black identity, then certainly of dark Black skin. It is especially problematic when *all* of the light-skinned, biracial actors in the film—Patton, Mariah Carey, and Lenny Kravitz—serve in savior or humanizing capacities, where darker-skinned actors are villainized.

3. It's worth mentioning that Obama had multiple "controversies" surrounding his "dad jeans," but none were so prominently discussed or, arguably, so egregious as the one occurring in 2009.

4. This may be one of a few reasons why films starring African American actors rarely receive Academy consideration unless they are dealing with issues of slavery or civil rights. Even films that address racially nonspecific themes have been labeled "race-themed" by virtue of the racial makeup of the cast, possibly in an effort to alert white potential viewers that the subject matter will be distant or somehow incomprehensible because of perceived inherent racial difference that need not be fully articulated—that "race" itself as theme is signifier enough.

5. Again, it is important to mention that this event does not emerge simply from Everett's imagination, as both *Push* and *Precious* were immense successes.

6. His most well-known work of satire is his 2004 novel *Soul City*.

7. This is, of course, the same Touré who, as Daphne Brooks rightly reminds us, called the Rolling Stones' "Brown Sugar" a song on both literal and figurative levels about white masters having sex with black slave women, "one of the great love songs written to black women" (106). Touré does seem prone to incendiary comments meant to sensationalize his arguments.

8. In "You Touch My Black Aesthetic and I'll Touch Yours," Julian Mayfield works to articulate the reality of a Black aesthetic sensibility. He explains, "There is a Black Aesthetic which cannot be stolen from us, and it rests on something much more substantial than hip talk, African dress, natural hair, and endless, fruitless discussions of 'soul.' It is in our racial memory, and the unshakable knowledge of who we are, where we have been and, springing from this, where we are going" (27). This definition offers some context suggesting what kaleidoscopic Blackness might contain.

9. An earlier version in a different form of the section on *Erasure* appeared in

Post-Soul Satire: Black Identity after Civil Rights, ed. James J. Donahue and Derek C. Maus (Jackson: University Press of Mississippi, 2014).

Chapter 3. "When Keeping It Real Goes Wrong"

1. In *Cultureshock,* Chris Rock says about his set, "I thought I was allowed to criticize hip hop, because I *loved* hip hop . . . these are my guys." I similarly criticize out of a deep, abiding love for comedy.

2. Interestingly, this was shortly before Chappelle did in fact walk away from his contract with Comedy Central.

3. A noteworthy shift is his 2018 Netflix special, *Tambourine,* in which Rock displays a great deal of vulnerability and nuance not seen since his earliest stand-up routines before *Saturday Night Live.* In this special, Rock performs in a (relatively) small theater at the Brooklyn Academy of Music and allows himself to be the target of many of the jokes. This special comes on the heels of his infidelity and divorce and seems to indicate not only that Rock's comedic persona may shift in response to his social situatedness but also that he remains eager to beat us to the punch line, cleverly attacking himself before we have the wherewithal to do it first.

4. *Bring the Pain* was filmed at the Takoma Theater in Washington, D.C., which Rock refers to as a "chocolate city," a term stemming from at least as early as the 1970s and meant to describe cities with a large black population.

5. The NBC sitcom *The Office* does an excellent send-up of this troubling situation in an episode titled "Diversity Day" (2005) where socially clueless boss Michael Scott (played by a pitch-perfect Steve Carrell) performs this set for his horrified employees, ultimately resulting in the entire office being forced to attend mandated racial sensitivity/diversity training.

6. Chris Rock himself is aware of the impossibility of this frame holding. In an episode of *Comedians in Cars Getting Coffee,* Rock discusses with Jewish American comedian Jerry Seinfeld his concerns surrounding police officers. Rock explains quickly his own sense of reimagined double-consciousness, saying to Seinfeld "I'm famous. Still black."

7. I am reminded here of a similar situation in which actor Morgan Freeman asserts that the best way to move to a post-racial society is to "stop talking about" race, and the ways that this quotation and video clip have been bandied about as the *final word* on race relations as if Freeman were the most credible source by virtue of his Blackness, fame, and robust and resonant voice.

8. This is ironic given his distinction between "niggas" and "black people" more than a decade earlier.

9. Spike Lee's film *Bamboozled* (2000) contemporarily utilizes blackface to reception that skewed negative. Lisa Schwarzbaum remarked, "So acrid is the indictment, yet so muddled the arguments, that Lee feels compelled to include the dictionary definition of the word *satire.*" The reviews seem to anticipate the failed satires undertaken in the metanarratives of the twenty-first century where the implication is that the writer must be condemned for a supposed imprecision and for an overde-

termined satirical frame. It also seems a widespread misunderstanding not only of Lee's authorial intent to unsettle our understanding of the satirical object but also of Lee's own satire as deliberately provocative and purposefully subtle.

10. "Weekend Update" historically offers performers the opportunity to pull from their stand-up bits and perform them in this abbreviated form. It often comes off clumsily, particularly for new performers who are learning the format. During a stand-up routine, the performer can control the tone and pace. During "Weekend Update" the pace is predetermined and mediated against the straight man with whom the conversation is held.

11. This is a significant effort at vulnerability on her part.

12. Black Twitter refers to the perceived collective interests and bargaining power of Black Twitter users. It often is identified by unified trending topics and points of conversation.

13. Pharoah and Zamata left the show in 2016 and 2017, respectively. Jones herself left in 2019.

14. Aaron McGruder is most famous for his comic strip and cartoon series *The Boondocks.*

15. It is worth noting that Chappelle has a strong background in stand-up comedy. He began performing in clubs as a teenager, and while he is gifted as both an actor and comedian, he seems more comfortable in a comedy club than other performance venues.

16. This joke seems to take its roots from Ralph Ellison's *Invisible Man,* in which the narrator remarks upon eating a sweet yam, "I walked along, munching the yam, just as suddenly overcome by an intense feeling of freedom—simply because I was eating while walking along the street. It was exhilarating. I no longer had to worry about who saw me or about what was proper. To hell with all that, and as sweet as the yam actually was, it became like nectar with the thought. If only someone who had known me at school or at home would come along and see me now. How shocked they'd be! I'd push them into a side street and smear their faces with the peel. What a group of people we were, I thought. Why, you could cause us the greatest humili-ation simply by confronting us with something we liked. Not *all* of us, but so many" (264).

17. He has somewhat moved away from this frame of self-reproach in his return to comedy, addressed at greater length in the conclusion.

18. After Chappelle left the show, he and Brennan had a very public falling-out. Both say they are on friendly terms now, more than a decade thereafter.

19. And despite Chappelle's later protestations, addressed in the conclusion.

20. In 2015 I saw Dave Chappelle perform in Rochester, New York. While his renewed enjoyment of joke telling was palpable, the vulnerability that marked his comedy was absent. My confusion surrounding his lack of vulnerability was short-lived, as an inebriated audience member began to loudly and belligerently heckle Chappelle, concluding by shouting "I'm Rick James, bitch!" Chappelle mildly hu-mored the man until finally speaking back and having the man removed. I no longer

had any questions about Chappelle's rationale for disallowing his own vulnerability on the comedic stage, although (as addressed in the conclusion) I am disheartened by his shifting articulations of identity and his fading role as focused satirist.

Chapter 4. "How Long Has This Been Goin' On, This *Thang*?"

1. I think much of this cynicism stems from a feeling of racial frustration. The reduction of de jure race-based oppression and an increase in visible members of Black communities with power—culminating, of course, with the Obamas' place in the White House—has served to offer encouragement but not full satisfaction. The frustration can perhaps be best described in the feeling of having a Black man as commander in chief and yet still feeling acutely aware that one's rights of citizenship are routinely ignored and disrespected. This has only been heightened with the election of Donald Trump and the chronological linking of these two legacies.

2. In other genres, her death might be more easily presumed, as we *seem* to see Rose take her last breath in the street, fatally wounded from a gun blast to the abdomen. However, the horror genre relishes in the ambiguity between life and death. Her death, particularly if there is a sequel in the works, cannot be a forgone conclusion. The genre loves nothing more than a "jump scare," where audiences are lulled into a false sense of tranquility only to be frightened out of it.

3. Peele has said in interviews that he initially wrote the script so that the approaching lights were, in fact, law enforcement officers and audiences would end with the knowledge that Chris was going to die at the hands of the police. He says that, after the election of Donald Trump, he felt the ending would be too intense and unfair, and that audiences deserved a sense of cinematic optimism (Nigatu and Clayton).

4. I use "Afromillennial" as a subcategory of the post-soul era to gesture to those individuals who were born (1981 and later) in the post-soul era but did not experience its inception and instead came of age during the 1990s and beyond.

5. See a comprehensive analysis of Leslie Jones's relevant work in chapter 3.

6. It seems that this focus on female homosocial relationships as a permanent fixture, rather than, traditionally, a bond that audiences expect to be broken once the women are paired off with men and inevitably scattered in different directions to begin their "real" lives, is emerging in millennial narratives. I think here of the British comedy *Chewing Gum* (2015), in which the friendship between Tracey and Candice is the linchpin of the entire second season, and their resolidification—indeed, the season ends with the two women holding hands—forms the cathartic payoff for viewers. Similarly, season 1 of *Insecure* ends with Issa and Molly sitting together on Issa and Lawrence's couch, Issa held by Molly.

Conclusion

1. Although, it is worth noting, BET was sold to Viacom in 2003 and is, quite infamously, no longer Black owned.

2. While both *Chappelle's Show* and *Saturday Night Live* are sketch comedies, their

structures differ significantly. *Saturday Night Live* is quite formulaic in the vein of a variety show or *Rowan and Martin's Laugh-In,* in which sketches are short and play to the immediate and obvious laughs desired for filming in front of a live audience. While *Chappelle's Show* utilized an audience, the sketches were filmed separately and offered more flexibility and the possibility for risk taking.

3. The frequent erasure of Black women from narratives that engage race and gender as discrete topics and refuse intersectionality is addressed at length in chapter 4.

4. The similarities between Donald Trump and Flavor Flav as wealthy, womanizing, and seemingly "laughable" reality show figures notwithstanding, of course.

5. Against Chisholm's 1972 campaign, prominent Black political leaders such as Jesse Jackson, Louis Stokes, and Alcee Hastings offered their support to white male candidates.

WORKS CITED

Alexander, Elizabeth. *The Black Interior.* Minneapolis, Minn.: Graywolf Press, 2004.

Anderson, Jourdon. "To My Old Master." Received by Colonel P. H. Anderson, *Letters of Note*, August 7, 1865, www.lettersofnote.com/2012/01/to-my-old-master.html. Accessed February 19, 2014.

Andrews, Helena. *Bitch Is the New Black: A Memoir.* New York: Harper Perennial, 2010.

Appiah, Kwame Anthony. "Is the Post- in Postmodernism the Post- in Postcolonial?" *Critical Inquiry*, 17, no. 2 (1991): 336–57.

Avilez, GerShun. *Radical Aesthetics and Modern Black Nationalism.* Champaign: University of Illinois Press, 2016.

The Awkward Comedy Show. Directed by Victor Varnado, performance by Marina Franklin, Supreme Robot Pictures, 2017.

ayo, damali. *How to Rent a Negro.* Chicago: Lawrence Hill Books, 2005.

Baker, Houston A., and Merinda Simmons, editors. *The Trouble with Post-Blackness.* New York: Columbia University Press, 2015.

Baldwin, James. Interview with Kalamu ya Salaam. "Interview: James Baldwin: Looking Towards the Eighties." *Black Collegian* 41, no. 1 (January 1979): 38.

Baldwin, James. "Freaks and the American Ideal of Manhood." 1985. *Collected Essays.* New York: Literary Classics of the United States, 1998. 814–29.

"B.A.N." *Atlanta*, created by Donald Glover, season 1, episode 7, FX Productions, October 11, 2016.

Bell, Derrick. *Faces at the Bottom of the Well: The Permanence of Racism.* New York: Basic Books, 1993.

Bell, W. Kamau. *The Awkward Thoughts of W. Kamau Bell: Tales of a 6'4", African*

American, Heterosexual, Cisgender, Left-Leaning, Asthmatic, Black and Proud Blerd, Mama's Boy, Dad, and Stand-Up Comedian. New York: Dutton, 2017.

Brooks, Daphne. "Burnt Sugar: Post-Soul Satire and Rock Memory." In *This Is Pop: In Search of the Elusive at Experience Music Project,* edited by Eric Weisbard. Cambridge, Mass.: Harvard University Press, 2004, pp. 103–18.

Carpenter, Faedra Chatard. *Coloring Whiteness: Acts of Critique in Black Performance.* Ann Arbor: University of Michigan Press, 2014.

Carpio, Glenda. *Laughing Fit to Kill: Black Humor in the Fictions of Slavery.* Oxford, U.K.: Oxford University Press, 2008.

Chappelle, Dave, performer. *Chappelle's Show: The Complete Series.* Comedy Central, 2012.

Chappelle, Dave, performer. *Chappelle's Show: The Lost Episodes.* Comedy Central, 2003.

Chappelle, Dave, performer. *For What It's Worth.* Sony Pictures Home Entertainment, 2005.

Chappelle, Dave, performer. *Killin' Them Softly.* HBO. 2003.

Child, Ben. "Will Smith Rejected Django Unchained Role Because It Wasn't Big Enough." *Guardian,* March 26, 2013, https://www.theguardian.com/film/2013/mar/26/will-smith-django-unchained-role. Accessed August 10, 2018.

"Chris Rock's *Bring the Pain.*" *Cultureshock.* A&E, October 15, 2018.

Cobb, William Jelani. *The Devil and Dave Chappelle: And Other Essays.* New York: Thunder's Mouth Press, 2007.

Coel, Michaela. *Chewing Gum.* E4, 2015–2017. *Netflix,* https://www.netflix.com/title/80130911.

Colbert, Soyica Diggs, Robert J. Patterson, and Aida Levy-Hussen, editors. *The Psychic Hold of Slavery: Legacies in American Expressive Culture.* New Brunswick, N.J.: Rutgers University Press, 2016.

Coleman, Robin R. Means. *Horror Noire: Blacks in American Horror Films from the 1890s to Present.* Abingdon-on-Thames, U.K.: Routledge, 2011.

Corsianos, Marilyn. "Freedom versus Equality: Where Does Justice Lie?" In *Interrogating Social Justice: Politics, Culture and Identity,* edited by Marilyn Corsianos and Kelly Amanda Train. Toronto, Ont.: Canadian Scholars Press, 1999, pp. 1–22.

Craft, Ellen, and William Craft. "Running a Thousand Miles for Freedom; or, the Escape of William and Ellen Craft from Slavery." 1860. In *The Long Walk to Freedom: Runaway Slave Narratives,* edited by Devon W. Carbado and Donald Weise. Boston: Beacon, 2013, pp. 205–28.

Crawford, Margo N. *Black Post-Blackness: The Black Arts Movement and Twenty-First-Century Aesthetics.* Champaign: University of Illinois Press, 2017.

Crawford, Margo N. "The Inside-Turned-Out Architecture of the Post-Neo-Slave Narrative." In *The Psychic Hold of Slavery,* edited by Soyica Diggs Colbert, et al. New Brunswick, N.J.: Rutgers University Press, 2016, pp. 69–85.

Crawford, Margo N. "'What Was Is': The Time and Space of Entanglement Erased by Post-Blackness." In *The Trouble with Post-Blackness,* edited by Houston Baker and K. Merinda Simmons. New York: Columbia University Press, 2015, pp. 21–43.

Crucchiola, Jordan. "In Get Out, Allison Williams Makes 'Good White People' Terrifying." *Vulture,* New York Media, February 22, 2017, www.vulture.com/2017/02/in-get-out-allison-williams-makes-good-white-people-scary.html. Accessed February 22, 2017.

"Dave Chappelle/A Tribe Called Quest." *Saturday Night Live,* season 42, episode 6, NBC. November 12, 2016.

Dawkins, Marcia Alesan. *Clearly Invisible: Racial Passing and the Color of Cultural Identity.* Waco, Tex.: Baylor University Press, 2012.

DesRochers, Rick. *The Comic Offense: From Vaudeville to Contemporary Comedy.* London: Bloomsbury Academic, 2014.

Dickson-Carr, Darryl. *African-American Satire: The Sacredly Profane Novel.* Columbia: University of Missouri Press, 2001.

"Diversity Day." *The Office.* NBC, WNCN, Durham, N.C. March 29, 2005.

Django Unchained. Directed by Quentin Tarantino, Weinstein Company, 2012.

Douglass, Frederick. *The Life and Times of Frederick Douglass.* 1892. Mineola, New York: Dover, 2003.

Douglass, Frederick. *The Oxford Frederick Douglass Reader,* edited by William L. Andrews. Oxford, U.K.: Oxford University Press, 1996.

Douglass, Frederick. "What to the Slave Is the Fourth of July?" Ladies' Anti-Slavery Society, July 5, 1852, Corinthian Hall, Rochester, N.Y. Teaching American History. https://teachingamericanhistory.org/library/document/what-to-the-slave-is-the -fourth-of-july/.

Dyer, Richard. *White.* Abingdon-on-Thames, U.K.: Routledge, 1997.

Ebert, Roger. "Danson's Racist 'Humor' Appalls Crowd at Roast." In *Roger Ebert's Journal.* October 10, 1993, www.rogerebert.com/rogers-journal/dansons-racist -humor-appalls-crowd-at-roast. Accessed August 18, 2015.

Elam, Harry, and Douglas Jones Jr., editors. *The Methuen Drama Book of Post-Black Plays.* London: Bloomsbury, 2012.

Ellison, Ralph. *Invisible Man.* New York: Random House, 1952.

Emerson, Jim. "Precious Based on the Film Female Trouble by John Waters." *Scanners with Jim Emerson,* December 22, 2009. https://www.rogerebert.com/scanners/precious-based-on-the-movie-female-trouble-by-john-waters. Accessed August 5, 2018.

English, Darby. *How to See a Work of Art in Total Darkness.* Cambridge, Mass.: MIT Press, 2007.

Everett, Percival. *Erasure.* Boston: University Press of New England, 2001.

Everett, Percival. *Percival Everett by Virgil Russell.* Minneapolis, Minn.: Graywolf Press, 2013.

Frankenberg, Ruth. "Introduction: Local Whitenesses, Localizing Whiteness." In *Displacing Whiteness: Essays in Social and Cultural Criticism,* edited by Ruth Frankenberg. Durham, N.C.: Duke University Press, 1997, pp. 1–34.

"Freeman on Black History." Interview with Mike Wallace. *60 Minutes,* June 14, 2006, https://www.cbsnews.com/video/freeman-on-black-history/. Accessed July 8, 2014.

Gates, Henry Louis. *Figures in Black*. Oxford, U.K.: Oxford University Press, 1987.

Gates, Henry Louis. *The Signifying Monkey*. Oxford, U.K.: Oxford University Press, 1988.

Gay, Roxane. *Bad Feminist*. New York: Harper Perennial, 2014.

Get Out. Directed by Jordan Peele, performance by Daniel Kaluuya, Universal Pictures, 2017.

Goldberg, Whoopi. *Book*. New York: William Morrow, 1997.

Gray, Richard J., and Michael Putnam. "Exploring Niggerdom: Racial Inversion in Language Taboos." In *The Comedy of Dave Chappelle: Critical Essays*, edited by. K. A. Wisniewski. Jefferson, N.C.: McFarland, 2009, pp. 15–30.

Harper, Phillip Brian. *Are We Not Men? Masculine Anxiety and the Problem of African-American Identity*. Oxford, U.K.: Oxford University Press, 1998.

Hartman, Saidiya. "Venus in Two Acts." *Small Axe* 12, no. 2 (2008): 1–14.

Haymes, Stephen Nathan. "Pedagogy and the Philosophical Anthropology of African-American Slave Culture." In *Not Only the Master's Tools: African American Studies in Theory and Culture*, edited by Lewis Ricardo Gordon and Jane Anna Gordon. Boulder, Colo.: Paradigm, 2006, pp. 173–204.

Hobson, Janell. "The Batty Politic: Toward an Aesthetics of the Black Female Body." *Hypatia*, 18, no. 4 (2003): 87–105, doi:10.1353/hyp.2003.0079.

hooks, bell. "Representing Whiteness in the Black Imagination." *Displacing Whiteness: Essays in Social and Cultural Criticism*, edited by Ruth Frankenberg. Durham, N.C.: Duke University Press, 1997, pp. 165–79, doi.org/10.1215/9780822382270-006.

Hurston, Zora Neale. "What White Publishers Won't Print." 1950. In *Within the Circle: An Anthology of African American Literary Criticism from the Harlem Renaissance to the Present*, edited by Angelyn Mitchell. Durham, N.C.: Duke University Press, 1994, pp. 117–21.

"The Interview: 'Boondocks' Creator Aaron McGruder." *The Interview: "Boondocks" Creator Aaron McGruder*, Washington Post Company, July 22, 2008, http://voices .washingtonpost.com/comic-riffs/2008/07/the_interview_aaron_mcgruder.html. Accessed June 9, 2016.

Insecure. Created by Issa Rae and Larry Wilmore, produced by Issa Rae et al., seasons 1, 2, and 3, HBO, 2016–2018.

James, Kendra. "'Get Out' Perfectly Captures the Terrifying Truth about White Women." *Cosmopolitan*, February 28, 2017, www.cosmopolitan.com/entertainment/ movies/a8990932/get-out-perfectly-captures-the-terrifying-truth-about-white -women/. Accessed February 28, 2017.

Jarrett, Gene Andrew. "Loosening the Straitjacket: Rethinking Racial Representation in African American Anthologies." In *Publishing Blackness: Textual Constructions of Race Since 1850*, edited by George Hutchinson and John K Young. Ann Arbor: University of Michigan Press, 2013, pp. 160–74.

Johns, Gillian. "Percival Everett's Erasure: That Drat Aporia When Black Satire Meets 'The Pleasure of the Text.'" In *Post-Soul Satire: Black Identity after Civil Rights*. edited by Derek Maus and James Donahue. Jackson: University Press of Mississippi, 2014, pp. 85–97., doi:10.14325/mississippi/9781617039973.003.0006.

Johnson, Caleb. "Crossing the Color Line." 1931. In *Passing: A Norton Critical Edition,* edited by Carla Kaplan, New York: W. W. Norton, 2007, p. 121.

Jones, Leslie, performer. "Chris Pratt / Ariana Grande." *Saturday Night Live,* season 40, episode 1, NBC, September 27, 2014.

Jones, Leslie, performer. "Andrew Garfield / Coldplay." *Saturday Night Live,* season 39, episode 19, NBC, May 3, 2014.

Jones, Leslie, performer. "Chris Hemsworth / Zac Brown Band." *Saturday Night Live,* season 40, episode 15, NBC, March 7, 2015.

@Lesdoggg. "What part of this joke that wasn't true? . . ." *Twitter,* May 4, 2014, https:// twitter.com/Lesdoggg/status/463074782205190144.

Jung, Moon-Kie. *Beneath the Surface of White Supremacy: Denaturalizing U.S. Racisms Past and Present.* Palo Alto, Calif.: Stanford University Press, 2015.

Kee, Jessica Baker. "Black Masculinities and Postmodern Horror: Race, Gender, and Abjection." *Visual Culture & Gender,* 10 (2015): 47- 56.

"Keith Obadike's Blackness." *eBay,* August 8, 2001. http://obadike.tripod.com/ebay .html. Accessed April 10, 2016.

Key, Keegan-Michael, and Jordan Peele, performers. "Slave Fight." *Key & Peele,* season 3, episode 3. Comedy Central, October 2, 2013, http://www.cc.com/video -clips/03e835/key-and-peele-slave-fight. Accessed October 30, 2016.

Key, Keegan-Michael, and Jordan Peele, performers. "All Vandaveon and Mike (Chronological)." *YouTube,* June 23, 2014, https://www.youtube.com/playlist?list =PLFzansCaLiNcQaiB6zIvsx_Jxc7pmiYqp.

"Kids Need Bullying." *Comedians in Cars Getting Coffee,* season 2 episode 6, July 18, 2013. *Netflix,* https://www.netflix.com/title/80171362.

Krefting, Rebecca. *All Joking Aside: American Humor and Its Discontents.* Baltimore: John Hopkins University Press, 2014.

Lauer, Matt, and Rachel Dolezal. "Rachel Dolezal Breaks Her Silence on TODAY: 'I Identify as Black.'" *The Today Show,* June 16, 2015. https://www.today.com/video/ rachel-dolezal-breaks-her-silence-i-identify-as-black-465269315945. Accessed September 29, 2015.

Leung, Rebecca. "Chappelle's Trip to the Top: Comedy Central Comedian Talks about Using the 'N' Word in Jokes." *60 Minutes,* May 27, 2005. https://www.cbsnews .com/news/chappelle-an-act-of- freedom-19–10–2004/. Accessed May 25, 2014.

Leung, Rebecca. "Rock: Bring on Oscar 'Safety Net': Ed Bradley Talks to Oscar Host about N— Word, Minstrelsy." *60 Minutes,* February 17, 2005. https://www.cbsnews .com/news/rock-bring-on-oscar-safety-net/. Accessed May 25, 2014.

Lott, Eric. *Love and Theft: Blackface Minstrelsy and the American Working Class.* Oxford, U.K.: Oxford University Press, 1995.

Marable, Manning. "Living Black History: Resurrecting the African-American Intellectual Tradition." In *The New Black Renaissance,* edited by Manning Marable, Boulder, Colo.: Paradigm, 2005, pp. 3–13.

Mayfield, Julian. "You Touch My Black Aesthetic and I'll Touch Yours." In *The Black Aesthetic,* edited by Addison Gayle. New York: Doubleday, 1971, pp. 24–31.

McConnell, Mariana. "Interview: George A. Romero on Diary of the Dead." *Cinema Blend*, Gateway Blend Entertainment, https://www.cinemablend.com/new/ Interview-George-A-Romero-On-Diary-Of-The-Dead-7818.html. Accessed April 8, 2017.

Mitchell-Kernan, Claudia. "Signifying, Loud-Talking and Marking." In *A Reader in African American Expressive Culture,* edited by Gena Dagel Caponi. Amherst: University of Massachusetts Press, 1999, pp. 309–30.

Moten, Fred. *In the Break: The Aesthetics of the Black Radical Tradition.* Minneapolis: University of Minnesota Press, 2003.

Murray, Derek Conrad. "Post-Black Art and the Resurrection of African American Satire." In *Post-Soul Satire: Black Identity after Civil Rights,* edited by Derek C. Maus and James J. Donahue. Jackson: University of Mississippi Press, 2014, pp. 3–21.

Nielsen, Aldon Lynn. *Black Chant: Languages of African-American Postmodernism.* Cambridge, U.K.: Cambridge University Press, 1997.

Nigatu, Heben and Tracy Clayton, hosts. "Incognegro (with Jordan Peele)." *Another Round,* episode 83, Buzzfeed, March 1, 2017, https://play.acast.com/s/anotherround/ episode-83-incognegro-with-jordan-peele.

O'Neal, Patrice, performer. *Elephant in the Room.* Comedy Central, 2011.

"Palin: Obama Known for 'Mom Jeans.'" *Politico*, March 4, 2014, https://www.politico .com/story/2014/03/sarah-palin-president-obama-vladimir-putin-104218. Accessed February 2, 2017.

Parks, Suzan-Lori. *Venus.* New York: Dramatists Play Service, 1998.

Perry, Imani. *More Beautiful and More Terrible: The Embrace and Transcendence of Racial Inequality in the United States.* New York: New York University Press, 2011.

Phillip, Mary-Christine. Quotation from John Hope Franklin. "To Reenact or Not to Reenact. *Diverse Issues in Higher Education* 11, no. 18, (November 3, 1994): pp. 24.

Pierson, William D. "A Resistance Too Civilized to Notice." In *Black Legacy: America's Hidden Heritage.* Amherst: University of Massachusetts Press, 1993, pp. 53–73.

Precious: Based on the Novel Push by Sapphire. Directed by Lee Daniels, performance by Gabourey Sidibe, Lionsgate, 2009.

Pryor, Richard. *Bicentennial Nigger.* Warner Bros. Records., 2015. MP3.

Rae, Issa, creator. *The Misadventures of Awkward Black Girl. YouTube,* 2011.

Rae, Issa. *The Misadventures of Awkward Black Girl.* New York: 37 Ink, 2016.

Robinson, Marius. "Marius Robinson's Transcription: Published June 21, 1851 in *The Anti-Slavery Bugle.*" *The Sojourner Truth Project,* Leslie Podell. https://www .thesojournertruthproject.com/compare-the-speeches/. Accessed August 12, 2019.

Robinson, Phoebe. Interview with Rachel Martin. *No "You Can't Touch My Hair" and Other Lessons from Phoebe Robinson.* NPR, October 2, 2016.

Robinson, Simon. "On the Beach with Dave Chappelle." *Time,* May 15, 2005. http:// content.time.com/time/arts/article/0,8599,1061415,00.html. Accessed May 25, 2014.

Rock, Chris, performer. *Bring the Pain.* Dreamworks, 2002. DVD.

Rock, Chris, performer. *Good Hair.* Lionsgate Home Entertainment, 2010. DVD.

Rock, Chris. "Chris Rock Talks *CB4*." *SPIN Magazine,* February 1993, https://www
.spin.com/2018/02/chris-rock-cb4–1993/. Accessed March 5, 2018.

Ryan, April. *At Mama's Knee: Mothers and Race in Black and White.* Lanham, Mary-
land: Rowman & Littlefield, 2016.

Sapphire. *Push: A Novel.* New York: Vintage, 1997.

Schwarzbaum, Lisa. "Movie Review: 'Bamboozled.'" Review of *Bamboozled* directed
by Spike Lee. *Entertainment Weekly,* October 13, 2000.

Seacrest, Ryan, and Barack Obama. "Obama Calls 'On Air with Ryan Seacrest' to
Defend ACA, Mom Jeans." *OnAir with Ryan Seacrest,* Premiere Networks, 2013.

Seidel, Michael. *Satiric Inheritance: Rabelais to Sterne.* Princeton, N.J.: Princeton
University Press, 1979.

Shavers, Rone. "Percival Everett by Rone Shavers." *BOMB—Artists in Conversation.*
Bomb Magazine, 2004. https://bombmagazine.org/articles/percival-everett/. Accessed August 5, 2012.

Smith, Sidonie, and Julia Watson. *Reading Autobiography: A Guide for Interpreting
Life Narratives.* Minneapolis: University of Minnesota Press, 2010.

Stewart, Anthony. "Uncategorizable Is Still a Category: An Interview with Percival
Everett." *Canadian Review of American Studies* 37, no.3 (2007): 293–324.

Sykes, Wanda, performer and producer. *I'ma Be Me.* HBO Studios, 2010.

Tafoya, Eddie. *Icons of African American Comedy.* Santa Barbara, Calif.: Greenwood,
2011.

Tarantino, Quentin. Interview by Krishnan Guru-Murthy. "Tarantino Clashes with
Krishnan Guru-Murthy over Django Unchained." Channel 4 News, January 11,
2013. https://www.theguardian.com/film/2013/jan/11/tarantino-krishnan-guru
-murthy. Accessed April 8, 2017.

Taylor, Paul. "Post-Black, Old-Black." *African American Review* 41, no. 4 (2007):
625–40.

Taylor, Yuval, and Jake Austen. *Darkest America: Black Minstrelsy from Slavery to
Hip-Hop.* New York: W. W. Norton, 2012.

Thurston, Baratunde. *How to Be Black.* New York: HarperCollins, 2012.

Touré. *Who's Afraid of Post-Blackness?* New York: Free Press, 2011.

Wall, Cheryl. *Worrying the Line: Black Women Writers, Lineage, and Literary Tradition.* Chapel Hill: University of North Carolina Press, 2005.

Wallace, Maurice O. *Constructing the Black Masculine: Identity and Ideality in African American Men's Literature and Culture, 1775–1995.* Durham, N.C.: Duke
University Press, 2002.

"Walter White, 61, Dies in Home Here." *New York Times,* March 22, 1955. http://movies2
.nytimes.com/learning/general/onthisday/bday/0701.html. Accessed March 10,
2017.

Watkins, Mel. *On the Real Side: A History of African American Comedy.* Chicago:
Lawrence Hill Books, 1999.

White, E. Francis. *Dark Continent of Our Bodies: Black Feminism & Politics of Respectability.* Philadelphia: Temple University Press, 2001.

White, Walter. "I Investigate Lynchings." 1929. In *Witnessing Lynching: American Writers Respond.* New Brunswick, N.J.: Rutgers University Press, 2003, pp. 252–60.

Young, Kevin. "Blacker than Thou." In *The Fire This Time: A New Generation Speaks about Race,* edited by Jesmyn Ward. New York: Scribner, 2017, pp.101–116.

INDEX

misrepresenting the past, 22, 90, 102–13
Mitchell-Kernan, Claudia, 36
"The Monsters are Due on Maple Street"
  (*Twilight Zone*), 138
Mooney, Kyle, 112
morality, 37
moralizing works, 10. *See also* didacticism
Morrison, Toni, 39
Mos Def, 119
Moten, Fred, 8, 151
Muhammad, Elijah, 66–67
multiculturalism, 9
Murphy, Charlie, 118
Murray, Derek Conrad, 148

Native Son (Wright), 75–76
natural hair movement, 100–101
"negro," used as identifier, 41
neoliberalism, 9
Netflix, 158
Never Scared (Rock), 94
Nielsen, Aldon Lynn, 4
"Niggas versus Black People" (Rock), 90–91,
  95–98, 114, 121
Night of the Living Dead (1968), 125–26
Nyong'o, Lupita, 107, 109

Obadike, Keith and Mendi, "Blackness"
  (eBay auction), 22, 58–59, 61, 79–82
Obama, Barack, 9, 148, 152, 171n1(ch.4);
  "dad jeans" controversy, 59, 60, 71–75,
  168n3(ch.2); post-racial mythology and,
  47, 53
Obama, Michelle, 72
objectification, 44–46, 79, 128, 138
The Office (television series), 169n5
O'Neal, Patrice: *Elephant in the Room*, 47

Palin, Sarah, 72
Parks, Suzan-Lori, 21, 49; *Venus*, 28, 44–47
passing. *See* racial passing
Patton, Paula, 67, 168n2
Peele, Jordan, 51, 148; *Get Out*, 22, 123,
  128–36, 138, 139, 143, 149, 160, 171nn2–3;
  Mad TV, 128; "White Zombies," 124–25.
  See also *Key and Peele*
performance art, 40–44, 48, 58, 79
Perry, Imani, 69
Perry, Tyler, 67
Pharoah, Jay, 111, 170n13
phenotypic appearance, 19, 68–71, 80,
  114–15, 167n16, 168n2

Pierson, William D., 53–54
plausible deniability, 5, 9, 28, 55, 91, 153; in
  horror genre, 125; racism and, 130; slavery
  and, 35–37
police brutality, 11, 14, 148, 149
political commentary, 152–58, 160. *See also*
  social commentary
popular culture documentaries, 102
post-Blackness, 60, 81–85, 123–24
postmodernism, 10–11
post-racial mythology, 169n7; absurdity
  of, 2–3; emergence of, 9; failures of, 47;
  hypocrisy of, 74; kaleidoscopic Blackness and, 7–8; post-Blackness and, 81–85;
  power and, 52; racial essentialism and,
  8, 57; racism and, 136–39; refusal of, 122,
  149; rejection of, 123–24; satire and, 11;
  Trump and, 165n4
post-soul era, 171n4
power dynamics, 37, 43; articulation of, 9;
  consent and, 46–47; critiques of, 32; post-
  racial mythology and, 52; silences and, 33
Precious (2009), 59–68, 77
Pryor, Richard, 11, 93–94, 97, 113–15, 167n17;
  "Bicentennial Nigger," 19–21, 39, 153–54
psychic death: danger of, 55; escaping, 3,
  22, 23, 59, 124. *See also* laughing to keep
  from dying
The Psychic Hold of Slavery (Colbert, et al.),
  25–26
psychic trauma, 22; of chattel slave system,
  41, 50–51; denial of Black interiority and,
  59. *See also* trauma
psychic violence, 113. *See also* violence
punching-up laughter, 16, 19, 89–90, 96,
  154, 159
Push (Sapphire), 59–68, 75, 76, 79
Putnam, Michael, 91

race: absurdity of, 2–3, 61, 80, 81; critical
  understanding of, 22; as performative (*see*
  racial performativity); phenotype and,
  167n16; as political construct, 29; as social
  construct, 29, 61, 136
racial anxieties, 57–58; fears of Black masculinity, 71–81
racial binary, 11; instability of, 32, 61, 71. *See
  also* racial passing
racial choice, 17
racial difference, 18, 168n4(ch.2)
racial essentialism, 2, 11, 57–61; African
  American literature and, 7, 75; Black hu-

DANIELLE FUENTES MORGAN is an assistant professor in the Department of English at Santa Clara University.

The New Black Studies Series

Beyond Bondage: Free Women of Color in the Americas   *Edited by David Barry Gaspar and Darlene Clark Hine*

The Early Black History Movement, Carter G. Woodson, and Lorenzo Johnston Greene   *Pero Gaglo Dagbovie*

"Baad Bitches" and Sassy Supermamas: Black Power Action Films   *Stephane Dunn*

Black Maverick: T. R. M. Howard's Fight for Civil Rights and Economic Power   *David T. Beito and Linda Royster Beito*

Beyond the Black Lady: Sexuality and the New African American Middle Class   *Lisa B. Thompson*

Extending the Diaspora: New Histories of Black People   *Dawne Y. Curry, Eric D. Duke, and Marshanda A. Smith*

Activist Sentiments: Reading Black Women in the Nineteenth Century   *P. Gabrielle Foreman*

Black Europe and the African Diaspora   *Edited by Darlene Clark Hine, Trica Danielle Keaton, and Stephen Small*

Freeing Charles: The Struggle to Free a Slave on the Eve of the Civil War   *Scott Christianson*

African American History Reconsidered   *Pero Gaglo Dagbovie*

Freud Upside Down: African American Literature and Psychoanalytic Culture   *Badia Sahar Ahad*

A. Philip Randolph and the Struggle for Civil Rights   *Cornelius L. Bynum*

Queer Pollen: White Seduction, Black Male Homosexuality, and the Cinematic   *David A. Gerstner*

The Rise of Chicago's Black Metropolis, 1920—1929   *Christopher Robert Reed*

The Muse Is Music: Jazz Poetry from the Harlem Renaissance to Spoken Word   *Meta DuEwa Jones*

Living with Lynching: African American Lynching Plays, Performance, and Citizenship, 1890–1930   *Koritha Mitchell*

Africans to Spanish America: Expanding the Diaspora   *Edited by Sherwin K. Bryant, Rachel Sarah O'Toole, and Ben Vinson III*

Rebels and Runaways: Slave Resistance in Nineteenth-Century Florida   *Larry Eugene Rivers*

The Black Chicago Renaissance   *Edited by Darlene Clark Hine and John McCluskey Jr.*

The Negro in Illinois: The WPA Papers   *Edited by Brian Dolinar*

Along the Streets of Bronzeville: Black Chicago's Literary Landscape   *Elizabeth Schlabach*

Gendered Resistance: Women, Slavery, and the Legacy of Margaret Garner   *Edited by Mary E. Fredrickson and Delores M. Walters*

The University of Illinois Press
is a founding member of the
Association of University Presses.

University of Illinois Press
1325 South Oak Street
Champaign, IL 61820-6903
www.press.uillinois.edu